SHAPING TOMORROW'S NORTH:
THE ROLE OF TOURISM AND RECREATION

Margaret E. Johnston, G. David Twynam and Wolfgang Haider,
Editors

Lakehead University

Centre for Northern Studies

Northern and Regional Studies Series #7

Northern and Regional Studies Series #7

SHAPING TOMORROW'S NORTH: THE ROLE OF TOURISM
AND RECREATION

ISSN 1183-6857
ISBN 1-895939-21-6
Printed in Canada

Published by the Centre for Northern Studies, Lakehead University
Thunder Bay, Ontario, P7B 5E1.

TABLE OF CONTENTS

i

ACKNOWLEDGEMENTS

The editors wish to acknowledge the support of the individuals and organizations that were instrumental in the implementation of the conference and these proceedings. *Shaping Tomorrow's North* was sponsored by the Lakehead University Centre for Northern Studies and Canada/Ontario Northern Ontario Development Agreement. We thank the following individuals for their assistance in the running of the conference: Dr. Dave Kemp of Lakehead University and Dale Ashbee of Ontario Ministry of Northern Development and Mines, members of the organizing committee; Betty Salo, Teri Saraka, Stephanie Mann, and Lori Slobodian, office, logistics and registration; Dr. Brian Phillips, field trip leader; Dr. Tom Potter and Dr. Bob Payne, workshop leaders; and, Dr. Cynthia Stacey and Peter Boxall, panel session moderators. Special thanks to our keynote speaker, Ted Manning, who presented on *Tourism as a Catalyst for Environmentally Sound Regional Development*, and all those who participated in panel discussions, paper and poster sessions, field trips and workshops.

We are grateful for the assistance of the many reviewers: Dr. Jay Beaman, Ottawa, Ontario; Mr. Peter Boxall, Canadian Forest Service; Dr. Erik Cohen, The Hebrew University of Jerusalem; Dr. Russell Currie, Lakehead University; Dr. B. Dadgostar, Lakehead University; Dr. Terry Daniel, University of Arizona; Dr. Philip Dearden, University of Victoria; Dr. Robert Dilley, Lakehead University; Dr. Dianne Draper, University of Calgary; Dr. Paul Eagles, University of Waterloo; Dr. Jens Kristian Steen Jacobsen, Norwegian Centre for Transport Research; Dr. Bjorn P. Kaltenborn, Eastern Norway Research Institute; Dr. Bonnie McFarlane, Canadian Forest Service; Dr. Simon Milne, McGill University; Jeppe Mordhorst, Denmark; Dr. Tom Potter, Lakehead University; Dr. Peter Prokosch, WWF International Arctic Programme; Dr. Rick Rollins, Malaspina University College; Dr. A. John Sinclair, University of Manitoba; Dr. Valene Smith, California State University; Professor Tom Stevens, Lakehead University; and, Dr. Geoffrey Wall, University of Waterloo.

We also thank Cathy Chapin of Lakehead University for redrawing several figures.

We extend our deepest gratitude to Robbie Buffington of the Centre for Northern Studies for her tireless work in coordinating the organization of the conference and in managing the production of these proceedings.

Margaret Johnston   Dave Twynam   Wolfgang Haider

SHAPING TOMORROW'S NORTH: INTRODUCTION

G. David Twynam
Lakehead University

Wolfgang Haider
Simon Fraser University

Margaret E. Johnston
Lakehead University

INTRODUCTION

In 1995 Lakehead University sponsored a conference to explore issues in the management and experience of northern tourism and recreation. This three-day meeting, called *Shaping Tomorrow's North: The Role of Tourism and Recreation*, brought together a diverse group from industry, government and research communities to focus on patterns, issues and future prospects of tourism and recreation in the north. The conference aimed to facilitate an exchange of information, ideas and expertise, and to foster an understanding of issues faced in the development of tourism and recreation opportunities in the north.

Ninety registrants participated in the three day conference. Participants attended from within Ontario and from as far away as the Northwest Territories, Yukon, Norway, Britain and Russia. A total of 34 papers were presented in 13 sessions, and two workshops and three panel discussions were held. Though not all presenters submitted manuscripts for the proceedings, the 14 chapters in this volume illustrate the diversity of research conducted on northern tourism, resource-based tourism, outdoor recreation, and land use planning.

The organization of papers for these proceedings reflects the thematic divisions within the conference presentations. The first group contains papers on Arctic tourism and includes research on environmental and cultural impacts, the management of protected areas, the management of tourism activities, and the relationship between tourism and indigenous people.

In the first paper, Viken focuses on the effects of tourism on the indigenous people of Scandinavia, the Sami. From an anthropological perspective Viken describes both the Sami culture and the tourists as diverse and constantly changing groups. Postmodern tourists enjoy visiting traditional cultures for their simplicity, which has been lost in modern society, but will do so with different intentions, leading to variations in the intensity of contact. Individual Sami cope in varying ways with tourists' expectations and the associated economic opportunities. Accordingly, Viken discusses the approaches to tourism taken by Sami individuals using a continuum expressing traditional to modern identities.

The second paper in this section also explores tourism and recreation in the Scandinavian context. Recreation in and tourism use of protected areas has emerged as a contentious issue in Scandinavia and across the north. Fitje elaborates on the situation in Norway, where a long-standing social tradition, referred to as "Every Person's Right," forms the foundation for wilderness use, preservation, and discussions of compatible recreation activities in national parks. Fitje suggests that within national parks, the compatibility of adventure tourism with conservation goals should be examined and approved by the authorities in advance. Fitje admits that it might be difficult to establish a licensing system, but believes that it would prove beneficial for both parties.

Mason provides a summary of the impacts of the increasing effects of tourism on Arctic environments and traditional cultures. Mason reviews various approaches to establishing codes of conduct aimed at lessening such impacts. After explaining the difference between regulations, which have some form of legal status, and codes of conduct, which are voluntary and self-imposed, Mason describes codes of conduct in more detail and presents examples from Svalbard, Norway and the Canadian North, and then suggests one for the Arctic. Universal problems associated with the implementation of codes of conduct are monitoring and assessment of their effectiveness, their appropriate use as marketing tools, the need for co-ordination, and the balance between self-regulation and external regulation.

Butler reminds us of the significant contribution that tourism can make in the diversification of single sector or remote communities. Yet when tourism is used as a means of development, it brings change that might produce the desired development, but also might generate changes that alter the very base of that tourism. Butler argues that successful tourism development needs to align the diverse interests of four key players: government, the tourism industry, the local population, and tourists. Butler stresses that tourism is only one agent of change, advocating that communities should make conscious efforts to control tourism.

The final paper in the section serves as a good example of the typical issues encountered in the process of national park establishment in northern Canada. Seale emphasizes that local indigenous people and communities must support a park initiative or there will not be any park established. In this case study the situation is complicated further by the mineral potential of the candidate park area. Yet tourism opportunities would exist if a park were established, such as an expansion into park based ecotourism guiding by traditional hunting and fishing guides.

The second group of papers focuses more closely on tourism marketing and operating issues. The papers examine topics such as pricing structure, ecotourism potential, market segmentation and the greening of accommodations. The first paper, by Hunt and Haider, is an analysis of the pricing structure of remote fly-in fishing outposts across northern Ontario. The authors use brochures of individual operations as the information source. A multiple regression model is specified with price charged for a standardized one week package as the dependent variable, and a number of other product characteristics as the independent variables. Among several significant variables relating to the quality of the establishment, the authors also identify regional differences in pricing structure.

Wight's paper provides information from recent market surveys of ecotourism markets in North America, identifying ecotourist motivations, activity preferences and accommodation preferences. Wight suggests that the ecotourist is a discerning consumer who belongs to groups or organizations with a nature conservation focus. The author recommends that marketing efforts should match the preferences and trip characteristics of ecotourists in order to meet their expectations. Marketing to ecotourists should be focused on outdoor magazines and publications of conservation organizations.

Robinson, Twynam, Haider and Hunt quantified the demand for ecotourism opportunities in northern Ontario. The authors describe the potential northern Ontario ecotourists and present six profiles of the ecotourism market for northern Ontario to illustrate the potential market segments. The authors state that ecotourism on its own will not provide the panacea for economic growth and sustainable forest management without the support of regional diversification.

In a second paper, Wight provides information on how lodges can make their internal operations more environmentally friendly. The author gives illustrations of these practices and emphasizes the importance of appropriate marketing strategies to encourage public and operator acceptance. A key contribution of this paper is an overview of environmentally sensitive technologies that are currently available.

The five papers in the third group address recreation and tourism management issues in the wider context of land use planning and management in the near north. The first paper, by Maddock and Dickson, reports on the emergence of a regional tourism partnership. The authors highlight the background for this partnership and identify its mandate. The foundation for this regional partnership was grassroots participation in a series of community fora. Participants at these meetings provided the concerns that became the cornerstones in the development of strategic direction for the partnership.

Hawley, Robinson and Robson report on research conducted on the McGregor Model Forest in northern British Columbia in the context of integrating the widest possible range of stakeholders in the decision-making processes for sustainable forestry. Hawley, Robinson and Robson studied the basic values that stakeholders and forest users may have through semi-structured interviews of 77 people. Using the results they address issues raised relevant to sustainable forest management.

Richardson, Pitt, Lime and Martin apply theories of landscape aesthetics to park management using state-of-the-art digital imaging technology. The picturesque landscape is a composite of "the beautiful" and "the sublime" and was a defining approach for desirable landscapes of North American travellers and tourists in the nineteenth century, and also influenced the national park movement. The authors explore the beautiful and sublime by studying the perceptual responses of park users to digital image simulations of parkway design in Pictured Rocks National Lakeshore, Michigan. They observe that different user groups focus on different dimensions of the landscape aesthetic and conclude that management strategies should be user group specific.

In the next paper, Bruns advocates expanding the long established outdoor recreation paradigm of 'experience-based management' to a 'benefits-based management' paradigm. This approach shifts attention from the traditional perception of the recreation resources as opportunities, activities, and experiences, and incorporates the concept of value-added benefits. According to Bruns, the concept of value-added includes the benefits accruing to the participant, as well as to the host population. As such, this concept constitutes an extension to outdoor recreation management frameworks and links to various concerns of tourism researchers.

In the final paper, Haider, Anderson, Daniel, Louviere, Orland and Williams summarize the technical aspects of a project initiated by the Ontario Ministry of Natural Resources to investigate the effects of logging on remote fly-in tourism. The authors selected an experimental approach to identify reactions of fly-in anglers to potential changes of attributes of a fly-in angling experience. Digitally calibrated images were used in the choice experiments to obtain accurate evaluations about timber management attributes from anglers. This paper focuses on the technical aspects of survey design and the digital imaging technique.

The conference provided the opportunity for entrepreneurs, resource managers, and researchers to debate the role of tourism and recreation in the north and the future prospects for sustainable tourism. Papers in this volume address these points from a variety of perspectives and provide examples of current and ongoing tourism and recreation management in the north. It is our hope that this volume reflects the themes of the conference that were expressed in formal papers, panel discussions, workshops and field trips.

ADVENTURE TOURISM AND NATURE CONSERVATION: THE NORWEGIAN CASE

Anders Fitje
Hogskolen i Sogndal

INTRODUCTION

This article deals with the possible conflicts between adventure tourism and nature conservation. The words tourist and tourism have been part of the English language for almost two centuries; still there is no single accepted operational definition of either (Smith 1990). Consequently, adventure tourism also lacks a consistent definition. However, Hall (1992), among others, points out that adventure tourism is categorized by a deliberate seeking of risk and danger by participants in outdoor activities. Hall proposes the following definition of adventure tourism:

> A broad spectrum of outdoor touristic activities, often commercialised and involving an interaction with the natural environment away from the participant's home range and containing elements of risk; in which the outcome is influenced by the participant, setting and management of the touristic experience (Hall 1992: 143).

This is a rather broad definition, but it seems that the definition includes only organized activities, so that outdoor touristic activities carried out by an individual or a group of individuals, single-handedly and self-supported, do not fall within the concept. The degree of engagement in formal, commercialized adventure-based activities is indeed regarded as the distinguishing factor between adventure recreation and adventure tourism. Moreover, adventure tourism is characterized by presenting a "danger in safety" concept, as Anderson (1983) puts it, meaning that the activities carried out by tourists are supervised by guides. In other words, adventure tourism may be characterized as an active use of nature in an organized setting, involving elements of skill. How real the risk needs to be in order to fall within adventure tourism depends on an individual's personal assessment of risks. Backpacking in parts of the Norwegian mountains is a touristic activity that demands skill, and for many foreigners not familiar with the activity it is probably also regarded as hazardous if carried out alone. Generally speaking, one may say that pursuing activities which require skill always involve elements of risk if this skill is lacking.

In Hall's (1992) definition, adventure tourism may also occur in non-commercialized forms, since he defines the phenomenon as often but not always commercialized. In this essay, I will focus on commercialized adventure tourism because the conflict of interests regarding use or protection of nature may be most evident here.

The year 1995 was the European Year of Nature Conservation. In this connection the Norwegian Government launched a policy program based on two main topics: preserving biological diversity and protecting the public right to free access to land. The fact that the policy program had this double-track goal indicates that the Norwegian Government did not regard the two objectives as contradictory or incompatible. On the contrary, both represented, in the view of the Norwegian Government, complementary contributions to conserving nature for the future. This policy program contained several measures ranging from preparing parliamentary bills to disseminating knowledge of and attitudes towards nature conservation through extensive information programs.

It is reasonable to assume that some of these measures, at least in the long run, will affect adventure tourism enterprises. The rationale for this assumption is first and foremost the intentions behind today's legislation regulating nature conservation and outdoor recreation. The bills were introduced by the government and considered by the Parliament in the spring of 1996 (Ot prp nr 27 [1995-96] Om lov om endringer i lov av 28. juni 1957 nr. 16 om friluftslivet, [Proposition to the Odelsting no. 27 (1995-96) on revision of the Open Air Recreation Act], and Ot prp nr 30 [1995-96] Om lov om statlig naturoppsyn, [Proposition to the Odelsting no. 30 (1995-96) on passing a new law, establishing a Governmental Nature Supervision Body]).

THE EUROPEAN YEAR OF NATURE CONSERVATION
AND NORWEGIAN GOVERNMENT POLICY

As far as the first topic, preserving biological diversity, is concerned, the Norwegian government is already obliged to protect the wildlife following several international conventions (for instance, the Rio convention, ratified by Norway in 1993, the Bonn Convention 1983, the Bern Convention 1982, and the Ramsar Convention 1974), as well as national legislation. *Lov om naturvern av 19 juni 1970 nr. 63, Naturvernloven* (The Conservation of Nature Act) provides the formal framework for this purpose, authorizing the establishment of different categories of preservation areas, among which national parks are the most important.

Even though national parks in Norway are supposed to serve both nature protection and to provide recreational opportunities, the main reason for their existence is to preserve biological diversity. However, the importance of national parks as arenas for public recreation, offering people the beauty of scenery in a quiet and peaceful setting, has probably increased since the first national park was established in Norway in 1962. In St.meld. nr. 62 (1991-92) *Ny landsplan for nasjonalparker og andre større verneområder i Norge* (Parliamentary White Paper, [No. 62, 1991-92]), the authorities divide the national parks into two groups: those that have outdoor recreation as part of their objective clause for regulation and those that do not. It is reasonable to assume that this classification was done for the purpose of emphasizing the aspect of nature conservation as the predominant reason for establishing national parks. However, some parks also serve as important outdoor recreation areas. The reason for this is first and foremost that some areas, deserving of preservation, have long traditions as areas of use. For centuries the natural resources in outlying areas were important for the very survival of many rural agrarian communities in Norway, and even today many of these resources have been utilized by small farmers as part of their economic basis. Some areas within different national parks, particularly in southern Norway, have in fact been used also for purely recreational reasons for more than 100 years. However, so far these outdoor recreation activities have been exercised in the form of enjoying the privileges connected to *Allemannsretten* ("Every Person's Right").

This leads to the second main topic: the safekeeping of the public right to free access to land. The right for public access constitutes a time-honoured common law permitting everybody to move freely in the wilderness and conduct activities such as picking nuts, mushrooms, wild berries and flowers on uncultivated land. The right also includes the opportunity to camp in outlying areas with only minor restrictions. In other words, one may, without permission, use other people's property. This latitude is granted as long as no damage is inflicted on the owner's property. The system works simply because it is based on a set of cultural land ethic rules (Hultkrantz and Mortazavi 1992). Since there is normally no permission required, no inquiry is needed.[1] Hence, the use of the right presupposes that the rules are commonly known. Therefore, the land ethic rules must be commonly shared and similarly exercised by everyone in the society in form of a cultural code. In Norway these rules were passed by the legislation of *lov av 28. juni 1957 nr. 16 om friluftslivet, Friluftsloven* (the Open Air Recreation Act). This was done, perhaps, as a consequence of uncertainty regarding the common knowledge of, or respect for, the old land ethic rules in the wake of the modernization of the country during the first half of the 20th century. Another, and perhaps more plausible explanation of this might be the development of the welfare state, and a dominant Norwegian Labour Government during the 1950s, providing a large working class with the wilderness life privileges as healthy forms of recreation.

The origin of the land ethic rules and the exercise of "Every Person's Right" are the basis of the wilderness life concept. As Pedersen (1993) points out, it is not easy to find an Anglo-American concept corresponding to the Norwegian term *friluftsliv*. The official English designation of *friluftsloven* is "the Open Air Recreation Act" (Cfr. "Translated laws," the Norwegian Foreign Department, Documentation Centre), but concepts like outdoor life or outdoor activities do not seem to convey the meaning of *friluftsliv*, since the latter actually only describes what you can legitimately do on other people's land and how you can do it in accordance with the old land ethic rules. Furthermore, this indicates that *friluftsliv* is synonymous with conventional, rather simple activities clearly reflecting elements of what might be called the Norwegian cultural heritage. In what follows, I will concur to Pedersen's (1993) concept of wilderness life when describing the phenomenon which in Norwegian is referred to as *friluftsliv*.

When using wilderness life as synonymous with traditional Norwegian recreation the intention is to apply a generic term for outdoor recreation activities which are favoured within national parks by the Norwegian authorities. It may be argued that the term is practically impossible to use in management because it builds on ideologies, history and individual perceptions of what constitutes the culturally correct use of outlying areas for recreation. However, when distinguishing desirable activities in national parks from unwanted ones, the term is in extensive use. Moreover, Norwegian authorities refer directly to traditional Norwegian outdoor recreation as preferential recreation activities in several official national documents also when discussing outdoor life in general (e.g. Det Kongelige Miljøverndepartement 1995; Direktoratet for naturforvaltning 1995; Flylkesmannen i Sogn og Fjordan 1994; NOU 1983).

The term wilderness life also reflects that the outdoor activities are exercised in outlying areas. Furthermore, wilderness life as traditional, simple, Norwegian recreation, includes only a limited number of activities, most of which are related to natural resource exploitation and passage, in other words, activities which in times past had a considerable utilitarian value. The concept also reflects the romantic conception of the independent wanderer, living a life in keeping with nature, an important Norwegian symbol in connection with the liberation of Norway as a sovereign state at the turn of the century. Still many Norwegians attribute the free individual in pristine nature as a symbol of Norwegian independence (Fitje 1996). Norway's first public hero, Fridtjof Nansen, admired the strong and independent child of nature, recalling in a speech in 1921 "a time when all a man should need to reside in the mountains for a few weeks was a matchbox and a fishing rod" (Frislid 1984: 164, [my translation]). However, wilderness life as an endurance test in the way Nansen emphasized it is not regarded as desirable today. In contrast to the extreme version, wilderness life in more common or light versions is often based on using different arrangements such as marked paths or tracks and tourist huts in connection with such activities as backpacking or cross-country skiing. These activities still reflect traditional Norwegian recreation, offer great nature adventures and are typical examples of activities encouraged by the authorities to be exercised in national parks.

Hence, when the Norwegian Government decided to focus on protecting the public right to free access to land as one main topic in connection with the European Year of Nature Conservation, the intention has been to safeguard the "Every Person's Right" and thereby stimulate more people to exercise the light versions of wilderness life. It seems that the Norwegian Government regards wilderness life as particularly well designed to promote knowledge of nature and strengthen the sense of responsibility towards nature conservation.

ADMINISTRATIVE PRINCIPLES FOR NATIONAL PARKS

In a Parliamentary White Paper (St.meld. nr 62. 1991-92), the government suggests conserving 46 new areas under the Conservation of Nature Act. At the end of 1993, 6.4 per cent of the total Norwegian territory was protected under the Conservation of Nature Act. The aim is to enlarge these protected areas to cover 12 to 13 per cent of Norway. None of the Norwegian national parks have been established as a direct measure to prevent an immediate threat to nature. The main objective for establishing national parks is to preserve untouched, or practically untouched, distinctive or beautiful landscapes for generations to come. As mentioned above, some national parks have the dual objective of protecting areas deserving of preservation, and offering recreation opportunities to the public. This does not imply that parks without a recreational purpose impose restrictions on the "Every Person's Right," but it is an important signal from the authorities that voluminous traffic is less desirable in some parks compared to others.

However, according to the preliminary strategy plan for the administration of national parks, (Direktoratet for naturforvaltning [Directorate of Nature Conservation] 1995), the "Every Person's Right," is to be considered in all parks and restrictions on wilderness life are only to be implemented for the sake of nature conservation when it is evident that recreational activities, although in correspondence with wilderness life, cause or threaten to cause damage to nature. As for new outdoor activities not related to traditional Norwegian wilderness life, restrictions within national parks will be strict. Founded on the Nature Conservation Act, such activities may be denied within national parks solely on the basis of presumptive evidence of harmful effects on nature, based on a "better safe than sorry" principle. This can be done without getting in conflict with the provisions of the Outdoor Recreation Act, since many of these activities do not represent elements of "Every Person's Right."[2]

The Norwegian Government is implementing an administrative regulation of the national parks reflecting the policy of balanced use and protection of nature reserves. One way of handling different user interests is to apply the principle of zoning. This principle distinguishes different areas within a national park that allow, or should we say invite, different use. However, zoning does not suggest a value grading of areas from a nature conservation point of view as every part of a national park is considered important to preserve (Direktoratet for naturforvaltning 1995: 76). It reflects the vulnerability of the areas as far as traffic carrying capacity is concerned.

The Norwegian administration of national parks operates with four different zones, but not all parks have to contain all four categories. However, when all the parks eventually have their own management plan the principle of zoning will represent a common framework and contribute to a uniform national management. This is believed to provide a more comprehensive picture where differences between the national parks become evident.

The first zone, described as the special preservation zone, represents areas in which admittance may be regulated and, if necessary, prohibited. Such zones normally represent relatively small, particularly vulnerable areas within a park. Until now no national park areas in Norway have been permanently closed for entrance; however, some areas are closed for limited periods, such as bird reservations during the nesting season and reindeer calving areas. In Hardangervidda National Park, Norway boasts the southernmost reindeer herd in the world. Norway has an international obligation to protect this herd, and one means to do so is to prevent contagious bovine abortion among reindeer which is caused by disturbances particularly from cross-country skiers. Obviously, in such areas traffic is unwanted. The second zone, the zone without any arrangements and encroachments, is open to traditional Norwegian wilderness life in the rough version. These areas are suitable for purists who want to experience unqualified wilderness. In such areas there are no arrangements to facilitate visitation. Visitors are supposed to get the feeling of entering an untouched area. Hence, the hikers in these areas must be very careful not to leave behind any traces. In order to maintain the impression of unspoiled wilderness, hikers are supposed to remove any provisional arrangements that might be required for crossing rivers, tenting, or building a fire; in other words, passage is based on the principle of trackless traffic. Such zones cover usually larger areas of national parks, particularly those parks without recreational use as a partial objective in its object clause. The third zone, labelled the user zone, implies that a certain amount of development is permitted, providing it supports traditional Norwegian wilderness life in the common or light version. Typical examples here would be marking paths or erecting cabins within a planned network of simple overnight stops. These arrangements are established first and foremost for the sake of safety, but also contribute to making hiking or cross-country skiing less fatiguing and more comfortable. Such user zones may cover small or large areas, and include fields traditionally used for trade, such as wood cutting or pasture. This type of zone is primarily to be found in parks with recreational use as a partial objective. The last zone, the zone with arrangements and encroachments, indicates that adjustments to special user interests are possible, for instance, larger tourism facilities such as well-appointed tourist hostels. Such zones cover only small areas, and are often found at the edge of a national park, usually with easy access to highways. As previously mentioned, it is important to emphasize that even though an area is categorized as the zone with arrangements and encroachments the area is regarded as valuable from a nature conservation point of view by the authorities. However, in most of these areas, various constructions were present previous to the establishment of the national park, and the policy in Norway has not been to demolish buildings, dams, power transmission lines and the like within areas which have been designated for conservation of nature including national parks.

The zoning is based on a set of criteria which reflects both the present environmental condition and the desirable future state, taking into account the accessibility to the area, topography, the traditional use of the area and its location and size. Preservation of biological diversity is always given primary consideration, and development is permitted only as long as no vital nature conservation interest is at stake.

Damage to nature from a nature conservation point of view has so far been reported to the authorities by ordinary users of the area, or by different supervision bodies superintending private interests in outlying areas. Hence, the supervision has until now been executed more or less by chance. However, the government proposed the establishment of a

Governmental Nature Supervision Body (Ot prp nr 30 1995-96). The aim is to make supervision of nature conservation more effective, and thereby attend to national environmental values, including preventing and opposing different forms of environmental crime in a more effective way. Supervision of national parks is supposed to constitute a considerable part of the duties for this body, but supervision may be executed also outside protected areas.

In the DNC 1995 strategic plan, recommendations are also given to implement zoning of adjacent areas. Outside national parks or other areas protected pursuant to the Nature Conservation Act, proposals to zoning are only guidelines for the land owners, whether they are private or public. This means, nevertheless, that further land might be subordinated to regulation, not under the Nature Conservation Act, but, as proposed in the strategic plan, introduced in regional planning by local authority pursuant to *Plan og byggningsloven av 14. juni 1985 nr. 77* (the Planning and Building Act). As mentioned, activities within these areas may also be supervised by the Nature Supervision Body.

ADMINISTRATIVE PRINCIPLES FOR WILDERNESS LIFE

The principles under which national parks are managed influence the opportunity for wilderness life but not to a very considerable extent. Some areas that were previously open to free traffic and prepared for light wilderness life might have become regulated or in some cases temporarily closed. Recently, a tourist hut owned by the Norwegian Travel Association was torn down and the path de-marked in order to prevent traffic in this particular area. By and large, the possibilities to pursue wilderness life within the national parks also in the light version remain good, but the national park administrative principles, warranted by the Nature Conservation Act, enable strict regulation if necessary. Over the last years it has become evident that sometimes there may be a clash of interests between preservation of the natural environment and wilderness life. Even if the land ethic rules are followed, the number of people enjoying the privileges of the "Every Person's Right" might become so large that environmental effects will gradually appear. Legal regulation is possible if the density of traffic is too high. Nevertheless, the Norwegian authorities seem to be reluctant to limit the "Every Person's Right" by establishing a set of criteria upon which potential visitors may be filtered, allowing some users into the area, while refusing others. The Norwegian authorities are more in favour of using selective information, deliberate layout of paths and other arrangements to channelling the traffic into areas already in use for recreational purposes and with a more robust natural environment.

These measures reflect a discussion on whether traffic should be concentrated in certain areas or dispersed. In the DNC 1995 strategic plan, the Directorate of Nature Conservation advocates concentration. From a nature conservation point of view it is preferred to concentrate nature tourism around the existing infrastructure, for instance marked paths, rather than to open virtually pristine wilderness to traffic. What is decisive for the choice of strategy is the extent, level and type of activity, in proportion to the vulnerability of the natural environment.[3] The proposed Governmental Nature Supervision Body is likely to be instructed to undertake responsibility for this kind of information and guidance within national parks.

Wilderness life is not only undertaken within national parks. Norway has large areas of uncultivated land not protected by the Act of Nature Conservation. In these areas the "Every Person's Right" is also in force, both the land ethic rules and the permission to use other people's land freely. In these areas activities are regulated by the Open Air Recreation Act. In the Open Air Recreation Act there is no direct reference to considerations of nature conservation. In a proposition to amend the Open Air Recreation Act, the government suggests a new first section, clearly stating that recreational activities must not be harmful to the natural environment (Ot prp nr 27 1995-1996). The government also suggests an amendment in Section 11 on traffic behaviour, enforcing a duty for everyone not to harm the nature environment.

The "Every Person's Right" takes effect on uncultivated land only. The difference between uncultivated and cultivated land is first and foremost how the land owner's right of disposal is managed. However, proprietary right does not give anyone a free hand as far as managing land is concerned. The Planning and Building Act demands management of land to be considered in a broader planning context by municipal authorities, and restrictions on the use of private land (e.g. alteration in use by cultivating uncultivated land) may be considerable. It is important to draw the attention to this act when discussing the framework for wilderness life in Norway. The Planning and Building Act is the most important tool for authorities to balance proprietary rights and public interests regarding the use of land outside protected areas under the Nature Conservation Act, including for the opportunities of pursuing wilderness life.

However, during the last years many people have claimed that areas particularly well-suited for wilderness life are sometimes managed by landowners in a manner not adequately favouring the interests of wilderness life. As early as 1986, the Norwegian Government addressed this topic. In a Parliamentary White Paper (St.meld. nr. 40. 1986-1987), the Department of the Environment discussed the need for a legal authority to protect areas for wilderness life. In a Hearing Document regarding a proposal for amending of the Open Air Recreation Act, January 1995, the Department of the Environment proposed the need for establishing more permanent protection of areas against different encroachments in order to improve the public's opportunities for hiking, tramping, hunting and fishing or for special arrangements for wilderness life purposes (Det Kongelige Miljøverndepartement 1995).

Particularly, as far as hunting and fishing are concerned, landowners regarded this proposal of legislation as a design against the proprietary right. The government accused landowners of excessive commercializing by pricing hunting and fishing so that the public at large is unable to enjoy these activities. The proposal raised political controversy, and it became uncertain whether the government would be able to convince the Parliament to pass a legal provision regulating the price level on hunting preserves or leasing fishing rights. Consequently, the proposal to amend the Open Air Recreation Act Section 34 to make it possible to protect private land for the sake of public recreation was not promoted in the proposition (Ot prp nr 27 1995-96). However, the suggested amendment of Section 34 is mentioned in the proposition, and the Department of the Environment announced that it will return to the matter at a later stage. Obviously, this is an important signal, and probably useful to be aware of, when discussing the prospects of executing wilderness life activities outside national parks in Norway.

NORWEGIAN NATURE CONSERVATION POLICY: IMPLICATIONS FOR ADVENTURE TOURISM

What implications does the framework described above have for establishing and operating adventure tourism products in Norway? Nature conservation, defined as preserving biological pluralism as well as safekeeping of the "Every Person's Right," both represents opportunities and limits for adventure tourism.

As a starting point, the Norwegian Government allows for a cautious exploitation of the national park system for the purpose of tourism (St. meld. nr. 62 1991-92). The national park system might for instance be used for the purpose of tourism by employing a number of selected parks in the marketing of Norway as a tourist destination. The existence of a national park in the region may be advantageous for the marketing of adventure tourism enterprises.

Before going further on the discussion of Norwegian nature conservation policy and its implications for adventure tourism, it may be useful to return to Hall's (1992) discussion of the concept. Hall offers an empirical classification of the concept, listing different adventure tourism activities (Hall 1992: 144):

backpacking (bushwalking, tramping)	bicycle-touring
cross-country skiing	fishing
hunting	mountain biking
hang-gliding	hot-air ballooning
mountaineering	orienteering
rappelling	river kayaking
rock-climbing	scuba diving
sailing	sky-diving
sea kayaking	spelunking
snowshoeing	whitewater canoeing
trekking	whitewater rafting

This list is incomplete as, for instance, glacier walking, a popular activity in Norway, should also be listed here. Some of the activities in Hall's list, also represent traditional wilderness life. Hunting and fishing, backpacking and rock-climbing, rappelling and cross-country skiing are all traditional activities deeply rooted in Norwegian culture.

Adventure tourism, understood as organized, commercialized activities, in the forms of traditional Norwegian wilderness life, and offering people an opportunity to challenge the natural forces, often calls for certain natural conditions, such as a physically demanding terrain, in order to present, for example, backpacking or cross-country skiing in a danger in safety concept. Within national parks, the opportunities to offer traditional Norwegian adventure tourism activities would consequently vary. Zones without any arrangements or encroachments would probably be the most suitable areas for exercising these activities, which in character usually are long-lasting, and require endurance and the ability to survive under primitive conditions. However, for some people hiking in Norwegian national park user zones might perhaps represent sufficient a challenge to be perceived as adventure tourism. From a nature conservation point of view, the latter would be preferred. The limitation on arrangements in the zones without any arrangements or encroachments intends, for one thing, to reduce traffic in the area. Hence, one might say that management arrangements to prevent traffic in a national park area paradoxically lead to making this area particularly well-suited for adventure tourism activities in the rough wilderness life version.

However, not all adventure tourism activities fall under the wilderness life heading in either the light or the rough version. Many popular activities such as para-gliding, hang-gliding and mountain biking, obviously do not have any relation to traditional Norwegian outdoor activities. Within national parks new adventure tourism activities are met with scepticism. Within national parks all activities requiring motorization (for instance, for transportation) are forbidden. According to the Management Plan for Jostedalen National Park the authorities are aware of the growing interest for new outdoor activities such as para-gliding, sky-diving, mountain biking, hang-gliding, whitewater canoeing and whitewater rafting. In the Management Plan it is explicitly stated that the authorities will examine to what extent such activities come into conflict with the rules of protection and the objective for establishing the national park as and when it becomes necessary. For that purpose overall use is monitored, especially the increase in new types of uses (Fylkesmannen i Sogn og Fjordane 1994: 55). Furthermore, the Jostedalen National Park management considers both para-gliding and hang-gliding as potentially harmful to nesting birds of prey, and mountain biking is considered to expose vegetation to hard wear (Fylkesmannen i Sogn og Fjordane 1994: 54-55). Hence, it is reasonable to presume that it will be somewhat difficult to obtain approval to offer new adventure tourism activities in Norwegian national parks. As already mentioned, recreational activities may be denied on the basis of presumptive evidence of harmful effects on the natural environment, based on the better safe than sorry principle.

The most important aspect about this classification of activities, as it appears in the Management Plan and in the DNC 1995 strategic plan, is that it expresses the opinion that all kinds of adventure tourism products within national parks should be examined and approved by the authorities in advance. Today regulations on this matter are insufficient in many national parks. What the authorities want is to establish a license system, which not only is based on an examination of the activities offered, but also involves an assessment of the operator's competence and skill. Within this system the authorities can ensure that all licensees possess adequate knowledge and the right attitude towards safety and nature preservation. Such a system obviously presupposes a national licence program which sets the standards against which the applicants can be measured. The need for a national licence program is, from the authorities' point of view, inevitable, and the establishment of such a program seems to have been given high priority in the DNC 1995 strategic plan for the administration of the national parks. Furthermore, it is suggested that a licence program also contain a training program. Moreover, the licence system should be based on annual reports from the licensees as a means of control, ensuring that the activities have been carried out in approved areas at the right time of year and with no more participants than allowed by the authorities.

In spite of the wish for a rather extreme regulatory system, the administrative authorities of nature conservation also express a positive attitude to commercialized nature-based tourist products within national parks. Adventure tourism may, as is pointed out in the DNC 1995 strategic plan, contribute to channelizing the traffic and disseminating knowledge about the natural environment as well as passing on the traditional Norwegian wilderness life culture. Hence, according to the DNC 1995 strategic plan, applicants with local connections will be favoured when it comes to the granting of licences for adventure tourism. Hence, in relation to the first issue, preserving biological diversity, the Norwegian Government seems to regard the adventure tourism industry as a potential partner with whom it can cooperate for the purpose of nature conservation. Commercial outfitters must therefore be prepared to accept both preceding assessment as well as succeeding control regarding the products offered and the persons implementing them.

It is reasonable to assume that most operators consent to the necessity of this kind of quality control. Furthermore, most people are also ready to accept that some areas have to be protected against use for the purpose of nature conservation. However, some of the operators may find the provision that licensees should preferentially have local connections somewhat unreasonable. The proposed regulation that is probably going to raise most disagreement is the stipulation of a maximum number of participants (tourists) in any one adventure tourism activity.

The clash of interests here appears obvious. In order to ensure that the adventure tourism enterprise is economic, operators need a certain number of paying participants. For the purpose of profit, it is reasonable to assume that operators want to attract as many tourists as possible. The number of participants might easily exceed what the authorities find acceptable from a nature conservation point of view. The problem is that when such disagreements arise it is difficult to define the limit for the carrying capacity of the natural environment, expressed in a fixed number of tourists participating in an activity. For this reason, it seems to be a good idea to encourage cooperation between the administrative authorities and the adventure tourism trade at an early stage, so that an agreement could be reached on the maximum number of participants in advance. Cooperation at an early stage could also contribute to appropriate channelling of the traffic, as well as developing adventure tourism products which offer guidance in relation to use and protection of nature.

In relation to the second topic, safeguarding the public right to free access to land, it is stated in the DNC 1995 strategic plan for the administration of national parks that adventure tourism products must not limit or come into conflict with the "Every Person's Right." Any adventure tourism arrangement within national parks must therefore not in any way hinder non-participants to enjoy the right to move freely in the area.

Obviously, the Norwegian nature conservation policy does not affect adventure tourism in the same way outside as inside national parks. However, for the sake of preserving biological diversity there are limits to the kind of activities that legitimately can be exercised. Generally, adventure tourism must in no way inflict damage on uncultivated land, whether inside or outside national parks. The use of motorized vehicles for transportation on uncultivated land is prohibited, and further regulations on the use of uncultivated land outside national parks are proposed. The Open Air Recreation Act protects, in Section One, the "Every Person's Right" by allowing everyone to walk on foot on other people's uncultivated land. Section Two establishes the right to ride and bike on roads and paths within uncultivated areas and everywhere in the mountain, if not prohibited on indicated stretches. Today the authority to regulate such traffic lies with the land owners, with consent from the municipal authorities. In the proposition on alterations in the Open Air Recreation Act, the government proposes that this kind of regulatory power be transferred to the municipal authorities, but in such a way that regulation demands consent from the land owner. The proposal emphasizes the importance of public involvement when reporting between conflicts such as different forms of traffic and nature conservation. It is explicitly stated in the proposition that the purpose of this amendment is to give the municipal authorities the possibility to intervene if riding or mountain biking causes damage to the natural environment (Ot prp nr 27 1995-96: 6).

Also with regard to safeguarding the "Every People's Right," Norwegian nature conservation policy holds implications for adventure tourism outside national parks. The most important signal is the intention of the Department of Environment to put a bill before Parliament to make expropriation of private land for the sake of public outdoor recreation possible. Although this proposal will not be passed this year, it is an important signal for the future. Fishing and hunting were the two first adventure tourism activities offered in Norway. For more than a century, the income from hunting preserves and leasing fishing rights has been of great importance for many farmers. The right to hunt and to fish in salmon rivers has been regulated since a long time, and has not been regarded to constitute parts of the "Every Person's Right." Hence, when the government in the longer term considers initiating measures which would not allow landowners to sell hunting preserves and leasing fishing rights at the full market value, in order to open up for the possibilities for everyone to enjoy these activities, this will certainly affect the prospect of running this kind of adventure tourism enterprises at a profit.

CONCLUSION

It seems obvious, as a starting point, to presume that conflicts between adventure tourism and nature conservation might easily arise. Within national parks the authorities may deny such activities for the sake of preserving biological diversity, without considering how well suited the area might be for establishment of an adventure tourism product. The differentiation of parks for various recreational purposes and the principle of zoning in order to protect biological diversity might have the opposite effect. For some forms of adventure tourism, an untouched and remote area is particularly attractive. Only adventure tourism activities which require motorization, for instance for transportation, are automatically prohibited within all national parks. Other forms of adventure tourism may be prohibited if substantial harm to the natural environment is foreseen. However, such judgments may be based on the better safe than sorry principle. According to official management documents, adventure tourism products based on traditional Norwegian wilderness life are to be favoured. It is also regarded an advantage if the operators in questions have a local connection. The authorities are currently preparing the announcement of a national licence program to ensure that the adventure tourism activities are exercised in accordance with the recommendations in the national park management plans, and that the operators possess adequate knowledge and skill. Under this program operators are expected to submit annual reports with information about when and where the activities took place and how many tourists participated in each activity. Providing these regulations are observed, the authorities regard adventure tourism operations as useful to preserve biological diversity. Adventure tourism could contribute to channelling visitor flow and disseminating knowledge about the natural environment. Some of these regulations, particularly the proposal to set a maximum number of participants in any one activity and the introduction of a compulsory annual report (which might easily result in much paper-work for the operators) are likely to raise conflicts. Arrangements for cooperation at an early stage in the process might bring about agreements on the issues.

As far as the safeguarding of "Every Person's Right" is concerned, this effort might also create a conflict with the adventure tourism industry. Reserving areas for such activities is not allowed, and the announced proposal to set the maximum price of hunting and fishing has produced a lot of bad feeling among landowners who depend on the income from rents. Nevertheless, "Every Person's Right" seems to be perceived as desirable also among the Norwegian adventure tourism operators.

All in all, it seems like the authorities are confronted with only minor tourism industry opposition to their attempts at establishing a set of regulations for the future administration of nature conservation. Although there will always be disagreements on how to weigh different interests, in the case of the Norwegian nature conservation policy, one must say that a general agreement seems to be prevailing.

There are many reasons for this general agreement. One reason is that most operators trading in adventure tourism today already have a local connection to the areas in which they are operating. Another reason is that adventure tourism based on traditional Norwegian "wilderness life" is favoured not only by the authorities, but also by the operators themselves. Last but not least, it is important to be aware of the fact that Norway has large areas of uncultivated land where adventure tourism, whether based on traditional wilderness life or not, may be practised providing, of course, the activities do not conflict with any of the regulations in the Nature Conservation Act. By implementing an overall national plan for the management of national parks that allow for local adjustments, improving the information system and ensuring cooperation between the different user interests at stake, the possibilities for preserving biological diversity, safeguarding "Every Person's Right" and giving commercialized adventure tourism enterprises acceptable working conditions in the future should be good.

NOTES

1. There are some exceptions to this general rule. Continuous camping for more than 48 hours must be permitted by the land owner in advance. Furthermore, on minor, limited areas prepared with arrangements for recreational activities, for instance a camping site, the Open Air Recreation Act recognizes the land owner's right to collect a site charge.

2. Some of these activities may actually be prohibited by other laws, such as: Lov av 29. mai 1981 nr. 38 om viltet, "Viltloven," (the Wildlife Act) and lov av 10. juni 1977 nr. 73 om motorferdsel i utmark og vassdrag, (the Act relating to motorized traffic in marginal land and water courses).

3. It is obvious that capacity levels are influenced by two types of factors: the characteristics of the touristic activities and the characteristics of the destination. Other researchers have focused on socio-demographic traits distinguishing the tourists when dealing with this subject (Gooding 1975; O'Reilly 1986; Aho 1994). However, the focus in this article is more on what tourists do, not so much on who they are. Of course, there is certainly a connection between the two, but in the end it is the human activities that matter as far as nature conservation is concerned.

REFERENCES

Aho, S.K. 1994. Nature based tourism in the framework of sustainable development. *Arktisen Keskuksen Julkaisuja 6*, 5-7.

Anderson, D.N. 1983. Packaging of the outdoor/wilderness experience: Does it hold implications for national parks? *Park News 19*(1) 5-7.

Det Kongelige Miljøverndepartement, 1995. Forslag til endringer i lov 28. juni 1957 om friluftslivet - høring.

Direktoratet for naturforvaltning, 1995. Strategiplan for forvaltning av nasjonalparker, (foreløpig utgave).

Fitje, A. 1996. *Naturbasert opplevelsesturisme på Bornholm - Produkttilbud, aktørstruktur og sammarbeidsprosesser*, Rapport 3/1996, Bornholms forskningscenter, Rønne.

Frislid R. in Semmingsen et al. (red.). 1984. *I velstandens tegn*, Norges kulturhistorie, (vol. 7), Oslo: Aschehoug.

Fylkesmannen i Sogn og Fjordane, 1994. Forvaltningsplan for Jostedalsbreen nasjonalpark, rapport nr. 3.

Gooding, E. 1975. *Effects of tourism upon the environment*, Paper presented at *Regional Seminar on Caribbean Tourism*, Nassau.

Hall, C.M. 1992. Adventure, sport and health tourism. In B. Weiler & C.M. Hall (eds.). *Special Interest Tourism*, pp. 143-144. London: Belhaven Press.

Hultkrantz, L. & R. Mortazavi. 1992. *Recreation, tourism and property rights to land: The economics of public access rights in Sweden*. Umeå Economic Studies No. 305, University of Umeå.

Lov av 29. mai 1981 nr. 38 om viltet.

Lov av 10. juni 1977 nr. 73 om motorferdsel i utmark og vassdrag.

Lov av 19. juni 1970 nr. 63 om naturvern.

Lov av 28. juni 1957 nr. 16 om friluftslivet.
NOU, 1983:45, *Friluftsliv og vassdragsvern*. Oslo: Universitetsforlaget.

O'Reilly, A.M. 1986. Tourism carrying capacity: Concepts and issues. *Tourism Management*, 7(4) 254-258.

Ot prp nr 27. 1995-96. Om lov om endringer i lov av 28. juni 1957 nr. 16 om friluftslivet.

Ot prp nr 30. 1995-96. Om lov om statlig naturoppsyn.

Pedersen, K. 1993. Gender, nature and technology: Changing trends in "wilderness life" in northern Norway. In R. Riewe & J. Oakes, (eds.), *Human ecology: Issues in the North*, Vol. 3, pp. 53-66. DeJong Printing Ltd. *Occasional Publication Series* No. 32.

Plan og byggningslov av 14. juni 1985 nr 77.

Smith, S.L.J. 1990. *Tourism analysis: A handbook* (2nd ed.). Essex: Longman Scientific & Technical.

St.meld. nr. 62. 1991-92. Ny landsplan for nasjonalparker og andre større verneområder i Norge.

St.meld. nr. 40. 1986-87. Om Friluftsliv.

A RATIONALE FOR TOURISM CODES OF CONDUCT FOR THE ARCTIC REGION

Peter Mason
Massey University

INTRODUCTION

To a great extent it is still possible to view the Arctic as a resource frontier (Hall & Johnston 1995; Mason 1994; Hall 1987). As yet most development has been limited in areal extent and tends to be concentrated in relatively few locations, though here activity is often intensive (Macklin 1991; Sugden 1982). Although tourism development is relatively recent, Snowman (1993: 182) indicates its growing importance in relation to other Arctic activities:

> the older preoccupations of the Arctic rim—sovereignty, defence, mineral exploitation—appear to be receding as new issues take their place. Everywhere nowadays the talk is about . . . the movement and conservation of animals and of fish, environmental pollution, climatic monitoring, aboriginal rights . . . or how best to develop Arctic tourism.

The nature of the Arctic region and attractions for tourists

The Arctic region has been variously defined, but there is no single universally accepted definition (Sage 1986). A commonly accepted approach is to use the tree line to distinguish the Arctic from the sub-Arctic (Bone 1992). This boundary is based on climate and soil, with a fairly close link between the $10°$ C July isotherm and the treeline. North of the tree line is the treeless or semi-treeless tundra. The existence of permafrost, which is a product of the climate, is important in definitions in Siberia and Canada (Sage 1986). In Alaska and Europe the Arctic Circle tends to be used as the boundary (Johnston 1995; Snepenger & Moore 1989). Recently, in an attempt to classify areas at risk and in need of protection, definitions have used a combination of climatic and biogeographical data (CAFF 1994). As Johnston (1995) points out, definitions of the Arctic are culturally and historically based constructs. One important construct, which relates to climatic factors and is used in tourism marketing, is the idea of the Arctic region being the land of the midnight sun (Jacobsen 1994), although some areas marketed as Arctic, such as Iceland, are in fact sub-Arctic and do not enjoy the conditions of the midnight sun. A generally agreed definition, involving reference to biogeographical factors such as the treeline, could assist in the identification of key features of the Arctic and hence its marketing for tourism.

A major appeal of the Arctic region for tourists is its image as a polar wilderness (Johnston 1995). Sugden (1982) indicates that this perception of the region is based predominantly on a temperate view. This view sees the region as both hostile and fragile (Sugden 1989). Johnston (1995) indicates that the perception of the environment as clean and unsullied by human activity—a pristine environment—is an important attraction. Bronsted (1994) also claims that it is this notion of a vast wilderness, relatively unvisited by tourists and almost free of a human population, that leads to the perception that the region provides great scope for recreation, adventure and enjoyment. Viken (1993) indicates another attraction when claiming the Arctic is perceived as being at the end of the world both geographically and culturally and is viewed by tourists as a place to escape from their hectic urban existence to reflect on life. Lopez (1986) supports this view that the Arctic is a place to retreat from alienated western life styles and believes responding to Arctic nature offers visitors a way to have more contact with their inner selves. Johnston (1995: 29) argues the Arctic carries mystic symbolism and it encourages contemplation about the links between humans, the earth and the universe. As she states: "It can be an awe-inspiring reminder of the connectedness of the global environment...."

The indigenous peoples in the Arctic are part of the region's tourist appeal. The people themselves are attractions for visitors, as are their artifacts and the manifestations of their activity, such as the reindeer herding of the Sami. The indigenous people are usually viewed by visitors as part of the Arctic environment and living in harmony with it (Mason 1994). This view is summed up well by a British visitor who subsequently became a resident in the Norwegian area of Finnmark.

> What fascinates me . . . is the Sami's bond with the wilds. Nature has been strong enough to determine their lives. It has shaped their characters, their language, their work (Hay Jones 1989: 209).

The scale of Arctic tourism

Although tourism in the Arctic is not on the scale of the mass tourism of the Mediterranean region, hundreds of thousands of tourists visit northern circumpolar destinations each year (Johnston 1995). Table 1 provides an indication of tourist numbers for selected locations in the Arctic and the sub-Arctic in the early 1990s.

Table 1.   Tourist Numbers in the Arctic and sub-Arctic

Northern Scandinavia	500,000
Yukon (Canada)	177,000
Northwest Territories (Canada)	56,000
Iceland	129,000
Greenland	6,000
Arctic Alaska	25,000

(Source: Johnston 1995)

Tourism numbers are likely to increase in both the short- and long-term (Colin 1994; Butler 1994). Reasons for the increase in tourist numbers are linked partly to greater disposable income and more leisure time (Mason 1994). Also recent years have seen improvements in transportation allowing greater accessibility (Butler 1994; Johnston 1995). A very recent and important spur to increased tourism in the Arctic is the political change in what was the U.S.S.R. (Hall & Johnston 1995). These combined effects will lead to more international and domestic tourism in the Arctic. There is likely to be an increase in international air tourism to, for example, Greenland, Iceland, Alaska and Russia, cross border land-based and air borne tourism in Scandinavia and between Scandinavia and Russia, and also increasing amounts of domestic tourism in Russia itself.

Environmental impacts of tourism

The fragility of the Arctic and its sensitivity to tourism impacts is still a matter for debate. Colin (1994) provides a reason for this when he argues that insufficient monitoring of impacts of tourism has been conducted and there is a need for more data. A study of the recovery rate of Alaskan Arctic tundra, which was not focusing specifically on tourism impacts, concluded that most single-event disturbances result in recovery, but multiple-event or cumulative disturbances are far more damaging to ecosystems (Walker et al. 1987). Much tourism activity would seem to fit into this cumulative disturbance category. Sugden (1982) claims that the Arctic's sensitivity to environmental change has been overstated and is partly based on a temperate perception. Johnston (1995: 28) argues that despite the 'temperate' bias towards Arctic issues: "there can be no doubt that polar ecosystems are susceptible to change and/or degradation from excessive or inappropriate tourism."

Colin (1994) claims that Arctic vegetation is particularly fragile and recovery from damage is very slow and he also argues that the destruction to ecosystems usually occurs rapidly, but may take decades rather than years to redress. This view is supported by Macklin (1991) who indicates that the imprint of a school's expedition camp made in 1970 in Norway was still visible more than 20 years later, as bare patches on the Arctic heath, and by Viken (1995a) who claims, in relation to Svalbard, that it will take hundreds of years for vehicle tracks to disappear from the tundra. Despite the fact that tourism related environmental damage is presently very small in scale in comparison with the impacts of large industries such as oil extraction, Colin (1994) claims that because of the sensitivity of ecosystems, even the smallest change in some Arctic habitats could cause major long-term effects in plant and animal populations.

Tourist litter and waste are becoming a significant problem in the Arctic and this is partly due to the lack of a system for litter removal and/ or the unwillingness of visitors to remove their rubbish (Umbreit 1991; Mason 1994). As Valentine (1992) points out improper litter disposal can create health hazards for wildlife and people, cause behaviour changes in animals and reduce the quality of the tourist experience. One of the tourism management concerns in Canada's Yukon territory is the disposal of waste (Johnston & Madunic 1995). In a study of over 500 visitors to the Yukon in the early 1990s, as many as 28 per cent reported negative impacts of tourism on the environment, with litter specifically referred to as a negative impact by 14 per cent (Johnston & Madunic 1995). This survey also reported an awareness by some tourists of the incompatibility between the pristine polar environment and litter, and a recognition by them that they, as tourists, were contributing to the environmental damage. Johnston and Madunic (1995) indicate that the presence of litter and other negative effects has not yet reduced the demand for tourist experiences in the Yukon.

Damage can also be caused by vehicles crossing the sensitive Arctic land surface. There is growing concern on the Norwegian island of Spitsbergen about the unregulated use of the snow scooter (Umbreit 1991; Abbot 1991). There is only a small resident population of 3,300 on the Svalbard archipelago, but visitors during the short summer season can increase the population by more than ten-fold (Abbot 1991). Tourists make use of snow scooters to travel around and these can have a damaging effect on spring and summer plant growth, particularly where snow cover is thin. This largely unregulated use of snow scooters has led the Norwegian environmental organization, Naturvern Forbundett, to argue against any increase in tourist numbers (Abbot 1991). Viken (1995a) reports on a survey of over 200 visitors to Svalbard, in the early 1990s, in which 30 per cent indicated that pollution and evidence of human damage to the environment were problems that affected tourism, although visitors believed these problems were not predominantly caused by tourist activities. Viken (1995a) believes that as yet the damage caused by tourism is small, but supports the view of Kaltenborn (1991) that a widespread consensus exists that, in relation to future tourism development on Svalbard, ecological and cultural sustainability must be guiding principles.

Socio-cultural impacts of tourism

It is often the claim of governments and tour operators that tourism will bring economic gain to destination regions. This argument can be particularly significant in areas where older industries are dying—Svalbard with a declining mining industry would be an Arctic example—or in locations which are relatively new to tourism and where few alternative economic activities are seen to have potential (Johnston 1995). Greenland is an example of an Arctic location with a young tourist industry and it is attempting to expand this activity greatly in the next ten years, from about 5,000 to 35,000 visitors annually by 2005. The chief benefits for Greenland, it is argued, will be increased jobs and income (Bronsted 1994). Yet Smith (1989) claims that there is a good deal of evidence to support the idea of economic leakage of tourism revenue from the Arctic and indicates that much money paid for an Arctic visit goes to tour operators, carriers and package holiday providers outside the region itself.

Another problem relating to tourism impacts on indigenous culture is that tourists may view members of host populations in the same way that they view wildlife and scenery, as a commodity to be consumed. This has been discussed widely in relation to other parts of the world (see, for example, Urry 1990; Smith 1989; Krippendorf 1987). Hall (1987) suggests this process is happening in the Arctic and sees particular problems with the way indigenous people are viewed and then marketed by the tourist industry.

> The danger is that the peoples of the north will become human animals in a cultural zoo, mere objects of curiosity for adventurous southerners wealthy enough to enjoy the temptations of glossy travel magazines, luxury cruises through the icebergs, reindeer round-ups or photographic safaris amongst the walrus and polar bears (Hall 1987: 217).

Smith (1989) echoes this concern and discusses the need for local communities to maximize economic benefit from tourism and yet also to be able to accurately represent their culture. She discusses the use of non-native guides in a location in Alaska, during the 1970s, when traditional activities were being demonstrated. This occurred when tourism was not controlled locally; when a local indigenous group took control of tourism in the late 1970s there was far more encouragement for the use of locally-owned businesses and workers. This, Smith (1989) argues, enables not only more economic benefit to accrue to the community but also allows them to demonstrate their own culture, in the way that they wish, which should minimize cultural damage.

In relation to Norway, Viken (1995b) argues that over the last 20 years much of the presentation of Sami culture has been by those who have lost their Sami roots or by non-Samis. He claims this has led to more commercialization, the presentation of "faked" culture and economic benefits accruing to these rather than more traditional Sami groups. Hall and Johnston (1995) also discuss the annoyance caused to the Sami community, when on a rare and unusual occasion, non-Sami guides were used to interpret Sami lifestyles to tourists in Finland. Hall and Johnston (1995) use this example to indicate the need for local control of tourism in the Arctic.

Many forms of Arctic tourism appear to complement local lifestyles (Johnston 1995). Despite this, there is a potential problem in the differing ways tourists and local people view wildlife. Johnston (1995) illustrates this potential conflict through reference to anecdotal evidence in which it is suggested tourists may wish to shoot wildlife with their camera, while local indigenous people may wish to shoot the animal in question with a rifle. These differing value systems as demonstrated in this example are likely to be significant in relation to tourism development.

These examples indicate that any discussion about the future direction of tourism in the Arctic has to include not only reference to environmental concerns, but also must consider socio-cultural impacts and the role of indigenous people.

Codes of conduct

Codes of conduct are usually part of a process attempting to regulate tourism. There are, however, differences between regulations and codes of conduct. Regulations usually have some form of legal status (Stonehouse 1990). Codes of conduct, codes of practice and guidelines, although attempting to regulate tourism, tend not to have the legal status of actual regulations. They are more likely to be voluntary and may be self-imposed. There are few examples of legally-backed regulations pertaining specifically to tourism, but a variety of codes of conduct in tourism have existed for at least the last 20 years and this section of the paper investigates the nature and use of such codes of conduct.

There are a number of discrete target groups for codes of conduct (UNEP 1995; Mason & Mowforth 1995) and these groups are as follows: visitors, the tourism industry, and members of host communities. The most significant target audience in terms of sheer number of codes is the visitor; the World Travel and Tourism Research Council (1995), for example, lists almost 80 visitor codes in use around the world in 1994. A number of codes have also been prepared for use by those directly involved in the tourist industry and more recently codes have been prepared for the use of host populations.

In addition to there being a variety of target audiences for codes of conduct there are a range of different authors. A significant number of codes have been written by concerned individuals and non-governmental organisations, while government bodies and the tourism industry itself have until recently not been very active in producing codes (Mason & Mowforth 1995).

Codes of conduct frequently fail to specify either their broad aims or more specific objectives (Mason 1994). UNEP conducted a survey of voluntary environmental tourism codes in 1992 and received information on 30 codes used by countries and international associations, and was able to deduce a number of specific objectives (UNEP 1995). UNEP produced, in summary form, five objectives of codes, which are as follows:

- to serve as a catalyst for dialogue between government and other bodies involved in tourism;
- to create an awareness in government and the industry of the need for sound environmental management;
- to heighten awareness amongst tourists of the need for appropriate behaviour;
- to make host populations aware of the need for environmental protection; and,
- to encourage co-operation between governments agencies, host communities, industry and NGOs (UNEP 1995: 8).

Tourism codes are not only concerned with environmental issues. A number of visitor codes, for example, make reference to socio-cultural matters, such as respect for local religious beliefs, and codes with industry as the audience frequently refer to the need for appropriate training and honest marketing of tourism products (Mason & Mowforth 1995).

Tourism codes of conduct in the Arctic

A small number of tourism codes currently exist and are in use in the Arctic and sub-Arctic regions. Those that exist tend to be aimed at visitors although some exist with tour operators and governments as target audiences. These codes have been produced by a number of different authors. A selection of codes is discussed below.

A number of separate regions within the Arctic have codes of conduct. Probably the location with the strictest regulations is the Norwegian archipelago of Svalbard (Johnston 1995; Viken 1995a). The regulations, produced by the Norwegian Ministries of the Environment and Justice, have visitors as their target audience and were first developed in 1983. The regulations aim to protect the natural environment and historical remains of the islands, as well as to provide safety for visitors. Umbreit (1991) details the specific instructions contained in the Svalbard regulations. He indicates they relate to the conditions under which vehicles can and cannot be used, the need to remove all litter, advice on how not to damage vegetation, and instructions to avoid disturbing birds and other wildlife.

The Norwegian sub-Arctic region of Trondheim has a code which was also developed by the Norwegian Ministry of the Environment. This code appears on posters and in guide books to the area. The code is much less admonitory than that for Svalbard and suggests visitors should feel welcome in the environment of the region and make use of much of what it has to offer, before giving instructions on what visitors should not do there (Mason & Mowforth 1995).

Regulations affecting tourism have been developed in the Northwest Territories and Yukon of Canada. These regulations relate to activities such as hunting and access to and protection of designated sites of special environmental or heritage value, but they are aimed at residents as well as visitors. More specific regulations aimed at visitors are in use in national parks within the Northwest Territories where visitors are required to register and take part in a visitor orientation programme, while outside the park areas a voluntary system of travel registration is administered by the Royal Canadian Mounted Police (Johnston & Hall 1995).

There is particular concern about the impacts of expeditions in some parts of Arctic Canada. The Department of Indian Affairs and Northern Development publishes a 'Guide for Expeditions to Northern and Arctic Canada' which acts as a visitor code in that it not only gives visitors information and practical advice, but also brings together all legislation relating to hunting, wildlife and environmental protection (Johnston 1993). The Canadian government has also demonstrated that it intends to take the environmental effects of expeditions seriously enough to back up regulations with insurance or bond requirements, similar to the arrangements in place for travel on the Ice Cap in Greenland.

Tourism codes of conduct, developed for use in Svalbard, Trondheim and the Canadian Arctic, have been aimed predominantly at visitors. In Finland, however, the Finnish Tourist Board has produced a set of guidelines aimed at the tourist industry (UNEP 1995). These guidelines are not aimed specifically at tour operators in the Arctic but certainly have relevance to the region. The guidelines, it is claimed, are an attempt to promote sustainable tourism. They focus on a number of environmental, economic and social concerns and can be summarized as follows:

- the need to build environmental viewpoints into planning for new tourism development;
- the need to recognize the importance of local culture and traditions;
- the need to make use of local products and services where possible;
- the need to reduce traffic noise and related problems;
- the need to give attention to landscape management;
- the need to provide staff with appropriate training;
- the encouragement for the use of public transport where possible;
- the encouragement of 'human power' rather than mechanical power where possible;
- advice and instructions on following paths and avoiding sensitive environments; and,
- the need for honest marketing of tourist products.

As well as these key principles, the guidelines suggest a number of practical measures to achieve sustainable tourism. These measures refer specifically to the use of water and energy and to waste disposal, and they emphasize conservation, recycling and appropriate disposal of litter (UNEP 1995).

In 1993, WWF Sweden, in collaboration with the Swedish Environmental Protection Agency, established a working group within the Swedish Tourist Industry to investigate ecotourism and sustainability and this group produced 'Ten Principles on Ecotourism' (Sharp 1995). These principles do not apply solely to the Arctic but include recommendations on the need for tour operators to employ an environmental officer, the need to educate visitors, and statements on the need to ensure that tourism benefits the local economy and the need to promote socially and ecologically sustainable tourism. A Swedish ecotourism operator claims that these ten principles should be applicable not only to the Swedish Arctic, but also to the Arctic region as a whole (WWF Arctic Programme 1995).

A number of parallels have been drawn between the Arctic and the Antarctic in relation to tourism issues (Hall & Johnston 1995; Stonehouse 1990; Mason 1994). There are clearly environmental similarities, and despite the Arctic having indigenous peoples, whilst Antarctica does not, the nature of tourism activities and impacts in each area leads to parallels in management strategies (Hall & Johnston 1995). An important difference between the two regions relates to sovereignty. In the Arctic, a number of countries have sovereignty over land, coastal waters and open oceans, whilst sovereignty is disputed in Antarctica. The disputed sovereignty in the Antarctic has led to the creation of the Antarctic Treaty System (ATS) which has enabled management strategies in relation to a number of environmental issues to be developed. Hence unlike the Arctic, under the ATS, Antarctica has very detailed regulations and recommendations on tourism (Enzenbacher 1994, 1995).

The Antarctic has codes of conduct for both visitors and tour operators. The code of conduct for tour operators was developed by the International Association of Antarctic Tour Operators (IAATO) and provides detailed tourism management guidelines on the continent (Stonehouse 1994; Enzenbacher 1995). Instructions and advice are aimed at guides and those operators bringing ship-borne tourists to the Antarctic. They are in the form of an 18-point checklist which gives guidance on ways operators can manage visits appropriately to minimize environmental damage. IAATO has also produced guidelines for visitors in an attempt to ensure that tourists do not disturb wildlife, do not damage plants, remove litter, do not interfere with scientific work, pay respect to heritage sites, do not smoke, and that shore parties stay with their guides (Enzenbacher 1995). A simplified code aimed at both visitors and operators, 'The Antarctic Travellers Code,' has also been produced (Stonehouse 1994). This code is a useful summary of the main concerns in relation to tourism management in Antarctica (Figure 1).

The Arctic currently lacks tourism codes covering the whole region, although a draft visitor code has been produced (Mason 1994). This code (Figure 2) has some similarities with codes for the Antarctic. The message of the code focuses on a number of environmental and cultural issues, including instructions on the use of vehicles, prevention of disturbance and damage to wildlife and habitats, the control of fishing and hunting, the proper disposal of waste and the need to respect indigenous cultures.

The code has the following aims:
- to raise awareness amongst visitors of environmental issues in the Arctic;
- to generally inform and educate visitors;
- to make visitors aware of environmental and cultural issues; and,
- to be included as part of an overall tourism management strategy for the Arctic region (Mason 1994).

Figure 1. Antarctic Traveller's Code

Antarctic visitors
- MUST NOT leave footprints in fragile mosses, lichens or grasses.
- MUST NOT dump plastic or other, non-biodegradable garbage overboard or onto the Continent.
- MUST NOT violate the seals', penguins', or seabirds' *Personal Space*
  —start with a "baseline" distance of 15 ft (5 m) from penguins, seabirds, and true seals and 50 ft (18 m) from fur seals
  —give animals the right-of-way
  —stay on the edge of, and don't walk through, animal groups
  —back-off if necessary
  —never touch the animals
- MUST NOT interfere with protected areas or scientific research
- MUST NOT take souvenirs

Antarctic tour companies
- SHOULD apply the Antarctic Traveller's Code to all officers, crew, staff, and passengers
- SHOULD utilize one (1) guide or leader for every twenty (20) passengers
- SHOULD employ experienced and sensitive on-board leadership
- SHOULD use vessels that are safe for Antarctic ice conditions
- SHOULD adopt a shipwide anti-dumping pledge

Source: Stonehouse 1990.

Figure 2. A Draft Visitor Code for the Arctic

Conserve resources
- Please leave wildlife habitats alone; where this is not possible, keep disturbance to a minimum.
- Please do not take plants, animals, and other samples from nature—these must be left where found.
- Please limit damage by vehicles such as snowscooters.
- Hunting and fishing are under the strict control of national and regional authorities. Permits can be obtained from * * *
- Accessibility to nature reserves and national parks is strictly restricted through the use of permits. These are obtainable from * * * * * * * *

Stop pollution
- Please do not leave behind any equipment or litter—this will decay only slowly, may injure wildlife, and could cost you a fine!
- All materials that have been brought in, and not consumed during your visit, should be taken out.

Respect indigenous cultures
- Almost all indigenous cultures in the Arctic have developed in harmony with nature, without over exploiting resources or creating unnecessary waste. Pay respect to these cultures.

Be a Guest
- Please do not expect to come to a wilderness and find all home comforts supplied.
- Be a true guest—one who is welcome in the landscape and amongst the local people.

Enjoy yourself and remember:
Take nothing but photographs,
Kill nothing but time,
Leave nothing but footprints.

Source: Mason 1994.

Issues in relation to the use of codes of conduct

A number of problems in relation to the use of tourism codes of conduct have been noted. Mason and Mowforth (1995) discuss four main areas of concern and these are: monitoring take up and effectiveness; the use of codes as a marketing tool; the need for co-ordination; and, whether there should be self-regulation or external regulation.

The UNEP report on Environmental Codes of Conduct in Tourism (UNEP 1995) argues that codes must be implemented to be effective, but also indicates that most tourism codes tend to be poorly implemented. The UNEP report also claims that it is essential to measure the effects of codes and that those who develop codes should follow up the implementation with an assessment of effects and make sure findings are reported. Enzenbacher (1995) argues that as yet little is known of the effects of tourism or tourism management regimes in the Antarctic and states that a tourism observer programme as part of the ATS could be an effective method to monitor the implementation of tourism regulations. Perhaps there are also lessons here for the Arctic region, with the need to monitor take up and effectiveness of the few codes that exist. Mason (1994) for example suggests in relation to his 'Draft Visitor Code for the Arctic' that the monitoring of its implementation could be achieved by observation of tourist behaviour, interviews and postal questionnaires.

Colin (1994) indicates that many separate organizations, groups and individuals are attempting to protect the Arctic from tourism impacts, but argues the need for greater co-ordination. Colin claims that despite the fact that different communities have different concerns there is a real need for co-ordination as this would at least lead to the discovery of common ground. Johnston and Hall (1995) refer specifically to codes of conduct when calling for co-ordination of tourism regulation efforts and suggest that there may need to be some form of international agreement in the Arctic on regulating tourism development.

There seems little evidence at present, mainly because so few codes exist in the Arctic, that they are being used for marketing holidays in the region. As so few codes currently exist, the issue of self-regulation or external regulation is not yet of great significance. Johnston and Madunic (1995) report that the regional tourism industry in Canada's Yukon has undertaken self-regulation by adopting an operator code of ethics. Mason and Mowforth (1995) argue that the motivation behind self-regulation is the tourist industry either wishing to appear to be acting responsibly in advance of imposed regulation, or attempting to stave off external regulation. Evidence from locations outside the Arctic

(McKercher 1993; Forsyth 1993; Porritt 1995) suggests that external regulation is likely to be far more effective than self-regulation.

Valentine (1992) suggests another very important factor and argues that it will be necessary to employ a number of codes of conduct with different audiences, simultaneously. He believes a code aimed at visitors should be used in conjunction with another aimed at operators and that a code for one group on its own would not be effective. Valentine also suggests codes should be employed as a part of a wider tourism management strategy. Johnston and Hall (1995) support this view of code production and use in relation to the development of Arctic tourism.

CONCLUSION

The Arctic has important natural and cultural attractions for visitors. Tourism is already a significant activity in the Arctic region and is set to increase. There is evidence of damage to the environment and disruption to indigenous cultures as result of tourism in the region, but this is not as yet at the level to discourage visitors. Strategies will need to be developed to sustain tourism and, at the same time, sustain the Arctic environment and indigenous cultures. Codes of conduct in tourism can assist in this process and Hall and Johnston (1995) argue the need for continued development and implementation of codes of conduct for the Arctic. As they state "visitor and operator codes of conduct are and will continue to be an integral component of any polar tourism management regime" (Johnston & Hall 1995: 310).

REFERENCES

Abbot, S. 1991. The natural beauty that could turn ugly. *The Independent*. London, July 7 1991.

Bone, R. 1992. *The geography of the Canadian North: Issues and challenges*. Toronto: Oxford University Press.

Bronsted, H. 1994. Tourism activities in Greenland. In C. Kempf & L. Girard (eds.). *Le tourisme dans les régions polaires/Tourism in polar regions*, Colmar: Conseil Géneral du Haut Rhin.

Butler, R.W. 1994. Tourism in the Canadian Arctic: Problems of achieving sustainability. In C. Kempf & L. Girard (eds.). *Le tourisme dans les régions polaires/Tourism in polar regions*, Colmar: Conseil Géneral du Haut Rhin.

CAFF. 1994. *The state of protected areas in the circumpolar Arctic: Conservation of Arctic flora and fauna*, Habitat Conservation Report No. 1, Trondheim, The Directorate for Nature Management.

Colin, M. 1994. Ecotourism and conservation policies in Canada. In C. Kempf & L. Girard (eds.). *Le tourisme dans les régions polaires/Tourism in polar regions*, Colmar: Conseil Géneral du Haut Rhin.

Enzenbacher, D.J. 1995. The regulation of Antarctic tourism. In C.M. Hall & M.E. Johnston (eds.). *Polar tourism: Tourism in the Arctic and Antarctic regions*, pp. 179-216. Chichester: Wiley.

Enzenbacher, D.J. 1994. Tourism at Faraday Station: An Antarctic case study. *Annals of Tourism Research 21*(2), pp. 303-317.

Forsyth, T. 1993. *Sustainable tourism: Moving from theory to practice*. Godalming: World Wide Fund for Nature.

Hall, C.M. & M.E. Johnston. 1995. Pole to pole: Tourism issues, impacts and the search for a management regime. In C.M. Hall & M.E. Johnston (eds.). *Polar tourism: Tourism in the Arctic and Antarctic regions*, pp. 1-26. Chichester: Wiley.

Hall, S. 1987. *The fourth world: The Arctic and its heritage*. London: Hodder & Stoughton.

Hay Jones, D. 1989. *Night times & light times*. London: Hodder & Stoughton.

Jacobsen, J.K.S. 1994. *Arctic tourism and global trends*, Research Report No. 37, Lakehead University Centre for Northern Studies, Thunder Bay, Canada.

Johnston, M.E. 1995. Patterns and issues in Arctic and sub-Arctic tourism. In C.M. Hall & M.E. Johnston (eds.). *Polar tourism: Tourism in the Arctic and Antarctic regions*, pp. 27-42. Chichester: Wiley.

Johnston, M.E. 1993. *Tourism and the regulation of adventure travel in the Canadian Arctic*. Paper presented at the *Fifth World Wilderness Conference - Arctic Tourism Symposium*, Tromso, Norway, September 24-October 1.

Johnston M.E. & C.M. Hall. 1995. Visitor management and the future of tourism in polar regions. In C.M. Hall & M.E. Johnston (eds.). *Polar tourism: Tourism in the Arctic and Antarctic regions*, pp. 297-313. Chichester: Wiley.

Johnston, M.E. & D. Madunic. 1995. Waste disposal and the wilderness in the Yukon Territory. In C.M. Hall & M.E. Johnston (eds), *Polar tourism: Tourism in the Arctic and Antarctic regions*, pp. 85-100. Chichester: Wiley.

Kaltenborn, B. 1991. *Forvaltingsplan for turisme of friluftsliv på Svalbard*. Lillehammer: Norsk Institutt for Naturforskning.

Krippendorf, J. 1987. *The holidaymakers*. London: Heinemann.

Lopez, B. 1986. *Arctic dreams*. London: Picador.

Macklin, D. 1991. Footprints forever. *Geographical Magazine*, July 1991, pp. 121-4.

Mason, P. 1994. A visitor code for the Arctic? *Tourism Management, 15* (2), pp. 93-97.

Mason, P. & M. Mowforth. 1995. *Codes of conduct in tourism*, Occasional Paper 1, Department of Geographical Sciences, University of Plymouth, U.K.

McKercher, R. 1993. Some fundamental truths about tourism: Understanding tourism's social and environmental impacts. *Journal of Sustainable Tourism, 1*(1), pp 6-16.

Porritt, J. 1995. *Education and regulation for tourism*. Paper given at the conference *Managing tourism: Education and regulation for tourism*, Commonwealth Institute, London, November 16.

Sage, B. 1986. *The Arctic and its wildlife*. London: Croom Helm.

Sharp, H. 1995. WWF's Sweden's project "Eco-tourism." *Arctic Bulletin* (WWF) *3*, 11.

Smith, V. 1989. Eskimo tourism: Micro models and marginal men. In V. Smith (ed.) *Hosts & guests: The anthropology of tourism* 2nd ed. pp. 55-82. Philadelphia: University of Pennsylvania Press.

Snepenger, D.J. & P.A. Moore. 1989. Profiling the Arctic tourist. *Annals of Tourism Research 16*, 566-570.

Snowman, D. 1993. *Pole positions: The polar regions and the future of the planet*. London: Hodder and Stoughton.

Stonehouse, B. 1994. Ecotourism in the Antarctic. In E. Cater & G. Lowman (eds.). *Ecotourism: A sustainable option?* pp. 195-212. Chichester: Wiley.

Stonehouse, B. 1990. A traveller's code for Antarctic visitors. *Polar Record*, *26*(156), 56-58.

Sugden, D.E. 1989. *The Arctic and Antarctic: A modern geography*, (2nd. Ed). Oxford: Blackwell.

Sugden, D.E. 1982. *The Arctic and Antarctic: A modern geography*. Oxford: Blackwell.

Umbreit, A. 1991. *Guide to Spitsbergen*. Chalfont St. Peter: Bradt Publications.

UNEP 1995. *Environmental codes of conduct*. Technical Report No 29, Paris, United Nations Environment Programme.

Urry, J. 1990. *The tourist gaze*. London: Sage.

Valentine, P. 1992. Nature-based tourism. In B. Weiler & C.M. Hall (eds.). *Special interest tourism*, pp. 105-127. London: Belhaven.

Viken, A. 1995a. Tourism experiences in the Arctic-The Svalbard case. In C.M. Hall & M.E. Johnston (eds.). *Polar tourism: Tourism in the Arctic and Antarctic regions*, pp. 73-84. Chichester: Wiley.

Viken, A. 1995b. *Ethnic tourism - Which ethnicity?* Paper presented at the conference *Shaping Tomorrow's North*, Lakehead University, Thunder Bay, Canada, October 14.

Viken, A. 1993. *The Arctic tourist experience.* Paper presented at the *Fifth World Wilderness Conference - Arctic Tourism Symposium*, Tromso, Norway, September 24 - October 1.

Walker, D.A., D. Cate, J. Brown & C. Racine. 1987. Disturbance and recovery of Arctic Alaskan tundra terrain. *CRELL Report 87-11*, Hanover, New Hampshire: U.S. Army Corps of Engineers.

World Travel and Tourism Research Council. 1995. *Database on codes of practice for the travel and tourism industry.* Oxford: World Travel and Tourism Research Council.

WWF Arctic Programme. 1995. Arctic tourism: Challenges and opportunities. *Arctic Bulletin 3*, 8-9.

ETHNIC TOURISM - WHICH ETHNICITY?
Ethnic tourism between tradition and modernity - the case of the Sami

Arvid Viken
Finnmark College

INTRODUCTION

Ethnicity is a significant cultural trait these days, and ethnic differences are constituting an otherness on which tourism often is based. In a way, most tourism is more or less ethnic tourism. But as the notion is most widely used, ethnic tourism is limited to visiting indigenous people or so called minority groups. "Ethnic tourism," states Smith (1989: 4), "is marked to the public in terms of 'quaint' customs of indigenous and often exotic people." Harron and Weiler (1992) define it as a form of cultural tourism, with more intimate contacts between the hosts and guests than in other forms of tourism. One can also distinguish between primary and secondary ethnic tourism (Wood 1984), where the first includes real intercultural communication, and the second is restricted to gazing. Thus, there are different degrees of intimacy in ethnic encounters.

By calling something ethnic or ethno-, one makes a distinction from something else, something that is supposed to be culturally more neutral (Hviding 1995). The term is used to characterize a phenomenon which is found in a particular ethnic context. In this paper ethnic tourism is used to describe a type of tourism, as apposed to an approach to tourism as a theoretical field. However, the analysis is done within the Western knowledge paradigm, which definitely is not the only one (see Said 1978). This is a paradigm strongly influenced by modernity. Ethnic tourism involves travel away from modernity and into the past. Ethnic communities are supposed to be traditional, and may give people a glimpse of periods and modes of life which most places in the Western Hemisphere have moved beyond. This is the main perspective in this paper: ethnic tourism as a phenomenon between tradition and modernity.

Ethnicity can be used to distinguish a group of people from others, and is often used by smaller groups to distinguish themselves from bigger entities (A. Cohen 1989). It is of course only one of many ways to characterize people and is primarily a dimension used when no other dimension functions (A. Cohen 1989). To distinguish people according to race and ethnicity has been a way for many cultures to signify their own superiority. Race has been looked upon as a biological dimension, and as a tool for external categorization (Jenkins 1994). Ethnicity is basically a cultural concept, defined, according to Barth (1969), through an internal group process, and through interaction with external groups—with the other. Ethnicity is a kind of collective identity (Jenkins 1994), and like

other identities, ethnicity is always a matter of discourse and of change.
Thus, political negotiations about ethnicity are a means of fortifying ethnic
identities and of making ethnic distinctions known for the public and the
authorities (Howard 1990). This is not the only way; tourism may be
another. Tourism may be an appropriate arena for displaying cultural
identities, and for testing out and experimenting with cultural changes
(Kalstad & Viken 1995). Of importance, then, is which identities are to
be exposed.

In Scandinavia, the Sami are the only indigenous people. The most
significant trait of the Sami until recent years was reindeer pastoralism
and nomadism. Today the Sami society is in transition—and one of the
new economic sectors is tourism. The Sami are not unfamiliar with
tourism—they have for decades been selling souvenirs to tourists—nor are
they unfamiliar with displaying their culture. They were, for example,
exhibited at the World Fair in Paris in 1900, and at a circus in Germany
in 1930 (Hætta 1994). But tourism as an industry is new. This paper is
a discussion of how the Sami culture is presented to and interpreted by
modern tourists. To establish a frame for the analysis, there is a need for
a brief presentation of the Sami region and Sami tourism. This will
discuss the position which Sami culture holds between tradition and
modernity, and how this leads to different types of Sami identities.
Finally, the discussion will show how the different identities are exposed
through tourism, some dilemmas of such exposure, and some implications
for the authenticity of the tourist experience. The paper is primarily
based on data from a research project on Arctic ethnic tourism, where
both tourists and their Sami hosts have been interviewed. It is also
influenced by the fact that the author has lived in the Sami area for 15
years.

Sapmi - the land of the Sami

The Sami are spread all over the northern parts of Norway, Sweden,
Finland, and Northwest Russia. This was a land without borders, and in
Norway there are Sami settlements as far south as 300 km north of Oslo.
In the summertime many are scattered along the main roads all the way
up to the North Cape, the northernmost point of Scandinavia, mostly as
kiosk holders or in small Sami market places along the roadside. These
market places are normally situated near the summer sites of the reindeer
herders. The signs of Saminess become more frequent as one travels
northwards. Reindeer herding is frequently seen even south of the Arctic
Circle. As the Sami area is huge, the different Sami groups lived rather
isolated from each other until quite recently, and different Sami cultures

emerged. Today, there are at least four distinct Sami cultures: Southern Sami, Lule Sami, Skolt Sami, and Northern Sami which is the largest group today. The Northern Sami are split between inland reindeer nomads, inland settlers—most often farmers—and Coastal Sami who traditionally combined farming and fishery. There is also a modern version of the Sami, people who have modern jobs and who are integrated in different types of local communities. The reindeer herders are those who are most easily recognized as Sami by the outer world, as many of them are still daily users of the major Sami symbols, the traditional costume, the tent, and the reindeer. In recent years, new symbols of the Sami culture have emerged, for example, a flag and the name of their country, *Sapmi*.

No official number exists for the Sami population—only 4,806 were registered in the last census in Finnmark (Norway), as the county of the Sami core area officially is called. But the number is surely greater than this, depending on which definition one uses. A recent estimate for the entire Sami population was 35,000 people. The Sami constitute a minority in most of the places and regions where they live, only in two out of 19 municipalities in Finnmark do the Sami constitute a majority. Two or three more municipalities are officially proclaimed as Sami, with Sami names and with Sami as an official language together with Norwegian. However, in many northern municipalities there is a mixture of ethnicities, a mixture that creates problems and requires creativity, both on a political and a community level. For many this mixture is also a matter of personal identity having roots in both the Sami and the majority society, both genetically, culturally and identity-wise.

Tourism in Sapmi

Today, tourism is a significant industry in the Sami areas of Norway, Finland, and Sweden. There are different types of tourism in this area. For most visitors Sami culture is an exotic element on a tour to North Cape, a destination visited by 263,000 people in 1994. More than 80 per cent of them crossed through Sapmi. Tourism in the Sami inland districts is mainly a post-war phenomenon. Before World War II, tourists to North Cape were seaborne and the tourists mainly met the Sami nomads in a few summer camps along the coast. Once roads were built through Sapmi and to North Cape by 1956, the patterns of travelling changed, and Sami culture became a more important ingredient in summer tourism. Another source for tourism in Sapmi has been the emergence of the leisure society and leisure activities among local people (Pedersen & Viken 1996). These activities have in recent years created a basis for several small tour operators. The most successful activities have been hunting, fishing, snowmobiling, and dogsledding. Together with more traditional alpine and cross-country skiing these activities have given rise to a significant winter tourism, especially in Finland, and in the district of Kiruna in Sweden. Skiing tourism is less developed in Northern Norway. Of interest are also the Easter Festivals all over Sapmi, and Santa Claus tourism around Christmas time, mostly in Finnish Lapland. The volumes of the different types of tourism are not known, except for the North Cape tourism. Together these different types of visitors create a foundation for a year-round tourism industry, but with the summer as the peak season. In the core Sami area, which was almost exclusively used by the Sami nomads and farmers 50 years ago, there is a significant tourist industry as a source of employment today. This also implies that Sapmi, earlier an area dominated by reindeer herding and harvesting of natural resources, has been transformed to a playground for people from all over the world (Pedersen & Viken 1996). What makes this playground attractive is the mixture of modern and traditional ethnic activities, including nature-based experiences.

Sami culture between tradition and modernity

The concepts of tradition and modernity both have common-sense meanings, but at the same time they are theoretical categories which are widely discussed within different academic disciplines. Tradition is of temporal significance referring to the past, or as Giddens puts it ". . . an orientation to the past, such that the past has a heavy influence . . . over the present" (1994: 62). Traditions are believed by many to have been of greater importance in the past than today. According to Giddens (1994), traditions were the glue that held pre-modern societies together. Yet, traditions are constantly developing and changing, as "an ongoing interpretation of the past" (Handler & Linnekin 1984: 274), "they develop and mature, or weaken and die" (Giddens 1994: 62). When they die, they are no longer traditions. For most people traditions represent taken-for-granted knowledge and attitudes, including moral guidelines. Traditions discriminate between insiders and others, and as such they contribute to the constitution of people's identities.

Traditions are signified through artifacts, myths and rituals. These visual aspects of tradition are those that give a platform for tourism; however, there is no guarantee that the signs are interpreted in the same way by foreigners as they are by the locals. Focusing on the interpreter, Pierce claims that "A sign . . . addresses somebody, that is, creates in the mind of that person an equivalent sign, or perhaps a more developed sign" (cited by Bruhn Jensen 1994: 21). This is an essential limitation to all inter-cultural contact, and of course for the host-tourist encounter. The greater the cultural differences, the less is understood of the other culture, and the greater the risk that cultural markers are consumed as signs. Signs that merely represent themselves are a characterization of post-modern society (Harvey 1990), a society which is also said to be sign-consuming. Signs consumed as such are an iconic interpretation (Bruhn Jensen 1994), opposed to indexical or symbolic interpretations where signs have a particular meaning, cognitive or even empathic. Some people, will regard the *lavvu*, the Sami tent or tepee, surrounded by reindeers, merely as an exotic landscape and as a sign of tradition. Others will become interested in pastoralism and nomadism. A third group will interpret the view as a symbol of a traditional life, a simpler life, or of a way of life in close contact with nature.

Today, traditions are believed to have lost their hold on people's everyday lives, and in modern societies they seem to have been replaced by rational enquiry, scientific knowledge and expertise. Modernity is sometimes called the post-traditional society (Giddens 1994). More often the concept is used to characterize the industrial or post-industrial society, its institutions and cultures (Harvey 1990). Giddens (1991) elaborates on three main elements of modernity. The first is the separation of time and space. Whenever one wants to have a sun and swim holiday, another climatic zone is only a few hours away. The second element of modernity Giddens talks about is the disembedding of social institutions. Things which were done by people themselves in the past, have been taken over by experts. People do not build their houses themselves, the schools take care of the teaching, and even the raising of children, and travelling preparations are made by travel agents. The third element of modernity which Giddens emphasizes is reflexivity. By this he means that the modern society and its institutions are based on a kind of formal knowledge. In tourism this is obvious: the industry is a major user of advanced technology and formal expertise. However, knowledge is no longer looked upon as truth, but rather as an argument in a theoretical discourse. The key words of this paper—tradition and modernity, ethnicity and tourism—are all good examples.

Most aspects of the Sami culture are influenced by the tradition-modernity transition (Kalstad 1995). Even reindeer herding has become commercialized, regulated, technologized, and acculturated. However, the skills of reindeer herding are learned the traditional way: it is the fathers and mothers who teach their children. Still the herds migrate to coastal pastures in springtime; still it is common to live in extended families which include three to four generations at the summer site; and, still this site consists of small sod houses and *lavvus* (tents). Still Sami children learn to speak the Sami language and to *joik*—the traditional folk song; and, still many children are given the same name as the parents—the grandfather is called Three-Mathis, the father Mathis-Mathis, the son Mathis. However, the signs of modernity are significant. The time and space concepts have changed—only the jokes about the Sami time conception remain. Traditional migration of the herd to and from the coastal summer pasture is now done in a few days with lorries. And the outside world is pretty close. One Sami tourist host often says that his home has a central location—it is in the middle of Sapmi—three hours from Oslo, 10 from New York. Also, the disembedding process is obvious. The traditional *siida*, the reindeer herding administrative unit, and the extended family are institutions which today have minor importance. Many of the old traditions within health care and education are taken over by modern experts. This also implies that the Sami people are part of the reflexive world. There is even a separate Sami college which offers higher education in language and cultural subjects. As for most indigenous people, there exists a large body of anthropological studies of their culture. For tourism, the modernization of the Sami society is both an advantage and a problem. With a well-documented culture of reflexive inhabitants, the possibilities of creating interesting tourist products are promising—even the history of reflexivity is interesting. However, many tourists look upon such presentations as staged ethnicity (MacCannell 1989).

The tradition-modernity dimension and Sami identities

For several decades the Sami have been through a process of identity negotiation. The Sami past is a history of exploitation, suppression and suffering (Lorenz 1991). To make the history of the colonization of Sapmi short, one may say that the first step was when people from the south went northward to exploit fisheries—as early as in the 13th century. The second step was the introduction of the regulation of trade and taxation. The third step was the annexation of the land for traditional farming. The last step is the recent period of recreation and tourism in the 20th century (Pedersen & Viken 1996). The result of this history is a people without faith in their own culture—at least until recently—and according to Eidheim (1969) their ethnic identity has been socially stigmatized. In a census in 1970 only a small portion registered as Sami, and in an investigation made as late as in the 1980s many Sami denied having any Sami past at all (Bjørklund 1985). Despite these facts the Sami have survived, mainly because of a strong primordial or immanent culture. Today, the Sami represent a vital minority in the Nordic countries, particularly in Norway. Their position is the result of a strong revitalization process which started in the 1960s. This process is political and not only a result of their own struggle for power, but also a result of a greater consciousness about ethnicity, as well as bad conscience and regrets by the public and the national authorities (Eidheim 1992; Stordal 1994). In this process concessions and positions have been given to those who are looked upon as Sami, people who were closely connected to the well-known Sami symbols: the costume, the *lavvu*, and the reindeer (Olsen 1995). Thus, it was the inland reindeer herding culture which became the official Sami culture. This meant that other aspects of the Sami culture, the Southern Sami, the farmers and the Coastal Sami were neglected. For many of the latter the assimilation process had proceeded beyond the point of public attention. They are looked upon as Norwegians, even by other Sami. This is rather typical for such processes; what becomes the identity of a group is a reflection of the view of others, and for a minority (and inferior) group in particular, that of superiority (A. Cohen 1989; Linnekin & Poyer 1990; Olsen 1995). Today, there are signs of an uprising against this, particularly among the Coastal Sami. Thus, there is obviously more than one Sami culture, and a number of Sami identities.

Identity is both a collective and an individual concern. The individual identity is a reflection of collective values, but not solely. Identity is also influenced by roles and statuses, and by self-consciousness. A. Cohen (1994: 11) cites Epstein's statement: "identity . . . is essentially a concept of synthesis. It represents the process by which the person seeks to integrate his [sic] various statuses and roles, as well as his [sic] diverse experiences, into a coherent image of self." A. Cohen (1994) emphasizes that the individual has a self-consciousness, which implies that people perform differently in the same roles and within the same cultural context. This is obvious with the Sami involved in tourism. The self-consciousness is signified by the fact that personality is said to be a major success factor among the Sami tourists hosts, as it is in general. This is also emphasized by tourists. Self-consciousness also influences the way these hosts expose different aspects of their identity, and the way they interpret and mediate their culture. Thus, the awareness of which identity one exposes varies also.

Traditionally, individual identity has been part of the unconscious mind, and group identity has been an incorporated (Connerton 1989) aspect of the culture and was not discussed. Thus, there is a significant portion which is tacit within most identities (Polanyi 1983; Kalstad & Viken 1995). This is said to be about to change since for modern people identity and lifestyle is also a matter of reflexivity and choice

(Featherstone 1992). That trend also appears to apply to the Sami. In most parts of the Sami community the Sami question is on the public agenda in one way or another. A main theme in this discussion is how the tradition-modernity questions should be handled. There seems to be an agreement about the fact that parts of the Sami community have been less influenced by the modernization processes than others, leading to several identities along the traditionalist-modernist dimension. At least five categories of people who combine different types of traditions and modernity can be recognized:

Rejectionists are a category of people who reject, suppress or do not expose their Sami origin. They are more or less successfully assimilated. Some of them even contest the Sami being given any particular attention from the authorities. Many in this category are rather non-reflexive in rejecting their Saminess, as it was their parents or grand parents who changed from Sami to Norwegian. Others are aware of their Sami roots, but regard it as a lost background. They are modern people, and may be found in all types of sectors and positions.

A second group are the *traditionalists*, people who are not particularly integrated in the modern world, and with a life less influenced by modern technology and the market economy than the others. Their reality is Sami, and this has never been discussed as such. Their numbers are declining, partly due to the process of mechanization and integration into the market economy, partly due to an ongoing process of restructuring reindeer pastoralism initiated by the authorities, but also due to the fact that young people prefer other ways of living.

Traditional modernists are the group of Sami living in and for the Sami culture. These look upon their society as a modern Sami society. They have the latest in technology, and are confident with both a market economy and the political system. They may be educated to a certain level, and have a certain level of reflexivity. They tend to be active within the Sami organizations, and head for careers or hold vital positions within the Sami community. These people represent the middle and upper classes. Their family background and the family's place of residence influence their positions in the labour market, the status system, and their identity. The system of social order is strong, and an incorporated part of the traditions. Traditional modernists wear Sami costumes when there is something to celebrate, and are aware of the status of new and costly costumes.

Reflexive traditionalists are mostly academics. They have a Sami origin, but as academics they often have more in common with their professional colleagues than with other Sami. They are reflexive and self-reflexive (Lash & Urry 1994) and discuss Sami identity and lifestyles with their family, colleagues, and friends. Some of them grew up with parents who rejected their Sami background. Others grew up as visitors in their parents' culture (Stordal 1994) while spending their childhood in boarding schools. For many of these, Sami culture and identity is what they learned from their teachers, based on knowledge acquired from anthropologists or other scholars. This knowledge is not neutral: the scientists who constructed this knowledge are co-writers of the reality of others, as Hastrup (1988) has put it. When scientific knowledge goes back as truth to the culture where the fieldwork was done, the mediators function as a kind of social engineers (Levi-Strauss 1966; Eidheim 1993). The engineer version of Saminess, however, is probably not always consistent with the Saminess of their parents, or with that of people of the same age who were brought up within a traditional context, and who belong to the pragmatic traditionalist or traditional modernist category. To make the list complete there is a need for one more category, the *non-Sami*. This is the majority of people who live in the Sami areas, people who are Norwegian, Finnish, or Swedish. Many of these are involved in Sami businesses and with the development of Sami communities.

The traditional-modern dimension could also be treated as a continuum. People are more or less traditional, more or less modern. However, the categorization gives a more concrete and immediately comprehensive description. The categories are of course ideal types. Thus, most people will have a portion of each, and even be of one category in one context, and of another type in another context. The Sami culture is described as pragmatic, and Sami people will choose what they believe is the optimal combination of identities for the situation. As pragmatism is a tradition, it is mostly the habit of people in the traditionalist category. It is within this category one finds people who sell souvenirs that are produced in Korean or Taiwan. Pragmatism in the other categories can be seen when modern traditionalists and reflexive traditionalists play a more traditional role in their relationships with tourists who expect them to be so. The reflexive traditionalist may perform a pure traditionalist or a traditional modernist role while coping with his or her compatriots, and a modern professional role in negotiations with the central authorities. If they believe it gives power to their arguments most Sami will put on their traditional costume when going to such meetings. In this way they change between external identities. The Sami are not only modern, but also post-modern. In post-modernity the questions of ethnicity and identity are social and political options (Featherstone 1992). To change identities may be done by everybody these days, but the repertoire is bigger still for people with a foot in a traditional society.

Which identities are shown to tourists?

As indicated above, tourists come to the Sami area for different reasons. Confronted with the Sami culture, most visitors become curious. Besides the many souvenir kiosks along the road, there are also quite a number of museums and visitor centres where the Sami culture is displayed. Some people purchase a Sami experience or adventure package, or go to a Sami festival, such as the colourful Easter festival. Apparently, for many tourists the highlight seems to be the accidental encounter: the Sami bringing his herd across the road, a Sami coming out of the birch forest with poles for a new tent, a talk with a Sami in costume sitting by a fireplace.

The following list gives some indications on where and how the different identities will be exposed for tourists:

Rejectionists. They are all over, but not observable.

Traditionalists. They are situated along the roadside in the Sami core area. Their camps have primitive tents and huts of transparent plastic. They are selling self-made traditional products as souvenirs. Some of them also sell objects which are made in Korea. They are not particularly interested in the tourists or the tourism industry, only in the money this activity may bring.

Traditional modernists. This group may also be seen along the roadside. Their cabins are normally of somewhat better standard, and they often have a *lavvu*. They sell self-made souvenirs and handicraft called *duodji*. There are also established *duodji* centres and more general shopping centres where one can buy Sami *duodji*. They also play central roles in festivals and feasts. Some receive tourists in their homes or in the traditional *lavvu*. They care about the image given of the Sami culture.

Reflexive traditionalists. They operate the museums, are central in festivals, and are in general those who present the Sami traditions from a scientific perspective, and thus are found primarily in back stage roles. They take an active part in tourism policy-making and funding policies.

Modern non-Sami. They operate the hotels in the Sami area and run adventure tourism firms based on Sami traditions. They take care of the marketing of the Sami tourist products.

Many of the traditional modernists and the reflexive traditionalists experience dilemmas in deciding which identity to expose. There is an expectation that the Sami hosts shall perform in a traditional way. This is the image known from books and marketing materials. To satisfy their customers the Sami hosts try to fulfil these expectations and perform much more traditionally than they would usually. For example, they wear traditional clothing, use tents, and use reindeer transportation. At the same time they feel that their activities are counter-productive with regards to another important aim: to become a respected and integrated part of the modern world. Therefore, these hosts are often criticized by other Sami who accuse them of exposing the Sami culture of the past. This dilemma is discussed and for many the solution is to include the issue in the narrative they present their visitors.

Another aspect in the use of traditional artifacts and symbols in touristic and commercial relations is that they tend to be modified. Today, the *lavvu* is of a flexible size and made of light materials; some are even furnished with benches and a modern heating system, though traditionally people sat on the ground covered by birch branches and reindeer furs around a fire. Similarly, river boats have been made bigger, taking up to 40 passengers as opposed to the traditional six or eight, and have more comfortable seats. A modified Sami costume is used as a uniform for people in visible positions in hotels, restaurants and shops. In architecture the shape of Sami tents and sod-houses is used extensively in modern constructions. In modern design it is convenient to use elements from Sami culture as a model. Some of these adaptations are met with scepticism and cause public discussions within and outside the Sami society. Most people view this development as an indication of a vital culture, a culture in progress.

The differentiation between Sami identities probably constitutes a wholesome mixture, some innovative, some preservationist. The new versions of old cultural expressions are normally constructed by the traditional Sami assisted by non-Sami, and advocated by the traditional modernist and reflexive traditionalists. However, this process of cultural change extends the boundaries for what is culturally acceptable. Today, Sami people think that there should be more costume-like uniforms, a use of the costume they heavily contested less than a decade ago. In Finland, these boundaries have been moved much further. There, the Sami tourism development has mainly been taken care of by people who have lost their Sami roots, and by non-Sami. The result is a significantly more commercialized Sami exposure (e.g. Pretes 1994), often faked. Examples are the shaman, who makes noise and baptises the tourists by marking them with soot on the forehead and the Sami folk dance groups and drummers. Many tourists and particularly many Sami are not comfortable with this false picture. They look upon it as a commodified and Disneyfied culture.

Authenticity

The question of authenticity is as central within the field of tourism, as is the confusion about its meaning. According to E. Cohen (1988), earlier authenticity was used to characterize artifacts in museums, but over the last two decades, the concept has also been used in connection with intercultural encounters and tourism (e.g. MacCannell 1989; E. Cohen 1988; Sharpley 1994; E. Cohen 1995). The touristic meaning of the concept is normally what is real or true in one way or another. There are two trends in tourism which affect how authenticity is comprehended. One trend is that tourists are visually oriented (Urry 1990), and thus are consumers of signs. The other is that tourists are focused on learning and knowledge (Kalinowski & Weiler 1992). In many respects the distinction may represent two different ways of interpreting signs. In the first trend it is the sign as such which is in focus, in the other it is the meaning of the signs.

As sign interpretation, authenticity becomes a matter of perception. This is influenced by the tourists' expectations, and who the tourist is. Tourists who believe that Sami wear traditional costumes tend to find few authentic Sami. In fact, this is a frequently encountered matter of dispute as the tourists do not believe it when people tell them they are Sami. Beside the costume, the tent, the *joik*, the reindeer, and even the Arctic landscape are also considered elements of authentic experiences, reflecting the value of signs as such for many tourists. However, many tourists also think that the Sami costumes and tents represent a staging of the culture, and that the traditional Saminess is a role the Sami enters when he or she becomes a tourist host, when they are going to work, so to say. This is partly the fact. Within one family the mother may use the Sami costume all the time, while the father uses it as a "tourist uniform." Most tourists are aware of the fact that Sami culture mingles between tradition and modernity. Therefore, many still think of it as authentic, even if they believe it is staged. At least it refers to a culture that until recently was a reality.

The knowledge seeking tourists are of course different, and what they consider as authentic depends on the direction of their interest or scientific approach. For an archaeologically or ethnographically interested person it may be important to be shown the artifacts as they were, for a historian or a social anthropologist it is probably more important to be presented an accurate narrative about history or an event. For such cultural tourists, authenticity is a question of the quality of documentation found at heritage sites, museums, other cultural institutions and in books.

According to many tourists this aspect of the Sami tourism product is not well-developed yet.

Most tourists will be interested in meeting and knowing ordinary people. The scientific parallel is the social anthropologist and the sociologist. Tourists mention occasional encounters with Sami as their most authentic experiences. Particularly valued are encounters and chats with reindeer herders in a practical work situation. Bargaining with a traditional souvenir seller or an encounter in a bar may give the same feeling. For those who are not so lucky, the encounters take place within touristic contexts, where both tourists and hosts play roles. In such circumstances there are small chances that other aspects of the identity will be exposed. Roles block more intimate contact. Roles might have been the opposite of what they seem to represent, an intermediate stage in the process of defining the self and the other as Callero (1994: 239) has stated. The problem is that the tight time schedule of the tourists seldom gives room for such processes. It takes time to get acquainted with a Sami—the experience with the other is not particularly well-developed in the Sami past. Therefore, only a very small portion of the tourists will advance to what Wood (1984) call the primary and intimate type of ethnic tourism.

The tourists' perceptions of authenticity are, of course, influenced by their own identity. This is certainly also a stage along the tradition-modern axis. Most important is the level of reflexivity. The more reflexive the tourists are, the more they are familiar with a perspective of themselves as gazers or sign consumers. The more reflexive, the higher is the comprehension of the Sami as a complex culture and society in transition. The less reflexive, the greater is the chance is that the encounter confirms the tourists' prejudices about aboriginal people in general, both as traditionalists and as a burden for society. Tourists express this in more or less sophisticated ways. Perceptions of authenticity are also a question of cross-cultural distance between the sign and its interpreter. For people who come from other and distant cultures, there are three main interpretations of the Sami. One is that the Sami still are a typical pre-modern tribe, still living in tents and with their herds. The tents, people in costumes and the reindeer confirm this belief. Another common observation is that this can no longer be the case. By observing the modernity of the region, people understand that their expectations were naïve or incorrect, and are confused about what could be authentic Saminess. The third reaction goes in the same direction. Many tourists know that the Sami culture has been modernized, and that most signs are hidden, as long as they neither speak Sami or Norwegian

or can hear the difference. "How can I know what is a real Sami?" a
German tourist asked.

CONCLUSION

This paper has presented the Sami culture and identities along a
traditional-modern scale, emphasizing that the post-modern Sami probably
comprises bits of all, or changes between different identities. This is also
the case with the tourists. In fact, for post-modern people, tradition is of
significant interest as a nostalgic element in the chase for otherness (E.
Cohen 1995). There might also be other explanations, for example, that
people like to see how their ancestors lived. The only difference between
Sami culture and the Norwegian or European, a Sami intellectual has
said, is the late start of the modernization project. Modernity is by many
perceived as an unauthentic society (e.g. E. Cohen 1988). It is
unauthentic because of its lost traditions. Tradition is often connected to
a simpler life, and romantic perceptions of intimacy and proximity to
nature. Graburn commented on ethnic tourism in this way: "Another way
to get close to Nature's bosom is through her children, the people of
Nature, once labelled Peasant and Primitive peoples and considered
creatures of instinct" (Graburn 1989: 31). The encounter with indigenous
people may give some glimpses into this way of life that modern people
normally have no access to. Thus, for modern people the Sami culture
both represents continuity and contrast, roots, and otherness. This is
often what tourism is about in the post-modern world of lost traditions
and cultural globalization. For the tourist host these motives may
constitute expectations which are difficult to meet. Their activities have
both been seen as an attempt to transform their local communities into
museums, and as such, counteract progress. Today, however, the
modernization project has reached so far, also in the Sami areas, that
even traditions are modern. This amalgamation of traditions and
modernity within the Sami society, is another opening for community
adjustment to tourism. In order to be more attractive to visitors, people
seem to be willing to decorate their communities with traditional Sami
symbols. The opportunities are many and so are the pitfalls.

REFERENCES

Barth, F. 1969. *Ethnic groups and boundaries*. Oslo: Universitetsforlaget.

Bjørklund, I. 1985. *Fjordfolket i Kvænangen: Fra Samisk samfunn til norsk utkant 1500-1980.* Tromsø: Universitetsforlaget.

Bruhn Jensen, K. 1994. *Meaningful society: A theory of social semiotics.* Vol. 3. Congress of Nordic Association for Semiotic Studies.

Callero, P. 1994. From role-playing to role-using: Understanding role as resource. *Social Psychology Quarterly Vol. 57*(3), 228-243.

Cohen, A. 1994. *Self consciousness: An alternative anthropology of identity.* London: Routledge.

Cohen, A. 1989. *The symbolic construction of community.* London: Routledge.

Cohen, E. 1995. Contemporary tourism - Trends and challenges: Sustainable authenticity or contrived post-modernity? In R.W. Butler & D.G. Pearce (eds.) *Change in tourism: People, places, processes*, pp. 12-29. London: Routledge.

Cohen, E. 1988. Authenticity and commodization in tourism. *Annals of Tourism Research 15*, 371-386.

Connerton, R. 1989. *How societies remember.* Cambridge: Cambridge University Press.

Eidheim, H. 1993. Bricolage og ingeniørverksemd i Sapmi. *Norsk sosialantropologi 1993 - Et utsnitt*, pp. 225-265, Oslo: Norges forskningsråd.

Eidheim, H. 1992. *Stages in the development of Sami selfhood.* Working Paper No. 7, Oslo.

Eidheim, H. 1969. When ethnic identity is a social stigma, In F. Barth (ed.) *Ethnic groups and boundaries*, pp. 39-57. Oslo: Universitetsforlaget.

Featherstone, M. 1992. Postmodernism and the aestheticization of everyday life. In S. Lash & J. Friedman (eds.) *Modernity & identity*, pp. 265-290. Oxford: Blackwell.

Giddens, A. 1994. Living in a post-traditional society. In A. Giddens, U. Beck, & S. Lash (eds.) *Reflexive modernization*, Cambridge: Polity.

Giddens, A. 1991. *Modernity and self-identity*. London: Polity Press.

Graburn, N.H.H. 1989. Tourism: The sacred journey. In V.L. Smith (ed.) *Hosts and guests: The anthropology of tourism*, pp. 21-36. Philadelphia: University of Pennsylvania Press.

Hætta, O.M. 1994. *Samene. Historie, kultur, samfunn*. Oslo: Grøndahl Dreyer.

Handler, R. & J. Linnekin. 1984. Tradition, genuine or spurious. *Journal of American Folklore*, *97*(385), pp. 273-290.

Harron, S. & B. Weiler. 1992. Ethnic tourism. In C.M. Hall & B. Weiler (eds.). *Special interest tourism*, pp. 83-94. London: Belhaven.

Harvey, D. 1990. *The condition of postmodernity*. Oxford: Blackwell.

Hastrup, K. 1988. Kultur some analytisk begreb. In H. Hauge & H. Horstbøll (eds.). *Kulturbegrebets kulturhistorie*, pp. 120-139. Aarhus: Aarhus Universitetsforlag.

Howard, A. 1990. Cultural paradigms, history and the search for identity. In J. Linnekin & L. Poyner (eds.). Oceania. *Cultural identity and ethnicity in the Pacific*, pp. 259-279. Honolulu: University of Hawaii Press.

Hviding, E. 1995. Nature, culture, magic, science: On meta-language for comparison in cultural ecology. In P. Descola & G. Pålsson (eds.). *Nature and society: Anthropological perspectives*, pp. 165-184. London: Routledge.

Jenkins, R. 1994. Rethinking ethnicity, categorization and power. *Ethnic and racial studies*, *17*(2), pp. 197-222.

Kalinowski, K. & B. Weiler. 1992. Educational travel. In B. Weiler & C.M. Hall (eds.), *Special interest tourism*, pp. 15-26. London: Belhaven.

Kalstad, J.K. 1995. *Pastoralism and management of common land in Finnmark*. Fifth Common Property Conference of the International Association for the Study of Common Property, Bodø.

Kalstad, J.K. & A. Viken. 1995. *Sami tourism: Traditional knowledge challenged by modernity*. Second International Congress of Arctic Social Sciences, Session on Ethics of Eco- and Ethno-Tourism, Guovdageaidnu.

Lash, S. & J. Urry. 1994. *Economies of signs and space*. London: Sage.

Levi-Strauss, C. 1966. *The savage mind*. Chicago: University of Chicago Press.

Linnekin, J. & L. Poyner. 1990. *Cultural identity and ethnicity in the Pacific*. Honolulu: University of Hawaii Press.

Lorenz, E. 1991. *Samefolket i historien*. Oslo: Pax.

MacCannell, D. 1989. *The tourist*. New York: Shocken.

Olsen, K. 1995. *Utfordringer og reorienteringer i samisk selvforståelse*. Alta: Finnmark College.

Pedersen, K. & A. Viken. 1996. From Sami nomadism to global tourism. In M. Price (ed.) *People and tourism in fragile environments*, pp. 69-88. London: John Wiley and Sons Ltd.

Polanyi, M. 1983. *The tacit dimension*. Gloucester, Mass.: Peter Smith.

Pretes, M. 1994. Postmodern tourism: The Santa Claus industry. *Annals of Tourism Research*, *22*(1), pp. 1-15.

Said, E. 1978. *Orientalism*. New York: Pantheon Books.

Sharpley, R. 1994. *Tourism, tourists & society*. Cambridgeshire: ELM Publications.

Smith, V. 1989. *Hosts and guests: The anthropology of tourism*. Philadelphia: University of Pennsylvania Press.

Stordal, V. 1994. *Same i den moderne verden*. Tromsø: Universitetet i Tromsø.

Urry, J. 1990. *The tourist gaze*. London: Sage.

Wood, R.E. 1984. Ethnic tourism, the state, and cultural change in Southeast Asia. *Annals of Tourism Research*, *11*(3), pp. 353-374.

THE ROLE OF TOURISM IN REMOTE COMMUNITIES

R.W. Butler
University of Surrey

INTRODUCTION

As tourism spreads further into remote parts of the world (Hall & Johnston 1995), its participants increasingly are coming into contact with residents of remote communities. Two important issues which need to be addressed in this context are: the nature of the relationship between tourism and such communities; and, the most appropriate role for tourism within these communities. A short-term, and perhaps initially unsatisfactory, strategy is for the remote communities to provide tourists with a good holiday, so that they return home with a positive and wider appreciation of the host destination. Good is defined here as fair value for money, a safe and relaxing holiday (in a variety of ways), and positive memories, in other words, a beneficial experience. (This is not the same as suggesting that the host community is obligated to give the tourists everything they wish or demand.) To suggest anything else is tantamount to entering an ideological minefield, and more importantly, to misunderstand the basic function of tourism. This is not to argue that tourism is above criticism, far from it, but rather that criticism should be appropriate and specific, and not generalized and idealistic or ideological.

There are positive and negative forms of tourism, and they are often the same. What makes one form good in one location and bad in another often depends on a combination of scale, setting, and rate of development, rather than tourism as a phenomenon itself. Tourism is created by social and economic demands as well as the provision and marketing of opportunities, and tourism responds to changes in the settings in which it occurs. As the demand for and development of opportunities for tourism increases, some tourists begin to visit destinations elsewhere. It might be argued that the greater the pressure, not only the greater the numbers and flows, but also the further afield they can spread. The outflow of tourists may be gradual and more or less continuous, or may be sudden and somewhat unanticipated, for example, following the improvement or initial creation of access to an area. Tourism can provide a fertile base for growth and development, or can become a suffocating element which changes an area dramatically and eventually chokes other forms of activity. Tourism can and should be planned and controlled so that it yields far more positive than negative effects. In the context of remote communities, such as those in northern regions, both the cultural and physical environments as well as the economy can be put at risk by tourism development which is not planned, controlled and appropriate in type and scale.

It can be argued that mass tourist destinations, and certainly those aimed at conventional mass tourists are not and never were intended to be examples of the real world around the destination. A holiday destination to most visitors is not the real world; it is generally an imaginary world, a wishful world, or a Shangri-La. Few tourists think that a whole country is identical to the resort or community in which they have vacationed. This was not always so, and for the early tourist the tourist gaze (Urry 1990) was supposed to fall on the genuine article, whether this was local culture, buildings, language or the arts, and to assimilate it and take it back to use in the tourist's own locality. In the case of present day tourists, it would appear that most wish their gaze to fall on pleasant, even if artificial or staged, vistas. What they wish to take back home with them, most importantly, is themselves: intact, refreshed, happy, and with good feelings and memories. Other, less important, desires may be to acquire artifacts or souvenirs and, perhaps, knowledge and experience gained from the trip. For most people, lasting cultural experiences and relationships, such as permanent friendships, whether with locals or with other tourists, are rare, although there may be intentions of such in the flush of holiday exuberance. In the case of remote communities, the majority of the tourists who visit them do so because they perceive these places to be different from anywhere else, and particularly different from their own environment. In this case, the situation is closer to that which existed in the early days of tourism, rather than what is the norm for mass tourism today, and these tourists may have different preferences and motivations.

ROLE OF TOURISM

Society cannot and should not expect much from tourism, certainly not conventional tourism, as most tourists have no hidden or second agenda beyond having an enjoyable holiday. This statement is not intended as elitist or derogatory towards mass tourism. Mass tourism goes back to the original concept of recreation and leisure, which implied freedom from constraints (albeit not from obligations) of work, of time, of behaviour and, if possible, of financial considerations for the holiday period. This would allow the person to be re-created and, if not fitter for work, at least rested in some way and better able to face the pace and pressures of daily life. A vacation is both a privilege and an opportunity but, most of all, to most people it is a chance for a change from their daily lifestyle (Pearce 1993). This can be done in a number of ways and through different forms of tourism. It is important to note here that while there are many forms of tourism described in the literature, these specialized forms (such as cultural tourism) are all part of the general phenomenon of tourism and most show unmistakable signs of becoming part of conventional or mass tourism. This process of conversion of specialized forms of tourism to mass tourism can be observed in many established destination areas (Messerli & Brugger 1984; Lundgren 1987).

It is important to note that tourism represents different things to the four groups of players involved in this activity, namely, the government or public sector, the industry, the residents of destination areas, and the tourists themselves. Each of these groups is interested in tourism for different reasons. For most governments, especially at the national level, the main role of tourism is to provide foreign exchange and to create employment. By so doing, tourism may also bring political benefits. For industry, the primary purpose for involvement in tourism, as in almost any activity, is to make profits, normally in the form of return on investment. To local people, for the most part, tourism is seen as a form of development able to provide income and employment, and thus assisting local community viability and stability. Finally, for tourists, participation in tourism brings pleasure in the form of experiences and memories.

Tourism may also fulfil secondary roles for all or some of these groups. It may contribute to sustain regional economies, and improve a country's economic status for the governments; it might enable economic linkages between industries; and, it may help to preserve natural and cultural heritage at the local and other levels. It may also provide tourists with challenge and excitement and add to their knowledge of the world around them (Ewert 1993). Under certain conditions it may assist in stemming migration from peripheral to central areas, and alleviate social and cultural problems resulting from this process. The more these secondary benefits are turned into primary ones at the large scale, the more likely tourism in a specific location is to become irrelevant or unattractive to most tourists, and the destinations involved become divorced from tourism through playing the role of pawns in ideological chess games. The major problems for many remote communities tend to arise when the communities themselves believe that tourism will save a declining community without inducing further changes. In reality, if tourism is capable of saving a dying community, it can only do so by changing that community structure to a more viable form. To be completely successful tourism has to fulfil the roles expected by all of the groups involved, which is not easy given that the goals of the groups may not always be compatible. In the case of small remote northern communities, local needs and priorities may be overridden by the goals of external agencies, both public and private (Grekin 1994; Parker 1993).

It has been argued increasingly that tourism development in small and remote communities in particular should be responsible, sustainable, and follow principals of equity (Boo 1990). While those are admirable principals, it is important to recognize that there are at least the four groups noted above which are involved in tourism development, and to ignore the needs and preferences of any of them increases the risk of non-viable development. This is not to say that tourism should not be responsible, environmentally, socially and economically; it must be so (Nelson, Butler & Wall 1993), but so too should be all forms of economic activity, whether in the developing world or the developed world. Irresponsible development anywhere is inappropriate and undesirable, and it makes little sense to target tourism alone as something which should be responsible. It should be taken as given that all development should be responsible and, that existing development retroactively should be made as responsible as possible. In most cases it makes sense in every way for tourism to attempt to maximize local and national benefits from development while avoiding local and national costs and undesirable influences (Murphy 1994). But this applies to all forms of development and too often becomes a motherhood generalization which is not translated into real action.

There can be no doubt that tourism is an agent of change, which affects culture, economies and environment around the globe (Pearce 1989; de Kadt 1992; Mathieson & Wall 1982). These changes take many forms; in some cases an effect may be viewed as positive while in other cases as negative, often depending on where one is standing and what viewpoint one has. One of the major problems with tourism is that it is often claimed and expected to be too many things to too many people and is criticized for not being everything it is supposed to be. Tourism is often viewed as a soft option, that is, something which can be easily introduced into a region or a community in a supplementary role and will automatically be complementary and supportive to existing economic and social activities. It is sometimes viewed and promoted as making few demands on areas or communities, having only minor impacts, and presenting no problems if there is a measure of local control. In reality tourism is often quite different. If it is successful in a community it often becomes the dominant activity, and can prove not only to be highly competitive for resources but in many cases very incompatible with other activities (Murphy 1985). Tourism can make very specific demands in terms of space, capital, labour and other resources and, as its scale and nature change with development, may become unattractive to at least some local residents. Local control may well not resolve such problems (Pearce 1995), but may increase them, as well as increase division within a community, a particular problem in small and remote communities. Tourism brings about change in a number of ways, some of them identical to the way change is brought about by any form of development. Others arise because of the nature of tourism, particularly because it involves the direct and often personal contact between people, frequently of different cultures, beliefs and values as in northern settings (Nickels, Milne & Wenzel 1991; Grekin & Milne 1996). Instead of local residents automatically being supportive of tourism, some of them may be, or may become, opposed to tourism development and its associated impacts.

A major problem is with the existence of such varying viewpoints and attitudes towards tourism. They reflect, in part, differences in cultures. Tourism is a form of economic as well as social change, and in some cultures change is welcomed and in others it is not. Tourism, as it has been known from the 16th century, is primarily a western concept. Nowadays, the majority of international tourists originate in the western developed world or newly developed countries. Thus, in societies which have accepted and adopted the western philosophy and attitudes, tourism is generally seen as less of a problem with respect to real or imagined impacts on culture and society than it is in those societies which have retained distinct cultures and are more different to those of the developed world. It is a disturbing irony that many of those cultures which have maintained their distinctiveness are the ones most attractive to those tourists who are interested in culture and, therefore, are those cultures potentially most vulnerable to change from tourism. To tourists who visit remote communities one of the key attractions is the nature of the society being visited, and the greater the difference between the host and guest societies, the greater is likely to be the attraction of the community to these tourists (Alaskan Department of Community and Regional Affairs 1993; Eagles 1992). The greater the similarity between the societies, in general, the less the incentive to travel to a remote community to visit it, unless the physical setting is a major feature of the attractiveness of the community. In the particular context of northern Canadian communities, the image of Inuit culture and society is extremely attractive to some potential tourists, even if reality is perhaps less different and less enthralling than was expected (Hinch & Swinnerton 1993). In many cases also, the very different physical environment makes a significant addition to the overall attractivity of the destination (Hamley 1991; Milne & Tarbotton 1995).

Distinctive cultures are attractive to some tourists as phenomena to be seen, observed, sampled, and even experienced in some depth by some visitors. The degree to which the cultures are attractive varies with a number of factors such as similarity with the visitor's culture, understandability, accessibility, and marketing, as does the depth of the experience a tourist is likely to want to share. Increasingly the marketing of unique cultures has become a major feature of international tourism, in recent years to such a degree that one can argue that it is not a case of demand led tourism but rather the demand is being created by skilful and intensive marketing. "Collecting" rare or unusual cultures has become a major feature, especially of up-market tourism such as ecotourism, where the human component often is packaged and sold in the same manner as the wildlife element of a trip (Wheeller 1993). Part of the problem in understanding this process is the fact that relatively little is known about the true origins of tourism in many destinations and the primary purposes it was supposed to serve in its initial period.

DYNAMIC ASPECTS

Remote communities should not feel under any obligation to market or expose local culture to the tourism industry. If they decide to do so, they should be aware of the likely implications of such actions, and care should be taken to ensure that local residents of proposed destination areas are made aware of likely changes too. There is plenty of evidence to demonstrate that few areas with such cultural attractions have not experienced or begun to experience the problems of overdevelopment and overuse (Pearce 1989; Shaw & Williams 1994). These problems manifest themselves in a variety of ways, from relocation of communities to significant changes in behaviour and attitudes. To deny local, often impoverished, residents the opportunity to obtain employment and income from tourism is a difficult and perhaps politically unacceptable option. However, to allow unlimited development should also be equally unacceptable (Keller 1987).

In this context tourism and its effects, especially with respect to culture, have not changed very much. The earliest tourists laid the pattern followed by many tourists today of travelling to different and often exotic locations (at least exotic to the tourists) with specific purposes of learning about culture, language, behaviour, and customs partly or primarily with a view to bring these ideas back to incorporate in their own lifestyles. Cultural transfer was a specific and expected part of the Grand Tour. In many cases, as European tourism developed, the expectations of tourists with respect to lodging, food, transportation, and other services became more and more sophisticated and demanding, and local entrepreneurs began to offer somewhat standardized fare and services (Towner 1985). By the time Thomas Cook offered the first form of packaged and mass tourism in the mid-19th century, tourism was well on its way to becoming the industry of today, and the principles for homogenization of tourist facilities found in the Sheratons and Hiltons of today had been laid down. In this sense tourism has not changed appreciably in nature and is unlikely to do so in the future, except in a few specific cases and locations. In the Canadian north, tourists who visit this area are often particularly interested in the art and artifacts produced by local inhabitants, and regularly search out and purchase such art forms as carving and prints as souvenirs (Grekin 1994; Milne, Ward & Wenzel 1994).

Tourists at a specific destination cannot be characterized as being of one type and are not likely to remain in one category, because they evolve and change, as do the destinations (Butler 1980). Part of the problem is keeping the destination in tune with the demands and preferences of the tourists and the tourist market and at the same time maintaining what is appropriate for the destination. It must be realized that it is impossible to keep most, if any, destinations static and unchanging, and this is equally true in northern communities as it is elsewhere (Lundgren 1987). It is appropriate to note here, that in many cases local residents do not wish their communities to remain unchanged, but wish to enjoy the benefits of development (Grekin & Milne 1996). The changes that tourism brings about are often no more or less than would have occurred in the presence or absence of other agents of change. No culture is static; all cultures change and develop, not necessarily in ways which are always deemed appropriate or beneficial. Tourism is only one force for change and often the changes resulting from tourism are not direct but indirect and filtered by many other forces and agencies. The effects of tourism often pale in significance compared to the effects of such phenomena as movies and television.

What is of particular significance is the degree of change and whether the changes induced by tourism are irreversible or temporary (Cohen 1995). Relocation of villages may be a normal part of a culture's existence and occur regularly, in which case relocation for the purpose of taking advantage of tourism is not necessarily significant. If, however, a community has no tradition of relocation, and continual occupancy of one site is the norm, then relocation purely or primarily for tourism purposes, implying considerable implications for many social and economic activities, represents a major change in behaviour. In such cases, changes which result may be irreversible and deserve careful scrutiny and consideration before such a step is taken. The Canadian north has an unfortunate and often spectacularly unsuccessful history of community relocation for non-traditional reasons, and to continue this process because of perceived benefits from tourism should not necessarily be encouraged (Usher 1987).

To many tourists remote communities are seen as exotic and exciting locations for vacations. As noted earlier, most tourists go on vacation for pleasure, for change, for escape, and for relaxation (Pearce 1993). In early days the major changes between the home/work environment and the tourism environment were associated with such aspects as not working (for the man), having the family together for leisure, being in a different location, being in a different mindset, being in a different climate, engaging in different activities, and freedom from routine. All of these aspects are true today, but remote communities can offer an increased chance of change of climate (not a major factor in the case of northern visitors to northern communities except in the winter), and increased differences in culture and the visible environment. For certain types of holidays, therefore, they have unique advantages over more local and traditional destinations. Their disadvantages are cost and time of access and some tourists' fears or dislike of vastly different lifestyles and cultures. For one part of the Canadian north, at least, the difficulties associated with tourism development have been summarized by Anderson (1991), Grekin and Milne (1996), Hinch and Swinnerton (1993), and Pretes (1988).

What concerns many researchers in tourism, particularly on the academic side of tourism, is that many remote communities seem determined to follow (or are incapable of avoiding) the sequences which traditional tourist destinations have taken which have presented them with so many problems. A minor adaptation of the old adage "do as I say and not as I have done" is applicable here. One only needs to look at the poor condition of many established tourist areas to see an unattractive pattern or cycle of development and decline. Even in Switzerland, generally regarded as one country which has managed tourism successfully for many decades, there are concerns over the effects of ever larger numbers of tourists on Alpine slopes and in small communities (Messerli & Brugger 1984). While it may be argued that such patterns of overuse and overdevelopment are not inevitable, one cannot help feeling that for many destinations they are inevitable unless the destinations control their futures (Murphy 1994; Butler 1991) rather than trying to react to a changing market after the fact.

CONCLUSIONS

To return to the opening statements in this paper, tourism can contribute to the well-being of remote communities by allowing tourists to experience other parts of the cultural and physical world away from those places in which they live permanently. By witnessing the variety of the world visitors are enriched and educated. However, it would be a mistake to assume that most tourists want much more than that opportunity, or are prepared to change radically their preferences or desires for the sake of greater understanding of other peoples. Very few tourists wish to work during their holiday; for most it is a time to leave work and effort behind. Examples of local culture are often in high demand (Milne, Ward & Wenzel 1994), but to expect most tourists desire more than being entertained, and perhaps gaining a few insights into how the local community lives, is almost certainly optimistic. To expect most tourists to appreciate the nuances and subtleties of a strange culture during a few days of visitation is unrealistic. It should be emphasized here that this discussion is referring to most tourists, and by implications the various forms of mass tourism. By definition, most tourism is mass tourism, but it is appropriate here to emphasize that mass tourism itself is not homogeneous, contrary to the impression often given, especially by opponents of the phenomenon. It takes a variety of forms, ranging from budget package tours relatively close to home, to expensive cruises and excursions far from the place of residence (Marsh & Staple 1995).

The labels that are placed on different kinds of tourism can be extremely misleading. All aspects of tourism are part of the same phenomenon. Tourists are people, and people change. The so-called ecotourists or cultural tourists of today may well be mass tourists of yesterday or tomorrow, depending on where they are in their life cycle (Pearce 1993). The way ecotourism and cultural tourism are developing, they, too, will be part of mass tourism very soon (Wheeller 1993). Indeed, in some locations it can be demonstrated that this has occurred already, and access to some cultural and natural features such as Stonehenge and the Lascaux Caves has been closed because of the pressure and effects of too high visitation.

It is of critical importance that communities make conscious efforts to control tourism and to direct it in the ways in which they desire, rather than allow tourism to control and direct their development. For this to be achieved, however, two key elements need to be taken into consideration. One element is the ability of the community to control tourism, and the other is the capability of the community to withstand or absorb the effects of tourism. To be able to control tourism a community must, first and foremost, desire to control tourism, rather than be totally receptive to whatever form or scale of tourism is developed. If that desire for control exists, such control can be achieved if a community puts a set of strategies and policies into place designed to achieve these goals. In many cases the creation of such strategies and policies requires the establishment of institutional arrangements to implement these strategies and policies. Finally, if it is to be effective, the community must have, or must secure, the opportunity to implement and utilize these strategies and arrangements. This opportunity needs to be acquired early in the development process preferably before its initiation, as it is generally easier to create and implement policies before the fact rather than after (Keller 1987). The way in which community strategies and arrangements are operationalized should reflect the characteristics of the community, since each community is unique and a common formula will never guarantee the success of a community in handling tourist development.

The second element involves the capability of the community to withstand the effects of tourism. While definitive measures of this capability do not exist (Nelson, Butler & Wall 1993), it is possible to state that the capability or capacity of destination areas to withstand the impacts of tourism relates to at least four identifiable characteristics of a community. These are the environmental, cultural and economic patterns or arrangements, and the spatial pattern or design of the community. All of these characteristics affect the nature of the impacts and the ways in which they can be absorbed (Mathieson & Wall 1982). In northern settings the environment is often extremely fragile, and may be easily subjected to irreparable damage even due to minor use. The vegetation resources are more limited in terms of diversity than in many southern tourist destinations, and the presence of permafrost makes physical development more complicated and potentially more harmful than further south. While issues relating to the cultural component may not be very different from those which manifest themselves in other tourist destinations, the very small size of northern communities may mean that development impacts are felt more immediately by all members of a community than in larger settlements. In recent years the traditional hunting and trapping activities of the Inuit and Indian populations of the Canadian north have come under criticism, particularly from environmental lobby groups in western Europe. This criticism, and subsequent bans on seal products, has made some communities wary of accepting foreign visitors, and affected the way in which they are treated in the communities (Milne & Grekin 1996; Wenzel 1985). A similar situation exists in some northern Norwegian communities with respect to whale hunting.

Wildlife is of crucial importance to the cultural and, to a large extent, the financial survival of many northern communities, and traditional harvesting activities can rarely be changed to accommodate tourism needs. Limited consumption of wildlife by tourists, for example, the purchase and use of polar bear hunting permits by tourists, may be an appropriate and sustainable use of the resource, if kept within accepted limits. Non-consumptive use of wildlife (eg. viewing and photography) allows greater numbers of tourists to participate, for example, to view polar bears at Churchill during the migration period, or to engage in whale watching in the North Atlantic, but even with these activities there are limits to the amount of disturbance which wildlife can tolerate. Finally, the geographic patterns (of settlement, community activity, and tourist behaviour) also affect the capability of a destination to absorb tourism. The pattern of small nucleated settlements, with an often wide spatial pattern of transient local activity (for example, for hunting), implies that northern regions are not capable of absorbing large numbers of tourists at one time (Johnston 1995). The considerable distance between many settlements in the north, and the great difficulty in travelling between them, except by air, also has implications for tourism, as few tourists are able to visit more than one settlement on a vacation to northern regions. Finally, the seasonal pattern of climate, and the extreme nature of the climate in most northern parts of the world means that tourism almost inevitably is concentrated into a very short period of time during the summer months, when access to the areas is possible, daylight is present, conditions are bearable, and wildlife and vegetation are more easily visible. This severe peaking imposes additional pressure on local communities and also curtails the numbers of tourists who can be accommodated over the tourist season.

A key point made earlier was that one role which remote communities can play in tourism is to allow visitors to see examples of the local culture (history, art forms, communities, and nature) in a way which enhances the visitor's overall experience. It is the function and responsibility of local planners and decision-makers to ensure that only appropriate locations are developed for tourism, and that realistic figures are identified and adhered to in terms of maximum levels of development. As well, it is essential that local residents who will have direct contact with tourists, and whose culture will be exposed to tourism, be informed about and understand the likely changes which will be caused by tourism, and agree to accept these changes before they take place. In the context of the Canadian north, the community based tourism policy of the Government of the Northwest Territories (1983) represents an appropriate response to the above conditions, although the existence and implementation of such a policy does not ensure ideal and completely acceptable development (Grekin & Milne 1996).

Residents of the developed countries live in a world which is increasingly undesirous of long-term commitment and has a shorter and shorter attention span. Tourists in general are no different than other people and to try to force them to accept undesired forms of entertainment is to fail to understand the market. Any observer of industry will be aware that if producers of goods or services do not understand the market they will not be successful. A similar argument in the context of tourism has been made by Hohl and Tisdell, who noted that "If the overall goal of tourism is to achieve economic social and ecological sustainability, it must provide a first quality visitor experience, conserve natural and cultural resources, and bring substantial benefit to local communities" (1995: 533).

If success were to be measured in terms of satisfied visitors, rather than, as is more common, the total numbers of visitors, a destination would have to give tourists what they want in order to ensure their satisfaction. Of equal importance, it would have to convince them that it could do that before they made the decision on where they will go for their holiday. An appropriate, sustainable, responsible tourist community without tourists is neither appropriate, sustainable nor responsible. Attraction (marketing), delivery and management of tourism are of great significance to all tourist destinations, but are of crucial importance to small remote communities.

REFERENCES

Alaskan Department of Community and Regional Affairs. 1993. *Cultural tourism as sustainable development*. Anchorage: Government of Alaska.

Anderson, M.J. 1991. Problems with tourism development in Canada's Eastern Arctic. *Tourism Management 12* (3), 209-220.

Boo, E. 1990. *Ecotourism: The potentials and pitfalls*. Vols. 1 and 2. Washington, D.C.: World Wildlife Fund.

Butler, R.W. 1991. Tourism, environment and sustainable development. *Environmental Conservation 18* (3), 201-209.

Butler, R.W. 1980. The concept of a tourist-area cycle of evolution and implications for management. *Canadian Geographer 24* (2), 5-12.

Cohen, E. 1995. Contemporary tourism - Trends and challenges: Sustainable authenticity or contrived post-modernity? In R.W. Butler & D.G. Pearce (eds.) *Change in tourism - People, places, processes*, pp. 12-29. London: Routledge.

de Kadt, E. 1992. Making the alternative sustainable: Lessons from development for tourism. In V. Smith & W. Eadington (eds.) *Tourism alternatives*, pp. 47-75. Philadelphia: University of Pennsylvania Press.

Eagles, P.F. 1992. Motivations of Canadian ecotourists. *Journal of Travel Research 31* (2), 3-7.

Ewert, A.W. 1993. The adventure experience in the northern regions: description and case study. Paper presented at *Arctic Tourism and Ecotourism Symposium*, Tromso, Norway, September 18-21, 1993.

Government of the Northwest Territories. 1983. *Community based tourism: A strategy for the Northwest Territories tourism industry*. Yellowknife: Department of Economic Development and Tourism.

Grekin, J. 1994. *Understanding the community-level impacts of tourism: The case of Pond Inlet, NWT*. Unpublished M.A. thesis, McGill University, Montreal.

Grekin, J. & S. Milne. 1996. Toward sustainable tourism development: The case of Pond Inlet, N.W.T. In R.W. Butler & T.D. Hinch (eds.) *Tourism and indigenous peoples*, pp. 76-106. London: Routledge.

Hall, C.M. & M.E. Johnston. 1995. *Polar tourism: Tourism in the Arctic and Antarctic regions*. Chichester: Wiley.

Hamley, W. 1991. Tourism in the Northwest Territories. *Geographical Review 81* (3), 389-399.

Hinch, T.D. & G.S. Swinnerton. 1993. Tourism and Canada's Northwest Territories. *Tourism Recreation Research 28* (2), 23-32.

Hohl, A.E. & C.A. Tisdell. 1995. Peripheral tourism development and management. *Annals of Tourism Research 22* (3), 517-534.

Johnston, M.E. 1995. Patterns and issues in Arctic and sub-Arctic tourism. In C.M. Hall & M.E. Johnston (eds.) *Polar tourism: Tourism in the Arctic and Antarctic regions*, pp. 27-42. Chichester: Wiley.

Keller, C.P. 1987. Stages of peripheral tourism development - Canada's Northwest Territories. *Tourism Management 8* (1), 20-32.

Lundgren, J. 1987. Tourism development in the northern periphery. *Teoros 6* (1), 13-19.

Marsh, J. & S. Staple. 1995. Cruise tourism in the Canadian Arctic. In Hall, C.M. & M.E. Johnston (eds.) *Polar tourism: Tourism in the Arctic and Antarctic regions*, pp. 63-72. Chichester: Wiley.

Mathieson, A. & G. Wall. 1982. *Tourism: Economic, social and physical impacts*. New York: Longman.

Messerli, P. & E.A. Brugger. 1984. Mountain areas between self-reliance and dependency, between economy and ecology - A summary. In E.A. Brugger, G. Furmer, B. Messerli & P. Messerli (eds.) *The transformation of the Swiss mountain regions*, pp. 1-19. Berne: Paul Hupt.

Milne, S. & R. Tarbotton. 1995. *Visitors to the Baffin Region: An analysis of the MTRG surveys of 1992 and 1993*. McGill Tourism Research Group Working Paper No. 8, McGill University.

Milne, S., S. Ward & G. Wenzel. 1994. Linking tourism and art in Canada's Eastern Arctic: The case of Cape Dorset. *Polar Record 31* (176), 25-36.

Murphy, P.E. 1994. Tourism and sustainable development. In W. Theobald (ed.) *Global tourism: The next decade*, pp. 274-290. Oxford: Butterworth Heineman.

Murphy, P.E. 1985. *Tourism: A community approach*. London: Methuen.

Nelson, J.G., R.W. Butler & G. Wall. 1993. *Tourism and sustainable development: Monitoring, planning, managing*. Waterloo: University of Waterloo.

Nickels, S., S. Milne & G. Wenzel. 1991. Inuit perceptions of tourism development: The case of Clyde River, Baffin Island, N.W.T. *Etudes/ Inuit/Studies 15* (1), 157-169.

Parker, B. 1993. Developing aboriginal tourism: Opportunities and threats. *Tourism Management 14* (5), 400-404.

Pearce, D.G. 1995. *Tourism today: A geographical analysis*. London: Longman.

Pearce, D.G. 1989. *Tourist development*. Harlow: Longman.

Pearce, P.L. 1993. Fundamentals of tourist motivation. In D.G. Pearce & R.W. Butler (eds.) *Tourist research critiques and challenges*, pp. 113-134. London: Routledge.

Pretes, M. 1988. Underdevelopment in two norths: The Brazilian Amazon and the Canadian Arctic. *Arctic 41* (2), 109-116.

Shaw, G. & A.M. Williams. 1994. *Critical issues in tourism*. Oxford: Blackwell.

Towner, J. 1985. The Grand Tour - A key phase in the history of tourism. *Annals of Tourism Research 12* (2), 297-333.

Urry, J. 1990. *The tourist gaze*. London: Sage.

Usher, P. 1987. The north: One land, two ways of life. In L.D. McCann (ed.) *Heartland, hinterland: A geography of Canada*, pp. 482-531. Scarborough: Prentice Hall.

Wenzel, G. 1985. Marooned in a blizzard of contradictions: Inuit and the anti-sealing movement. *Etudes/Inuit/Studies 9* (1), 77-91.

Wheeller, B. 1993. Sustaining the ego. *Journal of Sustainable Tourism 1* (2), 121-129.

TOURISM AND NATIONAL PARK ESTABLISHMENT
CASE STUDY: WAGER BAY

Elizabeth Seale
Parks Canada

Establishing a national park in northern Canada is a complex process that involves many issues and many stakeholders. This paper addresses the role that tourism is playing in the discussions of a new national park proposal in the central Arctic.

The park proposal in question is Wager Bay, situated on the north-western shore of Hudson Bay in the Keewatin region of the Northwest Territories, which will soon be known as Kivalliq (Figure 1). A key stakeholder is the community of Repulse Bay, also on the west coast of Hudson Bay, north of Wager Bay.

A national park at Wager Bay was first proposed in 1978. At that time, a flurry of enthusiasm identified six potential national parks "North of Sixty" in the Northwest Territories and Yukon. A park at Wager Bay would represent the Central Tundra Natural Region of Canada, a region of granitic rock, tiny tough plants, abundant wildlife, dramatic coastline and much evidence of ancient peoples.

In 1980, Inuit requested that Parks Canada stop the public consultation phase of park establishment until their land claim was settled. This was a long process and the claim was not settled until 1993. In the intervening years, Inuit did agree that Parks Canada should conduct the background studies necessary for the establishment of a national park. During the 1980s and early 1990s, studies were conducted on landforms and glaciology, mineral and energy potential, vegetation and wildlife, archaeological resources, oral history, and visitor expectations of the Wager Bay area.

Consultations with Inuit in the five surrounding communities began in 1994 following settlement of the Nunavut land claim. The communities are: Repulse Bay, in whose traditional territory Wager Bay falls; Coral Harbour, where one finds many people who originally lived year-round or seasonally at Wager Bay; Rankin Inlet, also where many former Wager residents live; Chesterfield Inlet, second closest community to Wager Bay; and, Baker Lake where most tourists currently start their voyage to Wager Bay.

All of these communities have a stake in what happens at Wager Bay. Furthermore, unless Inuit want a national park, there will not be one. The *Nunavut Land Claims Agreement* requires that an Inuit Impact and Benefit Agreement must be negotiated between Inuit and Government before any national park can be created in Nunavut.

Figure 1. Wager Bay, N.W.T.

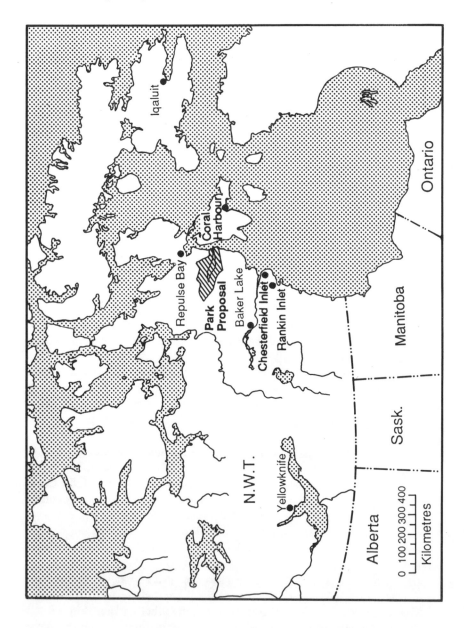

The key community that must be convinced of the desirability of a national park is Repulse Bay. Repulse Bay is a small, traditional community with a population of about 500. Many people still spend much of their time on the land hunting, fishing and trapping. Greatly improved health standards and a high birth rate have resulted, as in many northern communities, in a very large proportion of the population being under 15 (in some communities, 75 per cent of the population is under 15).

For many years, young people have had to leave Repulse Bay in order to attend high school. As these students come from very close family groups, this move is very difficult for them. Many drop out of school; many simply come home. I have been told that there has not been a high school graduate in Repulse Bay in 10 years. Gradually, that will change since the local school has been adding grades and is now up to grade 11. Next year, Repulse Bay should see the first local high school graduates.

Jobs are very limited in a community like Repulse Bay. Community leaders look everywhere for employment opportunities. They are particularly keen when they see interest from the mining industry because there might be jobs in exploration, expediting and mineral production.

A small part of the Wager Bay park proposal has been identified, through the federal government's own mineral studies, as having high potential for minerals. A consortium of mining companies is looking at a band of high mineral potential that stretches from Committee Bay southwest through the western tip of the national park proposal. Many people in Repulse Bay, seeing the interest of the mining companies and wanting to keep their options open, did not support the idea of a national park when Parks Canada began its consultations in November 1994.

Another factor in considering the Wager Bay area as a national park is the presence of Sila Lodge. The lodge caters to naturalists and offers an ecotourism experience to its visitors. Amidst an outstanding landscape, visitors can travel on land or water to observe and photograph wildlife accompanied by Inuit guides. Visitors also explore Inuit archaeological sites and many people find that they become as interested in the opportunity to interact with people of a different culture as in viewing wildlife.

Visitors to Wager Bay come largely from the United States, Canada and western Europe, at considerable expense, to enjoy a seven to 10 day experience at Sila Lodge. They then spend the rest of their two- to three-week vacation somewhere else in Canada. They travel to Wager Bay from Winnipeg, through Rankin Inlet and Baker Lake where they stay at least one day before going into Sila Lodge on a charter aircraft.

The people of Repulse Bay say that when the lodge was being established, they were told there would be many jobs for people of their community. They have watched the growth of Sila Lodge and feel that, despite promises from the lodge's owners, few people from their community have secured employment at the lodge. So they have difficulty seeing that tourism within a national park would benefit them more than mines might.

The challenge then in developing a proposal for a national park is to find ways of bringing benefits to Repulse Bay, a community that is out-of-the way in terms of transportation routes into Wager Bay.

During the course of public consultations about the park proposal, some influential elders began to say that Repulse Bay needed to stop waiting for some outside body to do something for the community. They emphasized that Repulse Bay should develop its own tourism offer so that it could take advantage of any increase in visitation to the Keewatin. Tourism has advantages to a traditional community like Repulse Bay. For example, guides can continue to live a lifestyle close to their traditional one, in touch with the land and its cycles.

Repulse Bay is a most attractive area and has many features that are not found elsewhere in the Keewatin. The community could draw tourists who have travelled a great distance to see Wager Bay and want to see other elements of the north. Repulse Bay is the community furthest north in the Keewatin and, in fact, it is right on the Arctic Circle. Tourists can see Bowhead whales, narwhal and walrus. None of these are found at Wager Bay. And within a short distance of Repulse Bay are fascinating archaeological and historic sites such as a major Thule archaeological site at Naujat and John Rae's cabin on the North Pole River, yet it is very difficult for an individual guide to make all the marketing contacts, to manage the financial side of a business, and to always be available should someone need a guide. Since spring 1995, the local Hunters and Trappers Organization (HTO) has begun working with the Department of Economic Development and Tourism (Government of the Northwest Territories) to help the community develop its tourism offer. The HTO will serve as the umbrella administrator for individual operators. That way guides can concentrate on working with tourists and not have to handle all the other elements of a business.

The HTO is also looking broadly at tourism. It can offer a much longer season to guides if it includes spring sport hunts and fall caribou hunts along with the summer ecotourism trips. Three trial trips have now taken place this year: one polar bear hunt, one caribou hunt, and one local ecotourism trip. All three trips worked out well and some spin-offs are already being felt. The four polar bear sport hunters left $8,000 in the community for carvings and caribou skin clothing.

The Government of the Northwest Territories requires that anyone guiding tourists have a guiding licence and be adequately trained. Yet, Repulse Bay has few trained and licensed guides. The NWT Tourism Training Group (TTG) is responsible for delivering guides' training courses. Parks Canada requested that the TTG consider offering a guides' course in Repulse Bay and a course was held in Repulse Bay in September 1995.

International tourists are often considered as the key targets for tourism offers in the north. However, Economic Development and Tourism conducted an innovative survey in Rankin Inlet, the largest community in the Keewatin and one with many civil service jobs. They found that many people in Rankin would consider going to Repulse Bay for their vacations. Inuit bureaucrats wanted to go out on the land with people whose skills are much more current than their own. They could also hunt species not found around Rankin. The non-Inuit travellers wanted to tour such places as Wager Bay and North Pole River.

If tourists travelling to a national park at Wager Bay will extend their visits to see complementary areas in the Keewatin like Repulse Bay and if a more local market like Rankin Inlet can be tapped, then the tourism potential for Repulse Bay is very good.

This new interest in tourism—both the hunting and ecotourism varieties—has resulted in a marked change in attitude in the people of Repulse Bay towards a national park. They are beginning to see that a national park could put the Keewatin on the international tourism map and could act as an anchor for their tourism industry. They know that Auyuittuq National Park Reserve has done this for the Baffin Region. They are enthusiastic about the upsurge in sport hunting due to changes in U.S. legislation about the import of polar bear skins. But they also understand that the ecotourism market is the one that is most rapidly expanding. Many of the people of Repulse Bay are now strong supporters of a national park.

Tourism will be around forever. Mines, if they are developed, will have finite lifespans. Repulse Bay is still examining possible compromises. For example, the mining potential of the area outside the proposed national park could be developed, while the area inside a national park would be protected forever. With this approach, the people of Repulse Bay may see a balance of opportunities for their young people for the near and distant future.

Postscript:

In the spring of 1996, the affected Keewatin communities asked their regional Inuit organization to begin negotiating a national park agreement with Parks Canada. At the request of Inuit, the area of the national park proposal at Wager Bay was withdrawn under the *Territorial Lands Act* in September 1996, effectively protecting it on an interim basis (three years), so that Inuit could determine their priorities for the area. Formal negotiation of an Inuit Impact and Benefit Agreement (the park agreement as required by the *Nunavut Land Claim*) commenced in May 1997 and Elizabeth Seale is Chief Negotiator for the Federal Government. Repulse Bay now has 12 grades in its school and is celebrating its first high school graduate.

APPEALING AND MARKETING TO THE NORTH AMERICAN ECOTOURIST

Pamela A. Wight
Pam Wight & Associates

INTRODUCTION

Until recently, ecotourism market information has been scarce. Whatever information has been collected usually was obtained from surveys of destination visitors, or of the travel trade. The primary purpose of this paper is to provide information about the characteristics of ecotourists, their preferences and motivations, with specific focus on those elements which may have practical relevance to market successfully to this group. The primary data of this paper are based on a recent major study of ecotourism markets (HLA Consultants & ARA Consulting 1994). The research was commissioned by Alberta Economic Development and Tourism, British Columbia Small Business, Tourism and Culture, Canadian Heritage and Industry Canada.

As part of the research, surveys were conducted of the ecotourism travel trade (companies that offer nature, adventure or culture tourism opportunities in North America); ecotourists who had experienced such a product offered by commercial ecotourism operators; and, travellers more generally interested in nature, culture, or adventure vacations (called general consumers). In this paper, information is extracted mainly from the consumer survey, with additional information from the ecotourist survey.

The general consumer survey focused on the residents of seven major metropolitan areas in North America: Winnipeg, Toronto, Los Angeles, San Francisco, Seattle, Chicago and Dallas/Fort Worth. The target was to complete 200 telephone interviews in each metropolitan area, providing a total of approximately 1400 interviews. Neighbourhoods were selected where the average household income was in excess of $45,000 (CDN) and $35,000 (US). Respondents were screened to include only those who had taken a vacation out of state or province in the last three years, and who had, or were interested in taking a nature/adventure/culture vacation in the countryside or wilderness in the future.

For the survey of experienced North American ecotourists, names of clients were requested as part of the travel trade survey, and a total of 1200 surveys were mailed to ecotourists located in the U.S. and Canada. Approximately 200 questionnaires were returned with incorrect addresses, and 424 surveys were completed, representing 42 per cent of those who received surveys.

ECOTOURISM MARKET PROFILES

For the purposes of the study, it was agreed by the clients and consulting team that a definition of ecotourism should not be provided to survey respondents, since individuals tend to have their own varied perceptions or definitions of ecotourism, which might predispose them to orient their responses accordingly.   Rather, respondents were asked questions about their activities and preferences. They were asked if they had taken, or were interested in a vacation which involved activities related to nature, outdoor adventure, or cultural experiences in the countryside or wilderness. These elements are well-recognized as having a relationship with ecotourism (Lindberg 1991; Ryel & Grasse 1991; Wight 1993; Stewart 1994).   The use of nature, adventure, and culture provided respondents with a common perspective, without requiring a lengthy preamble to ensure that the respondents understood and agreed with an ideal definition of ecotourism.

In the past, different studies have provided differing results on ecotourist characteristics (e.g., they have been said to be older than average [Fennell & Smale 1992] or younger than average [Yuan & Moisey 1992]; to have a tendency to be male [Backman & Potts 1993; Weaver, Glenn & Rounds 1995] or to be female [Reingold 1993]). In reality, there is no typical ecotourist, there are a number of ecotourism market segments; there are, however, characteristic tendencies. The current study examined the characteristics of general consumers interested in ecotourism, as well as those of more experienced ecotourists. These have been reported in detail elsewhere (Wight 1995c) together with preferred trip features.

MARKETS: WHERE ARE THEY?

Popular belief, as well as much of the established ecotourism research, locates the prime ecotourism destination in tropical and developing countries (Ziffer 1989; Ingram & Durst 1989; Boo 1990; Lindberg 1991; Yee 1992). In this survey, however, roughly one-third of those surveyed indicated Canada (33 per cent) and the U.S. (31 per cent) as their preferred future ecotourism destinations. In addition, when asked for a second choice of destination, the consumers again made similar choices: 38 per cent chose Canada and 25 per cent chose the U.S. Experienced ecotourists were even more interested in Canada as a destination for their next trip which involved nature, adventure or culture in the countryside or wilderness (47 per cent), while 28 per cent preferred the U.S.

Seventy-seven per cent of consumers had already taken a vacation which involved nature, adventure or culture in the countryside or wilderness. Of the 23 per cent of the consumers who had not taken such a vacation previously, only one of these respondents did not intend to do so in the future. If the seven metropolitan areas surveyed are representative of other metropolitan areas in North America, it can be concluded that ecotourism markets for Canada exist in virtually every major metropolitan area in North America. The challenge is to target those market segments which match the products offered.

PRODUCT PREFERENCES

The product provided should respond to the principles of ecotourism by catering to small groups, offering educational experiences relying on environmentally sensitive facilities, operations, and practices, teaching awareness of environmental fragilities, ensuring benefits to locals, and involving local communities (Andersen 1993; Brandon 1993; Wight 1995a; Selengut 1995; Russell, Bottrill & Meredith 1995). Ecotourists are well-educated. They want to know about many aspects of their trip, such as itinerary, location, times, activities, accommodation, and meals. It will be critical to provide the packages and product options that they are seeking. For example, Quest Nature Tours has at least two types of brochure: a coloured, glossy, lavishly illustrated brochure for more general interest markets; and a monochromatic, highly descriptive document for the more dedicated ecotourist. The key elements sought by ecotourists are detailed below.

Activity preferences

Both general consumers and experienced ecotourists were asked an open-ended question about the activities they preferred on their last vacation which involved nature, adventure or culture. Multiple responses were allowed. In addition, they were later asked what activities they would prefer in their next such vacation. Both groups are interested in a tremendous range of activities (Table 1). However, walking, hiking and trekking may not have been given as much emphasis as they deserve. In Indonesia, the most popular nature tourism activities (45 per cent of those surveyed) are trekking and hiking (Nababan & Aliadi 1993). In North Carolina, South Carolina and Georgia, the most popular nature-based activity was hiking/walking (22 per cent) (Backman & Potts 1993).

Table 1. Activities Enjoyed on Last and Intentions for Next Ecotourism Trip

Activity	General Consumer %		Experienced Ecotourist %	
	Last Trip	Next Trip	Last Trip	Next Trip
Hiking	24	37	45	60
Backpacking	1	2	10	11
Touring	24	20	10	11
Camping	11	19	23	21
Boating	13	17	5	9
Rafting			35	25
Canoeing			10	13
Kayaking			12	13
Sailing			10	7
Cruise boat			5	2
Walking	20	17	4	8
Fishing	11	16	9	12
Scenery other than mountain/ocean	13	14	9	13
Swimming	14	12	5	4
Other water activities	8	9	10	8
Local cultures	8	8	6	12
Cycling	4	8	18	25
Skiing	5	7	11	13
Wildlife viewing	6	7	14	15
Visiting museums	6	6	5	7
Historical ruins and sites	8	6	8	8
Horse/trail riding	4	6	5	8
Mountain scenery	6	4	2	2
Visiting popular attractions	10	4	3	1
Visiting parks	7	3	12	2
Ocean scenery	9	4	1	0.5
Total Respondents	1070	1372	402	402

Respondents proved multiple activities; therefore, percentages total over 100%.

Similarly, both the consumers and experienced ecotourists placed walking and hiking highest on the list of activities preferred. Table 1 presents percentages of respondents who expressed a preference for activities. What may be of even more interest is the activity preference for the next ecotourism trip: the intention to hike increases substantially with both groups. Thus, walking and hiking may currently be under-marketed as "activities."

Water-based activities are also important, particularly to the experienced ecotourist. It should be noted that the specialized nature of some of the travel trade providing client lists may have contributed to the ecotourists' strong interest in water-based activities. The travel trade's most popular activity list also includes a considerable number of water-based activities.

There are multiple activities mentioned by both general consumers and experienced ecotourists. This desire of ecotourists for multi-activity vacations echoes other findings that international tourists (particularly long haul) favour multiple stop vacations (Ayala 1995). Promotional activities should feature a variety of experiences and activity opportunities, whether or not a specialized market is targeted.

The open-ended questions about last trip/next trip preferences adds a dynamic element to ecotourism market research. Respondents indicate that not only would they prefer multiple activities, but also the number of activities increases from the last to the next trip. There are also changes in activity preferences, for both the consumers and the ecotourists. What is distinctive is that the consumers' preferences tend to be moving in the direction of the ecotourists' preferred activities. This supports some of the suggestions made in the literature (Reingold 1993).

Accommodation preferences

General consumers chose hotels/motel accommodation most often (56 per cent), but also selected a range of other options, from camping to fixed roof options. Each respondent volunteered 1.3 accommodation selections on average, (although they were asked for one only) which appears to indicate a willingness to use a range of types of accommodation. Experienced ecotourists seemed even more flexible, and made 3.5 selections of accommodation type. Hotels/motels accounted for only 41 per cent of the total number of responses for experienced ecotourists. Experienced ecotourists were far more likely than general consumers to select intimate, adventure-type accommodation, such as cabins (66 per cent), lodges/inns (60 per cent), camping (58 per cent), bed and breakfast (58 per cent), or ranches (40 per cent).

Of possibly greater significance than this desire for adventure-type accommodation is the number of responses made by each respondent. The travel trade interviews and other evidence (HLA 1994) supports the conclusion that the overall vacation experience seems to determine the accommodation; the accommodation is not the critical determinant.

In a Canadian survey of adventure travel operators (Tourism Canada 1995), the most popular form of accommodation was cabins/cottages (41 per cent) followed by tents (40 per cent). The literature also indicates a range of accommodation, with considerable emphasis given to smaller scale, rural and adventure-type accommodation, tending toward the more rustic, than the lavish (Ingram & Durst 1989; Wight 1995b; Reingold 1993).

With respect to luxury, the market demand study revealed that the main desire (over 90 per cent) is for mid-range (60 per cent) or basic budget (31 per cent) accommodation, by both general consumers and experienced ecotourists (56 per cent mid-range and 38 per cent basic budget). However, ecotourists often want a higher degree of comfort at the end of their trip. For example, after a week of hiking, hikers want amenities like a bed and a tub or shower (Sorensen 1993).

There are at least two relevant considerations related to ecotourism accommodations for promotional purposes: the type of accommodation and its greenness, implying how it demonstrates sensitivity to the environment (Anderson 1993; Bushnell 1994; Wight 1995c; Williams 1995). Ecotourism markets are interested in this information, witnessed by both media and ecotourism market interest in Selengut's Maho Bay operations in the U.S. Virgin Islands, as well as other environmentally sensitive properties (Selengut 1995; Hawkins, Epler Wood & Bittman 1995; Shundich 1996).

Other important elements of trip

General consumers and experienced ecotourists were asked to rate the importance of various features on a five point Likert scale, with one (1) being the most important and five (5) the least important (Table 2). A wilderness setting, including the wildlife, was the most important feature for the experienced ecotourism traveller, followed by wildlife viewing, hiking/trekking and visiting national park/other protected area. The features most important to the general consumer were very similar: casual walking, wildlife viewing, learning about other cultures, and visiting national parks/other protected areas.

Table 2. Importance Rating of Activities and Services

Service or Activity	Experienced Ecotourist Weighted Average	General Consumer Weighted Average
Wilderness setting	1.74	2.49
Wildlife viewing	1.83	2.02
Hiking/trekking	2.12	2.58
Visiting national park/other protected area	2.16	2.26
Rafting/canoeing/kayaking on a river or lake	2.24	3.08
Casual walking	2.32	1.84
Learning about other cultures	2.33	2.18
Participating in physically challenging programs	2.50	3.11
The importance of guides	2.67	2.76
Interpretive education programs	2.94	2.81
Ocean sailing/kayaking	3.00	3.37
Cycling	3.02	2.94
Trail riding (horse)	3.33	3.26
Cross country skiing	3.47	3.84
Mountain climbing	3.55	3.83

Ranked according to a 5 point scale, where 1=most important and 5=not important

MARKET MOTIVATIONS

Reasons for Trip

For both the ecotourist and the general traveller, the opportunity to enjoy scenery/nature was the primary reason for taking their next ecotourism vacation (Table 3). While 45 per cent of the general consumers gave this as a reason, this response rate is high, since only 22 per cent of general consumers gave enjoying scenery as the reason for their last trip. This result was identical to the responses of the experienced ecotourists.

The general consumers' reasons and interests are changing, as shown by differences in the last trip and the next trip preferences. For example, 40 per cent gave such conventional reasons for travel as to rest/relax/get away for their last trip, whereas only 13 per cent are interested in this as a reason for their next trip. Similarly, to visit family/friends as a reason for the trip has decreased, from 31 per cent for the last trip, to 11 per cent for the next trip. Both of these responses move strongly in the direction of the experienced ecotourists' responses (Table 3). Other distinct increases in interest (roughly a doubling) relate to travelling for new experiences/places, wildlife viewing, to see mountains, to experience cultural attractions/events/activities, and to study or learn about nature or cultures.

Table 3. Reason Why Trip Has Appeal

Reasons	Consumers		Ecotourist
	Last Trip %	Next Trip %	Next Trip %
Enjoy scenery/nature	22	45	45
New experiences/places	16	28	22
Land activities	9	8	16
Wildlife viewing	3	7	15
See mountains	7	15	14
Wilderness experience	0	12	11
Not touristy/crowded	0	1	11
Water activities	7	9	11
Cultural attractions	9	15	10
Study/learn nature/cultures	6	14	10
Rest/relax/get away	40	13	4
Been there/go again	14	16	3
Visit family & friends	31	11	1

N.B. Only the general consumer was asked the question regarding reason for last nature/adventure/culture trip. Multiple responses were permitted; therefore, total percentage will exceed 100%.

While wilderness did not rate as a reason for the consumers' last trip, it is a reason for 12 per cent for their next trip, and it is almost identical to the results of the experienced ecotourist. Also, the importance of cultural experiences or attractions on the next trip for the general consumer is more important than for the experienced ecotourist. Those in the industry should examine the experienced ecotourists' preferences, since there seems to be a tendency for the mainstream markets to follow the ecotourists' lead, and other literature supports this (Reingold 1993; Preece, van Ostersee & James 1995). Trends are helpful when considering what elements to make available in a package and what to promote.

Motivations

The literature reports that ecotourists have different motivations than the traditional travellers (Eagles 1992; Fennell & Smale 1992). Reingold (1993) refers to the growing dissatisfaction with traditional sightseeing, and how life enhancement was the chief vacation goal for 40 per cent of travellers interviewed. Hall and Weiler (1992: 8) discuss the special interest tourists' "common desire for authenticity, immersion in the cultural and/or physical environment, and the pursuit of environmental and experiential quality." These characteristics may be distinguished by educational and cultural motivations, and by a desire to experience novelty and uniqueness as part of the travel experience. Indeed, the latter element is a reason given by a quarter of all ecotourists for going on their next ecotourism trip (Table 3).

Ecotourists seek a range of products, but it is clear that the setting (which includes wildlife viewing) is of paramount importance to an ecotourism experience. It may be, however, that setting is also critical to other, more traditional types of travellers. Therefore, it is important to discover those features which distinguish between ecotourists and other types of traveller, so as to discover the benefits which ecotourists seek (Wight 1995a). These will be the elements to provide in a package, and also to feature in any promotional activities. Thus, it is important to differentiate products to respond to market segments in terms of type (e.g., adventure vs. historical interest), and also through a benefits sought approach.

HOW TO REACH THE ECOTOURIST

A marketing strategy can be non-segmented, and appealing to the overall spectrum of the market, or single-segmented, where a specific segment of the market is targeted. The latter may be chosen for a variety of reasons such as operator's expertise (e.g., ornithologist), the nature of destination resources (e.g., rare flora), or revenue potential (e.g., segment proven willing to pay). The following provides information on lead contact time, club membership, publications read, and information sources relevant to general consumers interested in ecotourism.

When to reach the markets

Most general consumers have a lead time for booking their trip ranging from zero to three months, as shown in Table 4. It would appear that the vast majority (71 per cent) of consumers decide within three months of the trip itself. There is no further information as to whether this is more likely to be months, weeks or even days before the trip. A six month lead time is usual for a further 15 per cent of respondents.

Information sources

The general consumers were asked about the sources of information used to find out and learn about their last ecotourism vacation. The responses are found in Table 5. Although multiple responses were allowed, it is clear that personal contacts (friends/family, personal experience from previous vacations, and word of mouth) are the major sources of information. In further support of these findings, an operator claimed that over 80 per cent of customers in 1991 were either repeat clients or had come as the result of a friend's recommendation (Wild 1992). Similarly, in Manitoba, in a survey of 24 ecotourism operators, 23 used informal, word of mouth modes of marketing. The effectiveness of this strategy can be confirmed since 22 operators asked their customers how they heard of the operation, and most customers (17) indicated word of mouth as critical (Weaver et al. 1995).

When such a large percentage of the decisions by the more mainstream ecotourism markets (consumers interested in nature, culture, adventure in the countryside or wilderness) are based on word of mouth recommendations or personal experience, delivering on product quality and expectation is an important aspect of future success. Thus, there is considerable need to ensure an appropriate match between markets and the products offered, as well as between market expectations and the experience provided.

Table 4. Lead Time For Booking Ecotourism Vacations

Lead Time	General Consumer %
0 - 3 months	71
4 - 5 months	6
6 months	15
7 - 11 months	2
1 year	6
> 1 year	1
Total Number of Respondents	1072

Table 5. Vacation Planning Information Sources

Information Source	General Consumer %
Friends/family	37
Personal experience/been there before	23
Books/magazine	16
Travel brochure	14
Travel association/bureau	14
Word of mouth	10
Travel agent	9
Television	2
Other	7
Total Number of Respondents	1072

Multiple responses were permitted; therefore, total percentages will exceed 100%.

Club membership

The experienced ecotourist exhibits a much greater propensity to belong to a nature-oriented club or organization (50 per cent) than the consumers (11 per cent). However, general consumers represent a huge target population, so the actual numbers of consumers who are members of nature-oriented organizations are by no means small overall.

The membership by type of organization is shown in Table 6. The most popular individual organizations to which both groups belong include the Sierra Club and the Audubon Society. It is interesting to note that the experienced ecotourism traveller, while tending to prefer activity-related magazines, belongs to more nature and wilderness-related organizations.

Table 6. Membership in Organizations/Clubs

Organization/Club	General Consumer %	Experienced Ecotourist %
% of total sample which belongs to club/organization	11	50
Club/Organization	153 respondents	189 respondents
Sierra Club	18	34
Outdoor activity club	13	11
Nature organization[1]	10	37
Audubon Society	5	17
Other wildlife organizations[2]	10	8
Fishing and hunting	6	0
Greenpeace	5	2
World Wildlife Fund	4	3
National Wildlife Federation	4	3
Boy/Girl Scouts	4	0

N.B. Multiple responses were permitted, therefore, total percentage may exceed 100%.
1. Refers to nature/naturalist/conservation/park organizations.
2. Refers to organizations such as Ducks Unlimited and wilderness societies.

Publications read by ecotourists

There has been an explosion in specialty publications, such as *Outside, Backpacker, Conde Naste, Escape, Eco-Traveller, Summit, Canoe, Diving, Snow Country*, and a whole range of outdoor and specialist monthlies. The degree to which the two groups read outdoor adventure or nature magazines and publications varies somewhat with 61 per cent of the consumers stating that they read these, compared to the 72 per cent of experienced ecotourists who read such publications. The results are shown in Table 7. Both groups mentioned the same publications, but their relative preference for each category of publication varied.

The most popular magazine for consumers was *National Geographic* (35 per cent); the preferred ecotourist magazines were classified as outdoor life (36 per cent), which included *Outdoor Life, Outdoors, Outside* and *Outdoor Canada*. Both these categories were more than twice as popular with their respective groups than the next most popular magazines. However, a range of other club publications and general activity sports publications were also reported. It is not surprising to find that double the percentage of experienced ecotourists read club publications, since many more experienced ecotourists (50 per cent) are members of organizations than general consumers (11 per cent).

Table 7. Publications Read

Publications	General Consumer %	Experienced Ecotourist %
% of total sample which reads such publications	61	72
Publication	540 respondents	271 respondents
National Geographic	35	17
Outdoor life[1]	10	36
Club publications	7	15
Fishing/hunting related	6	2
General nature[2]	5	3
Field & Stream	5	0
General travel	5	6
General activity/sport	5	14
Wildlife related	4	3

N.B. Multiple responses were permitted
1. Refers to *Outdoor Life/Outdoors/Outside/Outdoor Canada*.
2. Refers to nature/natural history publications.

PACKAGING AND PROMOTING

Products and services may be purchased separately or they may be packaged selectively. They are then offered as a single product at a single price, and are sometimes referred to as preset packages. The types of product combinations include transportation, guides, equipment, meals, and accommodation. The package components will vary by type of package. In addition, the length of package may have some relevance for package components. For example, the longer the package, the more likely it is that transportation, accommodation, and meals would be included. Tourism Canada (1995) surveyed adventure and nature operators and found that tour guides (79 per cent) and equipment (73 per cent) were the components most frequently included in packages.

PRODUCT PRICING AND WILLINGNESS TO PAY

There have been criticisms of ecotourism and nature-based tourism as being potentially elitist (Wheeller 1991; Weiler & Richins 1995), and on the other hand, that these forms of tourism have low earning capacity (Goudberg, Cassells & Valentine n.d.; Laarman & Durst 1993; Sayer 1981). In order to determine willingness to spend, respondents were asked how much they would be prepared to pay per person for their previously described nature, culture or adventure vacation in the countryside or wilderness. The cost per person was to include transportation, food, accommodation, and all other vacation costs. Table 8 shows that the experienced ecotourists were willing to spend more for their ecotourism experience than were the general consumers. For example, one-third (38 per cent) of consumers would pay over $1,500 per person, while almost half (45 per cent) of experienced ecotourists would spend this amount per person. There was, as expected, a strong relationship between expenditure and length of trip: as the length of trip increased, the willingness to spend increased.

In the market demand study, average expenditures per day were calculated for visitors who might be interested in Alberta or British Columbia. These figures should not be taken to equate to per diem package prices. In order to do this, certain assumptions, taken from the market research, were made, as follows:

• The destination will attract those who are prepared to pay over U.S. $2,000 per person for their total experience, as travel from destinations in North America will require higher expenditures than travel only a short distance within home state or province.
• With an exchange rate of $1.00 U.S. = $1.35 CDN, total expenditures are $2,700 or more
• Transportation to destination is $500 CDN
• Average trip duration is seven days

In this scenario, average daily expenditure per person will be $314. This seems to be reasonable, when compared with other findings (e.g., Lillywhite, Lillywhite and Johnson [1992], in Botswana, assumed an expenditure of $511/tourist/day for 10 days).

Since visitors will spend on items in addition to the ecotourism package (e.g., side packages, accommodation, meals, souvenirs, and tips), this should not be taken to represent the amount an individual operator can charge per person per day. This is not a price but rather an indication of what a percentage of the market indicate they are willing to pay per day for an average vacation that includes ecotourism experiences.

Table 8. Willingness to Spend

Expenditures	Consumers %	Ecotourists %
Less than $500	15	7
$501 - $1,000	25	22
$1,001 - $1,500	21	26
$1,501 - $2,000	16	21
$2,001 - $3,000	14	16
$3,001 - $5,000	6	7
Over $5,000	2	1
Total Respondents	1332	417

No currency adjustments are made, since an indeterminate proportion of expenditures may be incurred outside country of origin.

Given the diversity of the industry, prices naturally vary, sometimes dramatically, as shown on Table 9. Operators may have per diems which are quite low (the Canadian average for canoeing is $86.63 per day), and the lowest priced product is seal pup watching, which averages a meager $4.75 per hour. Prices can also be quite high (e.g., polar bear watching averages $312.81 per day), with an average high of $463.90 per day for other winter activities which includes heli-skiing (Tourism Canada 1995).

Expenditure is related to length of trip. Those who indicated a willingness to spend more typically also indicated a preference for a longer vacation. Of those who indicated a willingness to spend over $2,000, five per cent prefer a four to seven day trip, 14 per cent prefer an eight to 14 day trip, and 36 per cent prefer a longer than 14 day trip. Expenditures clearly vary with a variety of factors, including length of trip, origin of ecotourist, economic ability to pay, uniqueness, destination for ecotourism, type of accommodation, activities on vacation, opportunities for expenditure, and many others. There seems to be no typical pattern of expenditure.

INTEGRITY IN PROMOTION

Too often, ecotourism marketing has been charged with, or found guilty of a false green image or ecosell (Wight 1994). The ecotourist is likely to be highly educated and interested in his or her vacation and so is less likely to be deceived by ecosell. If operators or destinations developed a mission and goals statement which reflected the principles of ecotourism, they would be less likely to be charged with false green advertising (Wight 1993). This would also help with any marketing efforts. As Jean-Michel Cousteau (1993: 227) said, "It is my hope that tourists will demand ecological integrity from the airlines, hotels, and tour operators, and will ask different questions: what are you doing to support the local environment and culture? Are you using environmentally sensitive products and methods? Are you charging the real price it might cost to maintain and restore the environment?" A good transparent ethos for operations was used by Richard Bangs, partner in Mountain Travel Sobek, the largest adventure travel company in the world; his talk to the 1993 World Congress on Ecotourism was titled: "Clean, Green, and Meant to be Seen."

Table 9. Canadian Product Prices

Adventure Product	Average Price Per Day $	Average Number of Days
Nature Observation	172	5.3
Wildlife Viewing		
Bird watching	101	6.5
Polar bear watching	313	5.4
Seal pup watching	4.75/hr	2.5 hr
Other wildlife (bear, moose caribou, bison, etc.)	337.50	7.0
Water adventure products		
Canoeing	86.63	6.5
Sea kayaking	112.64	5.7
River kayaking	100	3.6
Rafting	135.28	4.3
Sailing	170.87	5.9
Scuba diving	194.33	4.2
Land adventure products		
Hiking	135.25	6.1
Rock/ice climbing	112.86	4.7
Trail riding	100.56	5.0
Bicycling	115.95	5.6
Winter adventure products		
Dog sledding	192.67	3
Cross-country skiing	109.53	4.5
Snowmobiling	179.05	4.1
Other winter (toboggan, snow-shoeing, heli-skiing)	463.90	5.7
Air adventure (hot air ballooning)	92.50/hr	2.5 hr
Other (e.g., native culture, jet skiing, motorcycling)	382.67	X

Source: Tourism Canada 1995

Success stories are helpful in promotional activities. Operators and destinations should consider mentioning any problems, issues or concerns for the locale. Providing such information within educational materials intended to help prepare the visitor for the experience would be a helpful approach. Oswaldo Munoz is a naturalist guide, consultant, and president of the Ecuadorean Ecotourism Association. He advises: "consider revealing some of your environmental problems in promotional brochures . . . Let's be honest with our guests, for they will quite often find out the truth for themselves" (1993: 62).

Consumers are concerned about the environment, and are likely to ask questions. They are interested in information indicating, for example, that local suppliers are used, or that a portion of the trip price goes to a conservation group, and skeptical about environmental window-dressing (Selengut 1993; Munoz 1993). But they are also likely to ask how many supplies are local and what proportion of fees go to which organization. It makes sense to partner with compatible organizations, whether conservation groups, research facilities, zoos, universities, or museums, for resource benefits, advice, and credibility in marketing (Morgan 1993; Mallett 1993). One of the fundamentals for a sustainable industry is conservation of the resource base, whether natural or cultural (Morgan 1993; Wight 1993a). It is not only a smart long-term approach to provide benefits to the resource (research, contributions, dollars, resource maintenance), but also it can add credibility to marketing efforts (Wight 1995c).

SUMMARY AND CONCLUSIONS

This paper indicates that North American ecotourists, whether specialists or more general interest travellers, share some common characteristics and preferences. They are very interested in Canada as a destination for nature, adventure, and cultural activities, with at least a third stating Canada as their next preferred destination.

In marketing the ecotourism product, it is helpful to be aware of the product preferences of the ecotourism markets. These include providing the activities which are desired, including forms of walking, hiking and trekking, and water-based activities, and ensuring that multiple activity opportunities are available; offering the type of intimate, more adventure-type accommodation that is increasingly in demand, and aiming to respond to the facility-based conservation that is increasingly desired; and offering the kinds of activities and services that are rated highly by ecotourists, such as remote settings, wildlife viewing, or opportunities to visit national or other parks/protected areas.

The reasons for taking a trip appear to be changing, with a significant increase of interest in scenery and nature, new experiences, wilderness, cultural attractions, and learning experiences.

Personal contacts of the ecotourist, their friends and family are the major sources of information when deciding on taking their trip. Since word of mouth can act negatively as well as positively, it is important to deliver the expected product, and to satisfy market expectations and preferences as much as possible.

For the purpose of reaching ecotourists, it is important to remember that a considerable number of ecotourists belong to organizations or clubs, such as the Sierra Club, a range of nature/conservation/parks organizations or the Audubon Society. In addition, marketing to ecotourists via the publications which they read might be a useful way to target this market. The main publications of relevance are outdoor-type magazines, as well as the club publications of those organizations to which ecotourists belong.

One of the fundamentals of ecotourism is conservation of the resource base. It appears that ecotourists are increasingly considering the activities of their host operator when they select their destination. Thus, building appropriate discussion of this aspect into promotional materials might also be beneficial to marketing efforts. The objective of operators and destinations should be not only to simply reach ecotourists successfully through marketing efforts, but also to use information about the market characteristics and preferences to provide appropriate product options, and to ensure that the overall experience matches the expectation of the market.

REFERENCES

Andersen, D.L. 1993. A window to the natural world: The design of ecotourism facilities. In K. Lindberg and D.E. Hawkins, (eds.) *Ecotourism: A guide for planners & managers*, p. 116-133. North Bennington, Vermont: The Ecotourism Society.

Ayala, H. 1995. From quality product to ecoproduct: Will Fiji set a precedent? *Tourism Management, 16* (1), 39-47.

Backman, K.F. & T.D. Potts. 1993. *Profiling nature-based travelers: Southeastern market segments*. South Carolina: Strom Thurmond Institute.

Bangs, R. 1993. Clean, green and meant to be seen: The ethos of eco-tourism. In *Proceedings of the 1993 world congress on adventure travel and eco-tourism*, p. 97-101. Manaus, Brazil. Englewood, Colorado: The Adventure Travel Society Inc.

Boo, E. 1990. *Ecotourism: The potential and pitfalls*. Washington, DC: World Wildlife Fund.

Brandon, K. 1993. Basic steps toward encouraging local participation in nature tourism projects. In K. Lindberg & D.E. Hawkins, (eds.) *Ecotourism: A guide for planners & managers*, p. 134-151. North Bennington, Vermont: The Ecotourism Society.

Bushnell, S.M. 1994. *The ecotourism planning kit: A business planning guide for ecotourism operators in the Pacific Islands*. Honolulu: The Pacific Business Center Program, University of Hawaii.

Cousteau, J-M. 1993. With best intentions. In *Proceedings of the 1993 world congress on adventure travel and eco-tourism*, p. 224-229. Manaus, Brazil. Englewood, Colorado: The Adventure Travel Society Inc.

Eagles, P.F.J. 1992. The travel motivations of Canadian ecotourists. *Journal of Travel Research*, *31* (2) 3-7.

Fennell, D. & B. Smale. 1992. Ecotourism and natural resource protection. *Tourism Recreation Research*, *17* (1) 21-32.

Goudberg, N.J., D.S. Cassells & P.S. Valentine. (n.d). *The prospects for an ecotourism industry in Northern Queensland wet tropical rainforests*. Townsville, Queensland, Australia: Institute for Tropical Rainforest Studies, Department of Geography, James Cook University.

Hall, C.M. & B. Weiler. 1992. What's special about special interest tourism? In B. Weiler & C.M. Hall, (eds.) *Special interest tourism*. p. 1-14. London: Belhaven Press.

Hawkins, D.E., M. Epler Wood & S. Bittman. 1995. *The ecolodge sourcebook*. North Bennington, Vermont: The Ecotourism Society.

HLA Consultants. 1994. *Tour operator market for Alberta ecotourism experiences*. Edmonton, Alberta: Alberta Economic Development and Tourism.

HLA Consultants and ARA Consulting. 1994. *Ecotourism - nature/adventure/culture: Alberta and British Columbia market demand assessment.* Prepared for Canadian Heritage, Industry Canada, BC Ministry of Small Business, Tourism and Culture, Alberta Economic Development and Tourism, and Outdoor Recreation Council of BC. Edmonton, Alberta.

Ingram, C.D. & P.D. Durst. 1989. Nature-oriented tour operators: Travel to developing countries. *Journal of Travel Research, 28* (2) p. 11-15.

Laarman, J.G. & P.B. Durst. 1993. Nature tourism as a tool for economic development and conservation of natural resources. In J. Nenon & P.B. Durst, (eds.), *Nature tourism and Asia: Opportunities and constraints for conservation and economic development,* p. 1-19. Washington, D.C.: USDA, Forest Service, USAID, USDA, Office of International Cooperation and Development.

Lillywhite, M., L. Lillywhite & K. Johnson. 1992. Development of a tourism-sustaining parks and wildlife conservation program for the Tibet Autonomous Region, China. In *Proceedings of the 1992 world congress on adventure travel and eco-tourism,* p. 77-78. Whistler, B.C., Englewood, Colorado: The Adventure Travel Society Inc.

Lindberg, K. 1991. *Policies for maximizing nature tourism's ecological and economic benefits.* World Resources Institute, February.

Mallett, J. 1993. Selling adventure travel new travelers - new techniques. In *Proceedings of the 1993 world congress on adventure travel and eco-tourism,* p. 127-130. Manaus, Brazil. Englewood, Colorado: The Adventure Travel Society Inc.

Morgan, D. 1993. Eco-Tourism, a reality at the end of the millennium. In *Proceedings of the 1993 world congress on adventure travel and eco-tourism,* p. 131-136. Manaus, Brazil. Englewood, Colorado: The Adventure Travel Society Inc.

Munoz, O. 1993. The ecotourism explosion: Is it radioactive? In *Proceedings of the 1993 world congress on adventure travel and eco-tourism,* p. 59-62. Manaus, Brazil. Englewood, Colorado: The Adventure Travel Society Inc.

Nababan, A. & A. Aliadi. 1993. Nature tourism profile: Indonesia. In J. Nenon & P.B. Durst, (eds.). *Nature tourism and Asia: Opportunities and constraints for conservation and economic development*, p. 43-54. Washington, D.C.: USDA, Forest Service, USAID, USDA, Office of International Cooperation and Development.

Preece, N., P. van Oosterzee & D. James. 1995. *Two way track: Biodiversity conservation and ecotourism*. Biodiversity Series, Paper No. 5, Canberra: Biodiversity Unit, Australia Department of the Environment, Sport and Territories.

Reingold, L. 1993. Identifying the elusive ecotourist. In *Going Green*, a supplement to *Tour and Travel News*, October 25, 36-39.

Ryel, R. & T. Grasse. 1991. Marketing ecotourism: Attracting the elusive ecotourist. In Whelan, T. *Nature tourism: Managing for the environment*, (ed). Washington DC: Island Press.

Russell, D., C. Bottrill & G. Meredith. 1995. International ecolodge survey. In Hawkins, D.E., M. Epler Wood & S. Bittman (eds.). *The ecolodge sourcebook* p. ix-xvii. North Bennington, Vermont: The Ecotourism Society.

Sayer, J.A. 1981. Tourism or conservation in the National Parks of Benen. *Parks*, 5 (4) 13-15.

Selengut, S. 1995. Foreword. In Hawkins, D.E., M. Epler Wood & S. Bittman (Eds). *The ecolodge sourcebook*, p. v-vi. North Bennington, Vermont: The Ecotourism Society.

Selengut, S. 1993. Responsible eco-tourism development. In *Proceedings of the 1993 world congress on adventure travel and eco-tourism*, Manaus, Brazil. p. 95-96. Englewood, Colorado: The Adventure Travel Society Inc., 95-96.

Shundich, S. 1996. Ecoresorts: Dollars, sense & the environment. *Hotels*, 30 (3) 34-40.

Sorensen, L. 1993. The special-interest travel market. *The Cornell H.R.A. Quarterly*, June: 24-30.

Stewart, W.P. 1994. Disentangling ecotourism. *Annals of Tourism Research, 21* (4), 840-842.

Tourism Canada. 1995. *Adventure travel in Canada: An overview of product, market and business potential.* Ottawa: Industry Canada.

Weaver, D.B., C.L. Glenn & R.C. Rounds. 1995. *Ecotourism in Manitoba.* RDI Report Series 1995-5, The Rural Development Institute, Brandon University, Brandon, MB.

Wheeller, B. 1991. Responsible tourism is not the answer. *Tourism Management, 12* (2) 91-96.

Weiler, B. & H. Richins. 1995. Extreme, extravagant and elite: A profile of ecotourists on earthwatch expeditions. *Tourism Recreation Research, 20* (1) 29-36.

Wight, P. 1995a. Ecotourism markets: Who are they and what are they seeking? Paper presented to *Sharing Tomorrow: Exploring Responsible Tourism.* Interpretation Canada National Conference. Riding Mountain National Park, Manitoba, September 24-27.

Wight, P. 1995b. Environmentally sensitive technologies/facilities: Responding to market demand for responsible travel and deriving economic benefit. Paper presented to *Sharing Tomorrow: Exploring Responsible Tourism.* Interpretation Canada National Conference. Riding Mountain National Park, Manitoba, September 24-27.

Wight, P.A. 1995c. Tapping into market potential for ecotourism. Keynote address prepared for workshop *Ecotourism in Ontario - New Business Opportunities.* Sir Sandford Fleming College, Haliburton Campus, Ecotourism Management Program, 24 - 25 November.

Wight, P. 1994. Environmentally responsible marketing of tourism. In E. Cater and G. Lowman, (Eds.), p. 39-55. *Ecotourism: A sustainable option?* Chichester: John Wiley & Sons and Royal Geographical Society.

Wight, P. 1993. Sustainable ecotourism: Balancing economic, environmental and social goals within an ethical framework. *Journal of Tourism Studies, 4* (2) 54-66.

Wild, C. 1992. The business of packaging adventure and ecotours. In *Proceedings of the 1992 world congress on adventure travel and eco-tourism*, p. 178-182. Whistler, B.C. Englewood, Colorado: The Adventure Travel Society Inc.

Williams, P. 1995. How green is my ecolodge: Eco-labeling evaluation issues and criteria. In Hawkins, D.E., M. Epler Wood & S. Bittman (Eds.). *The ecolodge sourcebook*, p. 87-93. North Bennington, Vermont: The Ecotourism Society.

Yee, J.G. 1992. *Ecotourism market survey: A survey of North American ecotourism tour operators*. The Intelligence Centre, San Francisco: Pacific Asia Travel Association.

Yuan, M.S. & N. Moisey. 1992. The characteristics and economic significance of visitors attracted to Montana wildlands. *Western Wildlands*, *Fall*, *18* (3) 20-24.

Ziffer, K.A. 1989. *Ecotourism: The uneasy alliance*. Conservation International, Washington: Ernst and Young.

IDENTIFYING DESIRED ECOTOURISM ACTIVITIES, SETTINGS AND EXPERIENCES

Dave Robinson
University of Northern British Columbia

Dave Twynam
Lakehead University

Wolfgang Haider
Simon Fraser University

Len Hunt
Ontario Ministry of Natural Resources

BACKGROUND TO THE STUDY

The concept of sustainable development necessitates consideration of three diverse components: environmental sustainability, economic sustainability and social sustainability. In this light, to achieve sustainable forest management the benefits derived from Canada's forests should be diverse and multiple, and forest management must adopt a multi-value management approach (Robson, Robinson & Hawley 1995). As such, the future success of forest managers in northern Ontario could well be judged by how well they develop policies that fulfil both timber and non-timber values. Such an approach must reflect the values and priorities of the public owners of Canada's forests, and must comprise truly integrated resource management that seeks to increase substantially the contact between people and the forest. Presently, the largest share of forest revenue in northern Ontario and across Canada in general comes from timber. Carrow (1993), a forestry economist, has argued that a greatly increased revenue base could come from non-extractive people-related activities in the forest.

The large tracts of forested landscape found in Canada provide a foundation for a multi-million dollar industry in outdoor recreation and tourism. Ecotourism[1] is now recognized as a viable, long-term use of Canada's forests that can contribute to the development of sustainable forestry policies that build upon the concepts of integrated resource management (Scace, Grifone & Usher 1992). Ecotourism is seen as an important supplementary means of providing local economic benefits and generating employment in local communities, while also contributing to the conservation and management of natural areas (Lindberg 1994). Nature-based tourism is now the fastest growing sector of both the Canadian and international tourism markets, and given the vast expanse of forest wilderness in northern Ontario, there exists in this region a potentially large market for forest-based ecotourism which to date has been relatively untapped.

An assessment of Ontario's speciality outdoor tourism projected that ecotourism is a major tourism market which awaits development (Marshall, Macklin & Monoghan 1991). The Ecotourism Opportunity Identification Study (1991) also indicated that ecotourism in Ontario has experienced constant and significantly higher growth than other areas of tourism, has been comparatively recession resilient, and has a potentially higher value added component than conventional tourism. A regional example is the remote tourism benefits accrued in 1988 to the region of North Algoma and to the province of Ontario. A study of this region by Economics Resource Limited and the Ministry of Tourism and Recreation (1990) indicated tourism expenditures of $8.1 million, $16.1 million in sustained gross output, $7.3 million in labour income, $3.1 million in taxes generated, 153 person years of direct employment from operations and capital expenditures, and 228 additional years employment through indirect and other direct effects.

These studies suggest that ecotourism could have a major financial impact on local economies and generate employment opportunities which may not otherwise exist in northern Ontario. If marketing strategies are devised which accurately target appropriate segments of the ecotourism market, the potential exists for forest-based ecotourism in northern Ontario to become an important industry that could supplement and strengthen existing economies. Beyond generating both economic and social benefits, ecotourism would promote multiple uses of northern Ontario's forests that support the sustainable use of the forests, and in so doing contribute to the conservation and preservation of those forests.

PURPOSES OF THE STUDY

In 1992, the Government of Canada, through its Green Plan of Canada initiative, entered into the Canada-Ontario Northern Ontario Development Agreement (NODA) with the provincial government of Ontario. NODA's primary objective is to support applied forestry research that will assist the forestry sector in developing policies to promote sustainable forestry in northern Ontario.

Traditionally, the forests of this region have been managed predominantly for timber extraction. This study was premised on the understanding that the use of a resource—in this case, extractive forestry in northern Ontario's forests—will have implications for all other competing uses. Seeking to support the objective of sustainable forestry, this project was designed to assess the viability of ecotourism as a multi-purpose non-consumptive component of integrated forest management in northern Ontario.

To develop a strategy which can promote successfully northern Ontario as a suitable destination for the ecotourist, it is necessary to identify and quantify the demand side of the ecotourism demand-supply relationship in northern Ontario. This demand side is defined as the desired ecotourism opportunities of the region's latent (i.e. untapped) ecotourism market. Recent northern Ontario research indicates that the latent ecotourism market of northern Ontario consists primarily of those individuals living in northern and southern Ontario, the bordering provinces of Manitoba and Quebec, and the northern states of the U.S.A., who have previously recreated in a wilderness or near-wilderness setting (Haider 1993, personal communication).

Focusing on forest-based ecotourism, the specific purposes of this study were:

• To identify the desired ecotourism opportunities of those visitors who make up the latent ecotourism market for northern Ontario; and,

• To develop ecotourism market segmentation profiles which, for marketing purposes, identify the desired ecotourism opportunities of specific socio-economic sectors of the latent ecotourism market of northern Ontario.

Once the demand aspects of ecotourism in northern Ontario are determined, it is then possible to match desired ecotourism opportunities with the supply side of the ecotourism demand-supply relationship. Supply is the region's existing ecotourism opportunities. This particular project dove-tails with a parallel study being conducted at the University of Western Ontario to develop a GIS data-base of northern Ontario's existing ecotourism opportunities.

Defining "desired ecotourism opportunities"

Over the past 20 years, the planning and management of ecotourism/ outdoor recreation opportunities has evolved into a consideration of three interrelated components: recreation/tourism activities, resource settings, and desired psychological experiences or benefits of the experience. These concepts form the basis of the behavioural approach, which suggests that recreation choices can be explained in terms of human behaviour which is goal directed (Driver & Tocher 1970). Desired ecotourism opportunities may be conceptualized as being of three interrelated types:

• User preferences for particular forest-based *activities* (for example, non-consumptive activities such as backcountry hiking, canoeing or bird watching, or cultural/heritage activities such as viewing traditional native community events);

• User preferences for particular forest *settings/environments* (for example, an unmodified pristine forest setting or a man modified forest setting); and,

• User preferences for particular forest-based *experiences* (for example, a remote wilderness experience where one encounters relatively few other visitors or a less remote forest experience where one frequently encounters with other visitors).

Tourist segmentation studies (e.g., McCool, Menning & Spettigue 1994) indicate that these desired opportunities will vary with specific socio-economic characteristics (e.g., age, gender, ethnicity, income, marital status, family make up, and rural/urban residence). This understanding forms the basis for the development of ecotourism market segmentation profiles that have marketing applications.

METHODS

Sample

The sample was comprised of 2000 potential ecotourists. These individuals were potential visitors to northern Ontario who were associated with either Mountain Equipment Cooperative [MEC] in Canada or Recreation Equipment Incorporated [REI] in the U.S.A. These two nature oriented recreation cooperatives were selected because they represent a clearly defined outdoor recreation/tourism related group which has marketing potential for ecotourism in northern Ontario. The random selection of participants from the mailing lists of MEC was based on a stratified sample of members in the provinces of Ontario, Quebec and Manitoba. REI submitted a random selection of member names based on those states which are in the vicinity of the Great Lakes.

Procedures

Surveys were mailed to a random sample generated from the MEC and REI mailing lists (1000 surveys each to U.S. and Canadian groups of potential respondents). Four weeks after the initial contact was made, a postcard reminder was sent to each participant. A follow-up letter and a copy of the survey questionnaire were then sent to non-respondents three weeks later.

Of the 2000 surveys sent 150 were returned to sender and 799 usable responses were received, resulting in a response rate of 43 per cent. The questionnaire contained a self-addressed envelope to facilitate the respondents' return of the questionnaire and to eliminate response bias resulting from direct mailing costs to the participant. To encourage response to the survey, participants were also given the option of including their name in a draw for 20 gift certificates worth $100.00. If the respondents opted to include their names on the ballot, this was immediately separated from the questionnaire to ensure the survey information remained anonymous.

RESULTS

The results have been divided into two sections; the first section outlines the general characteristics and preferences for the full (non-segmented) sample. The second section describes the market segmentation profiles developed from the full sample using a cluster analysis technique.

Socio-demographic characteristics, preferred activities, preferred settings, and preferred experiences

Socio-demographic highlights. The following summarizes the main social and demographic characteristics of the complete sample. Men comprised 64 per cent of the sample. The Canadian and American respondents were very similar with males comprising 65 per cent and 64 per cent respectively. A majority of the subjects, 58 per cent, were married/ common-law while 37 per cent were single and the remainder were divorced or widowed. Statistically significant differences existed between the Canadian and American respondents as a greater percentage of Canadians were single (42 per cent compared to 33 per cent of American respondents) and divorced (6 per cent compared to 4 per cent of Americans).

Respondents were well-educated, with 41 per cent having completed college/university and 31 per cent having some level of post-graduate studies. Statistically significant differences existed in education: 41 per cent of American respondents had attained post-graduate studies compared to 20 per cent of Canadian respondents.

Respondents were generally located in the higher income brackets (for example, almost one-third of the respondents had annual incomes of over $80,000). Over half (56 per cent) of the respondents reported annual incomes exceeding $50,001; 13 per cent were in the $40,001 - $50,000 bracket; nine per cent were in the $30,001 - $40,000 range; 10 per cent were in the $20,001 to $30,000 bracket and the remaining 11 per cent reported incomes of $20,000 or lower.

The majority of respondents were in the younger age groups with 59 per cent of the respondents aged less than 40 years: 22 per cent were between the ages of 20-29; 34 per cent were between the ages of 30-39, 27 per cent were between the ages of 40-49; and, 14 per cent were aged 50 or older.

Preferred activities.   An extensive list of ecotourism activities was generated inclusive of consumptive, non-consumptive, motorized and non-motorized land and water-based recreational activities (Table 1). Respondents were asked to score this set of possible activities on a scale of one (1) to three (3), with one being 'not at all interested' and three being 'very interested.' Table 1 shows the mean and rank for each activity. The highlights from this analysis are as follows.

The most preferred activities tended to be nature-based activities that were generally low risk, non-motorized, and non-consumptive in character. These include: visiting parks, visiting waterway parks, using interpretive services, viewing wildlife, nature photography, viewing local native culture, day hiking, cross-country skiing day trips, flatwater canoeing day trips, bicycling day trips, and swimming.

Preferred activities also included a variety of more physically demanding pursuits of a non-motorized nature. These include: multiple day hiking trips, multiple day flat water canoeing trips, multiple day cross-country ski trips, multiple day bicycling trips, whitewater canoeing day trips, and downhill skiing.

The least preferred activities included consumptive activities (e.g., hunting), motorized recreational activities (e.g., motorized water activities, snowmobiling), water-based activities (e.g., water skiing and water sports) and winter activities (e.g., ice climbing, ice fishing, dog sledding).

Table 1. Means and Rankings for Preferred Activities for the Full (Non-segmented) Sample

Activity	Mean	Rank
visiting provincial or national parks	2.56	1
hiking day trip	2.41	2
flatwater canoeing day trip	2.33	3
hiking multiple day trip	2.32	4
visiting waterway parks	2.32	4
flatwater canoeing multiple day trip	2.29	6
cross country skiing day trip	2.23	7
wildlife viewing	2.20	8
swimming	2.16	9
whitewater canoeing day trip	2.10	10
using interpretive services	2.08	11
viewing local native culture	2.07	12
bicycling paved roads day trip	2.05	13
cross country skiing multiple day trip	2.05	13
whitewater canoeing multiple day trip	2.02	15
interacting with local native culture	2.00	16
viewing human works	1.99	17
downhill skiing	1.98	18
bicycling paved road multiple day trip	1.93	19
mountain biking day trip	1.92	20
nature photography	1.92	20
viewing local activities	1.92	20
participate in educational nature tours	1.88	23
acquiring artifacts and crafts	1.82	24
snowshoeing day trip	1.82	24
sea kayaking day trip	1.81	26
sailing day trip	1.80	27
mountain biking multiple day trip	1.79	28
sea kayaking multiple day trip	1.78	29
tobogganing and snow play	1.78	29
bird watching	1.76	31
snorkelling	1.76	31

Table 1. (continued)
Means and Rankings for Preferred Activities for the Full (Non-segmented) Sample

Activity	Mean	Rank
winter camping	1.76	31
bicycling gravel road day trip	1.75	34
bicycling gravel and paved road multiple day trip	1.73	35
mountain/rock climbing	1.73	35
viewing roadside attractions	1.73	35
fishing catch within limit	1.72	38
fishing catch and release	1.72	38
sailing multiple day trip	1.72	38
horseback riding day trip	1.67	41
dog sledding day trip	1.65	42
ice skating	1.65	42
individual sports participation	1.62	44
participating in a guided nature tour	1.62	44
snowshoeing multiple day trip	1.60	46
spelunking/caving	1.60	46
scuba diving	1.59	48
horseback riding multiple day trip	1.54	49
dog sledding multiple day trip	1.51	50
wind surfing	1.50	51
water skiing and water sports	1.49	52
snowmobiling day trip	1.41	53
motorized water activities	1.39	54
outdoor art	1.35	55
ice climbing	1.32	56
ice fishing	1.32	56
snowmobiling multiple day trip	1.29	58
hunting	1.25	59

In general, respondent preferences spanned the full spectrum of land and water-based activities, as well as the full spectrum of pursuit-type activities and appreciative-type activities. Demand also exists for both summer and winter-based seasonal activities. However, emphasis was clearly given by this sample of ecotourists to activities which are non-consumptive, non-motorized and conservation oriented in nature.

Preferred settings. An exhaustive list of environmental settings was generated inclusive of all recreation opportunity spectrum (ROS) settings (Clarke & Stankey 1979; McCool, Stankey & Clarke 1985; Rollins & Rouse 1991) ranging from pristine forest wilderness to very human-modified environments (Table 2). Respondents scored these preferred settings using a Likert-type scale employing a one (1) through five (5) range, with one being 'very undesirable' and five being 'very desirable.' The overall mean for all settings was 3.2. Table 2 shows the mean and rank for each setting.

The large array of possible settings was reduced to a more manageable number of setting dimensions by the use of a principal component analysis with varimax rotation. The analysis on the setting variables led to the extraction of six significant dimensions accounting for 48.3 per cent of the data set variation. Interpretation of the six dimensions focused upon those variables containing factor loadings greater than 0.70 and to a lesser extent those with factor loadings less than 0.70 and greater than 0.40. The following dimensions were identified:

• Human influences: Items such as hearing and seeing all-terrain vehicles and powered water crafts loaded highly.

• Remoteness: Items such as travelling on low standard trails and being in areas with no facilities loaded most highly.

• Altered nature: Items related to developed trails and areas with interpretive signs loaded most highly.

• Flora and fauna: Items related to different types of bird, wild, and plant life loaded most highly.

• Geomorphology: Items associated with landscape features (e.g., presence of lakes) loaded most highly.

• Industry influences: Items related to such activities as logging and mining loaded most highly.

Table 2. Means and Rankings for Preferred Settings for the Full (Non-segmented) Sample

Setting	Mean	Rank
presence of lakes	4.83	1
presence of rivers and streams	4.82	2
area with views of undisturbed natural scenery	4.73	3
access to drinking water	4.67	4
view of waterfalls	4.63	5
variety of wildlife	4.59	6
view of gorges	4.55	7
large trees	4.50	8
variety of plants/trees	4.47	9
mostly undisturbed old growth forest	4.46	10
variety of birds	4.38	11
presence of rock outcrops	4.35	12
an area where trails have bridges over dangerous rivers	4.34	13
rare species of wildlife	4.23	14
area with developed side trails	4.23	14
area remote from towns or cities	4.22	16
access to good swimming	4.17	17
travel in the area on high standard trails	4.16	18
relatively large forested area	4.14	19
travel on lake/river systems	4.12	20
presence of beaches	4.12	20
rare plants	4.11	22
rare species of birds	4.10	23
area that has interpretive signs	4.03	24
access by gravel/forest road	4.00	25
areas with views of rural landscape	3.90	26
area where trails have bridges over creeks	3.89	27
area with historic sites and buildings	3.85	28
occasionally meeting other people	3.82	29
area with interpretive nature and cultural programs	3.80	30
access by boat	3.79	31
area with human waste facilities	3.78	32

Table 2. (continued)
Means and Rankings for Preferred Settings for the Full (Non-segmented) Sample

Setting	Mean	Rank
access to good fishing	3.75	33
access by paved road	3.70	34
travel on gravel/forest road	3.65	35
meeting no other people	3.58	36
moderate forested area	3.55	37
mostly second growth, single species younger forest	3.37	38
travel on low standard trails	3.37	38
access by float plane	3.31	40
area remote from food, equipment and supplies	3.28	41
travel on paved roads	3.19	42
area where camping is restricted to designated sites	3.12	43
no signs in the area	3.05	44
mostly dense, bush-covered areas	3.03	45
area with past naturally occurring forest fire	3.01	46
relatively small forested area	2.89	47
travel on low maintenance gravel roads	2.86	48
encountering anglers	2.78	49
area where trails have no bridges	2.77	50
area with no facilities	2.72	51
travel using hydro right-of-ways	2.67	52
area with a recent naturally-occurring forest fire	2.64	53
area where no fires are allowed	2.58	54
area remote from emergency assistance or rescue	2.56	55
recreating on a dammed lake	2.54	56
mostly selective cut forest	2.51	57
seeing dams in the area	2.43	58
continually meeting other people	2.14	59
seeing hydro lines in the area	1.94	60
area with view of residential development	1.83	61
area with no overnight camping	1.83	61
being in a logged area	1.79	63

Table 2. (continued)
Means and Rankings for Preferred Settings for the Full (Non-segmented) Sample

Setting	Mean	Rank
seeing powered water craft	1.79	63
seeing evidence of mining	1.75	65
seeing evidence of logging	1.75	65
seeing a gravel pit	1.73	67
hearing powered water craft	1.66	68
encountering hunters	1.63	69
mostly recent clear-cut forests	1.58	70
hearing sounds of vehicles	1.54	71
seeing all-terrain vehicles	1.51	72
encountering industrial vehicles	1.47	73
hearing gun shots	1.46	74
hearing all-terrain vehicles	1.46	74
area with views of industrial or commercial development	1.37	76
hearing sounds of logging	1.28	77

Findings on the preferred setting dimensions can be summarized as follows:

• The most preferred setting dimensions were those of geomorphology (e.g., presence of lakes, presence of rivers and streams and other natural features) and flora and fauna (e.g., a variety of wildlife and plants and trees). Ecotourists would appear, then, to have strong preferences for naturalness in terms of both landscapes/wild places and variety of flora and fauna.

• Also preferred was a consideration of remoteness from human development, including a willingness to confront more difficult forms of access (e.g., access by gravel roads, access by float plane or boat) and emergency support (e.g., remoteness from emergency assistance).

• Less preferred was the need for altered nature (e.g., travel on paved roads, areas with developed trails, areas with human waste facilities, views of rural landscapes).

• The least desirable settings included the dimensions of human influences (e.g., hearing and seeing all-terrain vehicles and powered water crafts, views of residential development, seeing hydro lines) and industry influences (e.g., scenes altered by evidence of logging, mining or dam-building).

• Audible contact with undesirable settings (e.g., hearing industrial activity, hearing all-terrain vehicles or motor crafts) is less desirable than visual contact (e.g., seeing a clear-cut area, seeing motorized vehicles).

Preferences for forest-based settings were most clearly focused on those environments which display the highest levels of naturalness and least focused on those environs which display human/industrial alterations.

Preferred experiences. A comprehensive list of possible desired outcomes was generated from existing studies and inventories (Crandell 1980; Driver 1975; Manning 1986; Rollins & Rouse 1991). Respondents scored preferred experiences on a five point scale, with one (1) representing 'not at all' and five (5) representing 'extremely important.' The overall mean for preferred experiences was 4.04. Table 3 displays the means and ranks for all of the preferred experience items.

For the purpose of developing a meaningful interpretation of the preferred experiences data, the large array of possible experiences was reduced to a more manageable number of preferred experience dimensions by the use of a principal component analysis with a varimax rotation. This analysis revealed five dimensions accounting for 52 per cent of all data set variation. Component interpretation focused upon those items with factor loadings greater than 0.70 and to a lesser extent those with factor loadings less than 0.70 and greater than 0.40. The following dimensions were identified:

• Interaction: Items related to learning about and meeting new people loaded most highly.

• Escape: Items related to relaxing mentally and physically and feeling an emotional release loaded most highly.

Table 3. Means and Rankings for Preferred Experiences for the Full (Non-segmented) Sample

Experience	Mean	Rank
enjoying the sights, sounds, smells of nature	4.73	1
enjoying the scenic beauty	4.61	2
getting away from civilization for a while	4.54	3
feeling an emotional release from my work	4.47	4
relaxing mentally	4.46	5
experiencing a feeling of freedom	4.44	6
doing something with my family or close friends	4.42	7
travelling to and exploring new places	4.41	8
learning about and appreciating nature	4.35	9
being physically active	4.34	10
being with people who enjoy the same things	4.32	11
avoiding hustle and bustle of daily activities	4.29	12
preserving the natural environment	4.28	13
having a stimulating and exciting experience	4.26	14
keeping physically fit	4.25	15
helping to safeguard forests and wilderness areas	4.22	16
experiencing new and different things	4.22	16
adding some variety to my daily routine	4.13	18
being self-reliant	4.09	19
making my own decisions	4.08	20
expanding my interests	4.07	21
feeling competent	4.05	22
developing my skills and abilities	4.05	22
doing something new and different	4.04	24
relaxing physically	3.98	25
doing something creative	3.86	26
thinking about personal or spiritual values	3.82	27
sharing experiences with others	3.78	28
feeling safe and secure	3.77	29
understanding myself better	3.76	30
sharing skill and knowledge with others	3.65	31
enjoying the sights, sounds, smells of nature	4.73	31

Table 3. (continued)
Means and Rankings for Preferred Experiences for the Full (Non-segmented) Sample

Experience	Mean	Rank
learning about the native culture	3.61	32
experiencing a feeling of control	3.51	33
meeting new and interesting people	3.45	34
learning about local communities	3.40	35
being daring and adventurous	3.16	36
chancing risky situations	2.76	37

• Adventure/skill improvement: Items such as being daring and adventurous and developing my skills loaded most highly.

• Nature/conservation: Items such as enjoying the scenic beauty, and learning about and appreciating nature loaded most highly.

Findings on the preferred experience dimensions can be summarized as follows:

• The most preferred dimension was nature/conservation (e.g., enjoying the sights, sounds, smells of nature, enjoying the scenic beauty, preserving the natural environment, helping to safeguard forests and wilderness areas). This finding is in keeping with the presumed conservation ethic that the ecotourism literature so frequently associates with the "true" ecotourist.

• Escape (e.g., getting away from civilization, experiencing a feeling of freedom) was also an important dimension. Again, this finding is in keeping with the urban base of the ecotourist characterized in the literature.

• Interaction (e.g., learning about native culture, learning about local communities, meeting new and interesting people) was also an important dimension. Again, this finding is in keeping with the literature's depiction of an ecotourist as someone who is interested in having strong cultural/

local community and educational/learning components to their eco-trip.

• Although still an important dimension, the least preferred dimension was that of adventure/skill development (e.g., chancing risky situations, being daring and adventurous, developing skills and abilities). The adventure aspect of ecotourism is often depicted as one of the fastest growing sectors of the ecotourism field; however, with this particular sample of ecotourists it appears to be only one important type of experience among several.

Discussion of Results Section 1. Summaries described above depict the general or undifferentiated picture of the potential ecotourism market for northern Ontario. In this light, the latent ecotourism market can be described in the following general narrative:

The market is male dominated, made up of people primarily between the ages of 30-50 years who often have children at home, who are well educated and have relatively high annual and discretionary incomes. These ecotourists tend to prefer nature-based activities that are generally low risk, non-motorized, and non-consumptive in character, and tend to have the least preference for consumptive and motorized activities. They prefer to pursue their chosen activities in settings which are natural in terms of both the physical landscape and wildlife and flora, and tend not to want to recreate in human/industrially altered environs (particularly those that include the sound of motorized/industrial activity).

The latent ecotourism market of northern Ontario is clearly not a homogeneous group; within this latent market are embedded a number of market segments or groups which may be usefully depicted in terms of their clustered socio-demographic characteristics and preferred activities, settings and experiences. This type of information would permit marketing efforts to more accurately target specific ecotourism groups. The segmentation analysis of the latent market is depicted in the following section of the results.

Section 2. Profiling the ecotourism market segments

The following market segmentation procedure was based on that developed by McCool et al. (1994). As reported in section 1 above, the principal component analysis conducted on the preferred experiences data identified the four factors of interaction, escape, adventure, and nature/conservation. A K-means cluster analysis on the factor scores for these

Identifying Desired Ecotourism Activities

four factors was then implemented. From this analysis, six segment clusters were selected (solutions with less than six groups yielded accelerating heterogeneity). Using these six clusters, an assessment of group means on the four preferred experience dimensions facilitated definition of the market segments (Table 4). These market segments were titled Enthusiasts, Weekend Warriors, Environmentally Friendly Tourists, Escapists, Naturalists and Adventure Naturalists.

Profiles for each of these market segments were then developed as follows. Using the six preferred setting dimensions (human influence, remoteness, altered nature, flora and fauna, geomorphology, and industry influence) identified through the previously reported principal components analysis, the item scores were subjected to a simple analysis of variance test. Significant findings were found for all settings and the differences are outlined within the following market segment profiles (Tables 5, 6, 7, 8, 9, and 10).

Table 4. Market Segment Mean Scores on Preferred Experiences Dimensions.

	Interaction	Escape	Adventure	Nature
Enthusiasts	0.92	0.66	0.61	10.28
Weekend Warriors	0.33	-0.38	-0.22	-1.17
Environmentally Friendly Tourists	0.59	-0.84	-0.99	0.41
Escapists	-1.26	0.49	0.58	-0.67
Naturalists	-0.59	0.57	-0.88	0.54
Adventure Naturalists	-0.43	-1.02	0.76	0.76

Note: overall component score means are zero with a standard deviation of one.

Table 5. Profile #1: Enthusiasts

Percentage of respondents belonging to this group: 22.9

Socio-demographics:
- aged between 16-30 and 50-59 years old.
- tend to have the fewest number of children at home.

Activities:
- Enthusiasts have a strong interest for almost all activities, particularly with regard to interacting with native and local communities, and pursuing nature-based activities (both low risk and adventure types) that have an educational component.
- the only real exception is hunting.

Settings:
- settings with human and industrial influences are viewed most negatively.
- most other settings are viewed favourably, including altered nature, flora and fauna, and geomorphology.

Other:
- more likely to travel in June and September.
- information sources are higher for newspapers, travel magazines, and from friends/relatives.

Activities to pursue during a northern Ontario outdoor recreation/ ecotourism trip: 1. hiking 15.6%, 2. canoeing 10.0%, 3. biking 7.9%, 4. fishing 5.9%, and 5. swimming 4.6%. Total of top five activities: 44.0%.

Accommodation preferences: Slightly higher preferences for luxury lodge (10.3% to 8.4%) and bed and breakfast (14% to 11.9%) accommodations for northern Ontario.

Main Marketing Considerations: Enthusiasts are generalists in terms of their preferred activities, and due to the high level of interest Enthusiasts have for most outdoor activities, this group may be most easily targeted for an ecotourism adventure in northern Ontario. This group is also fond of a variety of forest settings, with the notable exceptions of human and industrial influences. Their preferred travel period is typically the summer months. With fewer children, this group also tends to have higher discretionary income.

Table 6. Profile #2: Weekend Warriors

Percentage of respondents belonging to this group: 19.1

Socio-demographics:
- marital status is single.
- tend to under 30 years of age.

Activities:
- Weekend Warriors have a higher affinity for pursuing "artificial" activities, e.g., individual sports and water skiing, than do other groups, but also have interests in interacting with native and local communities.

Settings:
- Weekend Warriors are more tolerant of human influences and industry influences than most other groups.
- tend to see remoteness, flora and fauna and geomorphology as less necessary than do other groups, preferring less remote near-urban destinations.

Other:
- likely to use hotel accommodation when travelling to northern Ontario.
- likely to go with an organized group trip.
- higher likelihood of travelling to northern Ontario in March.
- higher likelihood of using travel agent, newspaper, and travel magazine for travel information.
- not likely to have pursued outdoor trips before.

Activities to pursue during a northern Ontario outdoor recreation/ ecotourism trip: 1. hiking 15.0%, 2. canoeing 9.2%, 3. fishing 6.4%, 4. biking 5.6%, and 5. water-skiing/water sports 4.4%. Total of top five activities: 40.6%

Accommodation preferences:
Weekend warriors appear to prefer hotels more than others groups (16.3% to 11.4%) and they appear to have less affinity for unorganized tents sites (22.5% to 29.5%).

Main Marketing Considerations:
The Weekend Warrior is a short-term visitor and is therefore not likely to be a frequent visitor to northern Ontario, with the possible exception of those living within fairly close proximity to the north. Their chosen activities are not conservation oriented nor do they contribute much business to local outfitters. They prefer near-urban destinations, and as such they are likely to contribute to local economies because of their hotel accommodation preferences. Being single, they will tend to have higher levels of discretionary income.

Table 7. Profile #3: Environmentally Friendly Tourists

Percentage of Respondents Belonging to this Group: 11.5

Socio-demographics:
- tend to be married with a number of children at home
- Age 40+
- highly educated and higher income bracket

Activities:
- Environmentally Friendly Tourists enjoy activities that are not too physically demanding, e.g., hiking day and horseback day trips.
- They also prefer activities that are nature-based, e.g., viewing wildlife and participating in nature tours, and native culture/local community based, e.g., viewing local native culture and human works.

Settings:
- This segment dislikes remoteness, preferring near-urban activities and experiences, but they also disdains industry influences.
- They also have a greater preference for altered nature-based settings which provide campsite amenities and interpretive programs. Settings that are altered to increase access and comfort are viewed positively by this group.

Other:
- prefer to travel in the high summer season, especially July (school holiday period).
- prefer not to travel in off-season periods, especially February, September, and December.
- main information sources are newspapers and automobile clubs.
- tend to belong to environmental groups.
- their primary residence has been mostly in non-city environments.

Activities to pursue in northern Ontario: 1. hiking 15.5%, 2. canoeing 9.2%, 3. biking 7.6%, 4. fishing 5.3%, 5. visiting parks 4.3%. Total for top five activities: 41.9%.

Accommodation Preferences: This group is likely to use organized campsites (24.9% to 16.3%) and much less likely to use unorganized campsites (18.9% to 29.5%). Hotels are also a preferred form of accommodation (14.7% to 11.4%).

Main Marketing Considerations: Environmentally Friendly Tourists desire an experience that is "environmentally correct," but which is not necessarily focused on pristine or remote nature. Given that they will often be travelling with children, they tend to prefer front-country type settings offering family oriented recreational opportunities (both activity and educational) and developed sites (e.g., provincial park sites or private camp sites with modern conveniences) or motel/hotel accommodations in local towns. Remoteness and difficult access are not attractive to this group. This group is important economically in that they are often established professional people with high discretionary income. They also tend to be the high-season traveller.

Table 8. Profile #4: Escapists

Percentage of Respondents Belonging to this Group: 13.1

Socio-demographics:
- this group has the highest male rank.
- tend to be single and also contain highest incidence of divorced or separated individuals.
- younger in age (20-40 years) and well educated.

Activities:
- Escapists are similar to Weekend Warriors in activity preferences, preferring physical and adventure type activities, although they have a lower affinity for nature-based activities.
- Escapists also prefer "artificial" activities, such as motorized water activities and downhill skiing, more than other groups.
Enjoy meeting with new and interesting people and other travel groups.

Settings:
- Remoteness is viewed positively.

Other (relative):
- tend to organize trips themselves.
- travel most often with friends.
- preferred accommodation is camping.
- travel more in the early spring.
- have lived more often in city environments.
- tend to be experienced travellers.

Activities to pursue during a northern Ontario outdoor recreation/ ecotourism trip: 1. hiking 18.3%, 2. canoeing 15.0%, 3. fishing 9.3%, 4. camping 6.6%, and 6. mountain biking 4.3%. Total of top five 53.5% (this is the highest of any of the groups).

Accommodation Preferences: Escapists appear to have lower preferences for hotels (7.1% to 11.4%) and higher preferences for unorganized campsites (39.1% to 29.5%).

Main Marketing Considerations: Escapists, like Weekend Warriors, are very outdoors oriented but tend to be attracted to a mix of vigorous activity and simply camping in remote areas. They are looking to meet and interact with new people. Northern Ontario's many remote fishing and canoeing lakes, wilderness backpacking areas, as well as opportunities for motorized water-sports would be appealing to this group. Prefer basic accommodation, preferably camping in unorganized campsites.

Table 9. Profile #5: Naturalists

Percentage of Respondents Belonging to this Group: 18.8

Socio-demographics:
- tend to be married
- fall into 30-40 age group
- high number of children at home

Activities:
- Naturalists prefer activities that are nature-based, e.g., wildlife viewing and moderately challenging activities, e.g., flat water canoeing day trip and cross country skiing day trip.
- They tend to dislike more than other groups artificial type activities, e.g., scuba diving and wind surfing, and difficult activities, e.g., white water canoeing and multiple day activities

Settings:
- This segment tends to view human influences and industry influences as more undesirable than the other groups.

Other (relative):
- tend to travel as a family unit more often than other groups.
- travel information sources lower for travel agents and newspapers.

Activities to pursue during a northern Ontario outdoor recreation/ ecotourism trip: 1. hiking 15.3%, 2. canoeing 11.7%, 3. fishing 7.4%, 4. biking 5.9%, and camping 4.7%. Total for top five activities 45%.

Accommodation Preferences: Naturalists prefer basic lodge (22.7% to 19.8%) accommodations above other groups. They are also less likely than others to use an unorganized tent (25.4% to 29.5%) or luxury lodge (5.3% to 8.4%).

Main Marketing Considerations: This group appears to be a good target for ecotourism in northern Ontario. This segment wants to have a true nature-based trip away from disturbing influences. Unlike Environmentally Friendly Tourists, alterations to natural environments would be considered a major detriment to this group. This type of group usually travels as a family unit with children, and as such appears to like activities that are physical and moderately adventurous in nature yet not too demanding. Finally, Naturalists prefer accommodations that will provide revenue to basic lodge or organized campgrounds.

Table 10. Profile # 6: Adventure Naturalists

Percentage of Respondents Belonging to this Group: 14.6

Socio-demographics:
- predominantly males
- single marital status
- young age group (16-30 years)
- low number of children at home

Activities:
- Adventure naturalists enjoy physical activities, e.g., biking and cross country skiing, and dangerous activities, e.g., white water canoeing and ice climbing, more than the average population.
- Whereas passive activities, e.g., viewing local activities and roadside attractions are seen by adventure naturalists as less desirable.

Settings:
- Adventure Naturalists prefer remote settings more than all other groups with the exception of Escapists.
- Also this segment sees flora and fauna and geomorphology as more desired settings than average.
- Finally, adventure naturalists perceive altered nature and human influences as less desirable settings.

Other (relative):
- travel accommodation usually is with a tent
- travel times are higher in February, May and September
- more likely to belong to environmental groups

Activities to pursue during a northern Ontario outdoor recreation/ ecotourism trip: 1. hiking 16.0%, 2. canoeing 11.9%, 3. mountain biking 7.7%, 4. mountain climbing 5.4%, and 5. camping 5.4%. Total for top five activities 46.4 %

Accommodation Preferences: Adventure naturalists have a higher affinity for basic lodge (23.6% to 19.8%) and unorganized tent (40.2% to 29.5%) accommodations than others.

Main Marketing Considerations: Adventure Naturalists may be among the truest ecotourists in terms of their preferences. This group prefers nature-based and remote settings, physical and educational activities, and very simple accommodation, i.e., unorganized tent for most summer activities. Combined with high interest in many activities, this group appears to be a good target for remote adventure trips in true nature settings.

The preferred activity data were then analyzed using the six market segments. Since the preferred activities were measured on a three-point ordinal scale (which does not mimic sufficiently interval/ratio scale), non-parametric Kruskal Wallis H tests were performed in place of analysis of variance tests. Almost all activities were significantly different when analyzed by the market segments except hunting, fishing catch within limit, and fishing catch and release. The activity differences among the segments are highlighted in the market segment profiles (Tables 5, 6, 7, 8, 9 and 10).

The socio-demographic data, as well as additional information on accommodation, trip planning information sources, and travel periods, were also analyzed in terms of the six market segments. These items were analyzed by Chi Square statistics and cross tabulation. Tables 5 through 10 portray the details of the six market segmentation profiles.

Discussion of Results Section 2. The six profiles developed for northern Ontario's latent market suggest that there are a number of identifiable facets in this ecotourism market of northern Ontario. This sub-divisioning of the green travel market has been generated to assist businesses and tourism marketers in their efforts to better understand the potential ecotourism market of northern Ontario, and to help them to position, promote, and perhaps change their products, services and practices accordingly. The six groups clearly overlap in some of the ecotourism preferences, yet explicit differences also exist that are important to the marketing of specific ecotourism opportunities to particular groups. Hiking, canoeing, fishing, camping, visiting parks, biking, mountain climbing, and water sports are the most attractive activities across these groups, although between group differences are evident. Differences exist between the groups in terms of family make-up, occupational background, and discretionary income, and these variables influence preferences for types of destinations/settings, activities, desired experiences, time of travel, and type of accommodation. The groups also have differing information sources. These profiles may be particularly useful to those marketers seeking to create a specific market niche.

CONCLUSIONS AND IMPLICATIONS

Ecotourism can act as an important pillar of economic stability for many rural areas of the world. Unfortunately, studies have shown that many communities and regions wait until other economic sectors are suffering and failing before turning to tourism as a solution to their economic problems (Hill 1995). In reality, for many areas of the world and most probably for northern Ontario, ecotourism on its own does not and will not provide a panacea for economic growth or stability. Rather, tourism development can act as an additional support to an existing economy by diversifying the economic base of communities which are largely dependent on forest or mineral extraction, agriculture or manufacturing. Communities that are dependent on a single industry or activity invariably suffer decline in the long-term.

The tourism industry itself is cyclical, and those businesses that depend on the changes of market preferences are particularly vulnerable. Rarely does tourism succeed as the only economic sector in a community or region. Those communities that have economic diversity are better positioned for long-term economic stability and hence community well-being (Field 1986). However, due to its labour intensive nature and large number of small businesses and entrepreneurs, tourism can be an excellent vehicle for economic development and economic diversification. By encouraging the local development of tourism businesses and supporting enterprises, economic developers can magnify the economic impact to an area significantly (Hill 1995).

Ecotourism, theoretically, has the added benefits of contributing to the sustainable use of a community's or region's resources in that it supports the preservation and conservation of the natural environment. In northern Ontario, traditionally a timber industry-oriented region, it is now being recognized that past forest management practices have resulted in unanticipated changes to the environment that are expected to cause growing hardship, and that we are now struggling to redress or cope with. Ecotourism could play an important role as a part of integrated forest management in this region.

The reality of the relationship between ecotourism and sustainable forestry will depend very much on how forest managers, economic developers and tourism businesses coordinate and implement their policies and programs. Forest managers are required to see ecotourism opportunities as an integral part of forest management, and not merely as an add-on to the traditional business of timber harvesting. This will require of them a far broader approach to the use of northern Ontario's forests than has traditionally been adopted. It should be remembered, for example, that three of four Canadians view the forest as a national treasure to be held in trust for future generations (Carrow 1993).

Economic developers must also acknowledge that planning for ecotourism at the local level is seldom adequate. Rather, a regional vision is required that identifies ecotourism opportunities and coordinates tourism development with existing industries in a broad regional economic development/diversity plan. Economic developers also must accept that tourism can be over-developed in an area. This leads to communities attempting to control tourism after social and environmental impacts have already occurred. To avoid this outcome, The Ecotourism Society and the World Tourism Organization have prepared guides to assist planners in the development and coordination of sustainable tourism projects.

Ecotourism businesses have an obligation to promote viable and honest ecotourism experiences: those which conserve the natural environment and improve the welfare of the local people (NODA 1994). As Hill (1995) states, some traditional tour operators have expanded into the nature-based market because it seems to be a profitable exercise; they are likely to be experts at marketing, but may lack the commitment to those clientele desiring a trip that meets their educational, cultural and ecological expectations. Thus, while the profiles generated in this study may assist ecotourism businesses to better market their products, it is paramount that these ecotourism enterprises never become merely ecosell, where business and profit concerns overshadowed environmental ethics and clientele needs.

FOOTNOTE

1. Ecotourism is defined as the use of an area for outdoor recreation travel experiences which conserve the natural environment and improve the welfare of the local people (NODA, 1994). Outdoor recreation is "all those activities of a recreational nature resulting from our interest in the environment and our relationship to its elements" (Sessoms 1984: 238).

REFERENCES

Carrow, R. 1993. *Integrated resource management in Canada: A case of unrealized potential*. Paper presented at the *Toward the 21st Century* Annual Meeting of the Canadian Institute of Forestry, Montreal, September.

Clarke, R.N. & G.H. Stankey. 1979. *The recreation opportunity spectrum: A framework for planning, management, and research*. General Technical Report PNW-98. Portland, OR: US Department of Agriculture, Forest Service, Pacific Northwest Research Station.

Crandall, R. 1980. Motivations for leisure. *Journal of Leisure Research*, 3, 45-54.

Driver, B.L. 1975. Quantification of outdoor recreationists' preferences. In B. vanderSmissen & J. Meyers (eds.), *Research, camping and environmental education*, pp. 165-187. Penn State University HPER Series 11, University Park, Pennsylvania.

Driver, B.L. & R.C. Tocher. 1970. Toward a behavioral interpretation of recreational engagements. In B.L. Driver (ed.), *Elements of outdoor recreation planning*, pp. 9-31, University Microfilms, Ann Arbour.

Development Consulting Limited. 1991. *Ecotourism opportunity identification study*. Report submitted to the Policy and Program Development Branch of the Ontario Ministry of Northern Development and Mines.

Field, D.R. 1986. *Community and natural resource development: Another look at tourism*. Paper presented at the 18th IUFRO World Congress, Ljubljana, Yugoslavia, September 7-21.

Haider, W. 1993. Centre for Northern Forest Ecosystem Research, Lakehead University, Ontario. Personal communication, May 24.

Hill, B. 1995. A guide to adventure travel. *Parks and Recreation*, September, 56-65.

Lindberg, K. 1994. Quantifying ecotourism - Are reliable statistics in sight? *The Ecotourism Society Newsletter*, 4, 1-7.

Marshall, Macklin & Monaghan Limited. 1992. *Ontario's specialty outdoors product: Strategic directions for its development, management and marketing background report*.

McCool, S.F., N. Menning & B. Spettigue. 1994. Segmenting the wildlife viewing market. Paper presented at the *Fifth International Symposium on Society and Resource Management*, Fort Collins, Colorado.

McCool, S.F., G.H. Stankey & R.N. Clarke. 1985. Choosing recreation settings: Processes, findings, and research direction. In G. H. Stankey & S. F. McCool (Compilers), *Proceedings - Symposium on recreation choice behavior*, pp. 1-8. General Technical Report INT-184. Ogden, UT: US

Department of Agriculture, Forest Service, Intermountain Research Station.

Robson, M., D.W. Robinson & A. Hawley. 1995. *The community of interests and social values related to the McGregor Model Forest*. Milestone Report #1 for the McGregor Model Forest Association. Prince George, B.C.: MMFA.

Rollins, R.B. & J. Rouse. 1991. Segmenting backcountry visitors by setting preferences. In J. H. Martin Willison et al. (eds.) *Science and the management of protected areas*, 485-497. Proceedings of a conference organized by the Science and Protected Areas Association, Nova Scotia, Canada.

Scace, R.C., E. Grifone & R. Usher. 1992. *Ecotourism in Canada*. Report to the Canadian Environmental Advisory Council. Hull, Quebec: Environment Canada.

Sessoms, D. 1984. *Leisure services*. Englewood Cliffs, NJ: Prentice Hall.

Shindler, B., P. List & B.S. Steel. 1993. Managing federal forests: Public attitudes in Oregon and nationwide. *Journal of Forestry*, 7, 36-42.

Stankey, G.H. & R.N. Clarke. 1992. *Social aspects of new perspectives in forestry*. Milford, Pennsylvania: Greytowers Press.

PRICING AND PACKAGING STRATEGIES OF REMOTE FLY-IN OPERATIONS IN NORTHERN ONTARIO

Len Hunt
Ontario Ministry of Natural Resources

Wolfgang Haider
Simon Fraser University

The vast, pristine landscape of northern Ontario provides an ideal setting for resource-based tourism. Most important among the various forms of tourism are the fishing and hunting resorts. However, the past 20 years have seen increasing land use conflicts between forestry interests and tourism, and the protection of the environmental qualities that constitute the foundation of resource-based tourism has become an integral part of Ontario's public land management debate. The many conflicts and the Class Environmental Assessment on Timber Management on Crown Land in Ontario (Environmental Assessment Board 1994) have made the decision-making process more open and participatory. Participatory decision-making also requires improved information and analyses of the various economic activities and their effects on one another. Surprisingly little information and, consequently, analysis exists about resource-based tourism in northern Ontario and it has proven difficult to collect relevant information about a diverse industry that is spread over a large land base and is dominated by small businesses.

This paper investigates differences among resource-based tourism operations in northern Ontario from a price perspective (Figure 1). Fundamental economic principles suggest that the price charged by an entrepreneur depends on the overall quality of the product. The tourism product is a complex amalgam of services, site characteristics, and less tangible experience-related attributes (Smith 1994). Thus, the challenge is to investigate the relationship between a wide range of these product components and to probe for a systematic relationship to price. The price charged by an operator and related information is readily available from brochures, which can be collected freely at information centres throughout the province, at travel trade shows, or from operators directly. To conduct the analysis presented below it must be assumed that most information relevant to price setting is presented in the brochures. Hence the focus of the analysis differs from the content analysis that is typically conducted on tourist brochures.

Figure 1. Map of Study Area and Regions Used for Analysis

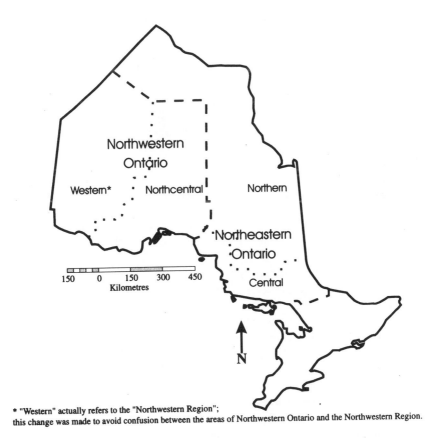

* "Western" actually refers to the "Northwestern Region";
this change was made to avoid confusion between the areas of Northwestern Ontario and the Northwestern Region.

The scope of this research is limited to the pricing structure for fishing packages of fly-in, outpost camps in Ontario. Remote lodges are not analyzed here because they are too few in number, they offer a heterogeneous product, and the brochures collected are incomplete. The analysis is limited to fishing since it is the main product of the remote tourism experience (Northern Ontario Tourist Outfitters Association [NOTO] 1987). The focused scope of this research permits this study to provide: a profile of the outpost product of northern Ontario; an analysis of the prices charged by these operations and the relationships between price and other characteristics listed in brochures; an examination of regional differences between operations; and, an examination of economies of scale.

To meet these objectives, the paper is structured into five sections. The first section describes the types of tourist establishments in northern Ontario and reviews previous studies on resource-based and remote tourism. The section on methods provides insights about the data sources and data collection. The section on results describes the information typically found in brochures and provides a detailed analysis of the relationship between price and other variables. The analysis concludes with a detailed investigation of regional differences. Finally, economies of scale are explored qualitatively, and an overview of the remote tourism industry is provided.

Resource-based tourism in Ontario: Structure and relevant research

Fundamental differences in resource-based tourist facilities in northern Ontario can be observed in terms of accessibility, structure, and available activities. Besides road-accessible facilities, remote tourism establishments are located in areas that can only be accessed by float plane. Between the extremes of road and remote operations one can also observe semi-remote operations. Semi-remote operations are accessible by boat or train, but the lakes on which these semi-remote operations are located are usually road-accessible. The remote and semi-remote operations exist in both lodge and outpost forms. Lodge operations are typically composed of several cabins grouped around one central unit and may accommodate between 10 and 100 customers at any one time. One further distinction among lodges is based on the meal plan offered with both American Plan and housekeeping packages available. Outpost camps are single cabins situated alone on a lake, or on isolated areas of larger lakes. The most common activities associated with both of these accommodation types are fishing and hunting. However, in some areas, non-consumptive activities are increasing in prominence.

The importance of remote tourism to northern Ontario's economy has been documented by studies on the economic impact of remote tourism in North Algoma (Econometric Research Limited & Ministry of Tourism and Recreation 1990), Red Lake (Hope 1987), and northern Ontario as a whole (Rushton/Shanahan & Associates Ltd. et al. 1979; NOTO 1987). These studies all found that remote tourism is an important contributor to the local and regional economy. In fact, it is estimated that approximately 15,000 people are directly employed in this sector (NOTO

1987). Although employment for 15,000 people appears insignificant, the entire labour force over 15 years of age, in Northern Ontario and outside the census metropolitan areas of Thunder Bay, Sault Ste. Marie and Sudbury is only 208,665 (Statistics Canada 1994a; Statistics Canada 1994b).

A study by Tindale (1986) focusing on resource-based tourism in northwestern Ontario provided a crude economic profile of the industry. Tindale's analysis, summarized in the top portion of Table 1, was based on three different *a priori* classifications of all operations: three strata based on volume of sales; three groups based on Ontario's star grading system; and, four operation types. For each grouping, Tindale examined sales, expenditures, and profitability and compiled the numbers separately by operation units and accommodation units. He concluded that an operation's financial success increased with quality, with higher employment, with higher marketing expenditures, with increasing specialization of the business, and with higher sales volume.

Several limitations of Tindale's study exemplify the problem associated with obtaining reliable and meaningful data about resource-based tourism in northern Ontario. When collecting financial or economic data, the unit of analysis ought to be the individual enterprise. Even if concerns about confidentiality of data can be overcome, the problem remains that any single tourism operation in northern Ontario may offer several distinct product types (e.g., mainbase lodges and outpost camps, road accessible and remote). None of the three classifications proposed by Tindale accomplishes any meaningful separation between product types. Instead, in each stratification, several product types are grouped.[1] One can, however, improve the analysis by investigating expenditures and profits as a ratio of sales per unit rather than relying only on overall expenditures and profits. The results from such a perspective reflect the actual proportion of sales accounted for by each of the respective expenditure or profit items. Despite the limitations imposed by the various segmentations, rather different, yet interesting and plausible trends emerge.

The segmentations by volume of sales and the star-rating system for quality display very similar results. As expected, employment expenditures as a percentage of sales increase for both operations with larger sales volumes and operations with higher quality ratings. However, expenditures per unit of sales for advertising and repairs decrease significantly with increasing sales volume. If the reasonable assumption that larger operations contain the highest sales levels on average is true, then the decrease in advertising and maintenance expenditures signifies the presence of economies of scale. Advertising expenditures for three-star operations are much higher than for two- or four-star establishments,

Table 1. Reanalysis of Tindale's Data

Segment	Sales			Star Grading			Type of Operation			
Variable	Bottom 1/3	Middle 1/3	Top 1/3	2-star	3-star	4-star	base/camps	base/outposts	base only	outposts
sales/unit	$7,263	$13,920	$35,831	$12,000	$12,000	$28,000	$17,471	$9,350	$18,068	$29,210
Expenditures/Profitability per unit of Sales										
employment	$1,051	$2,924	$9,108	$1,500	$2,100	$6,800	$2,823	$2,190	$4,124	$7,635
advertising	$381	$543	$1,024	$225	$680	$800	$549	$295	$563	$993
maintenance	$693	$1,086	$1,514	$610	$790	$1,440	NA	NA	NA	NA
profitability	$1,848	$2,849	$7,005	$2,200	$4,000	$4,900	$3,194	$2,094	$3,887	$5,880
Percentage of Expenditures/Profitability per unit of Sales **										
employment	14.5	21.0	25.4	12.5	17.5	24.3	16.2	23.4	22.8	26.1
advertising	5.3	3.9	2.9	1.9	5.7	2.9	3.1	3.2	3.1	3.4
maintenance	9.5	7.8	4.2	5.1	6.6	5.1	NA	NA	NA	NA
profitability	25.4	20.5	19.6	18.3	33.3	17.5	18.3	22.4	21.5	20.1

** - calculated by authors based on data published by Tindale (1986)

Source: Tindale (1986)

while the expenditures on repairs remain similar for all three quality levels. The unusual result that both the bottom third of operations in terms of sales and three-star operations have higher profits per unit of sales than the top third and four-star operations, respectively, defies explanation.

Finally, the segmentation by operation type shows, surprisingly, that the highest employment expenditures per unit of sales are made by outpost operations. Even if one considers the high cost associated with the mode of transportation, outposts employ no staff on site, except an occasional guide. The differences between the operation types for advertising expenditures and profitability are negligible.

Besides examining economic issues, several previously-cited studies provide some basic insights into the composition and origin of the remote tourism clientele. One important finding is that as one moves westward through northern Ontario, an increasingly larger proportion of the clientele is American (McKercher 1992). Further detailed examinations of the visitor differences between regions show that American clients to northwestern Ontario arrive from Minnesota, Wisconsin and Illinois, while for northeastern Ontario the American clientele originates from Michigan and Ohio (NOTO 1987). On a more detailed research level, a case study in the North Algoma region (Haider & Carlucci 1994) examined trip behaviour, attitudes, motivations and preferences of remote clients. Insights gained from this study provided a rationale for several crucial decisions made in this study, for example, what trip length should be used for analysis. Currently, a complex decision support system (DSS) is being prepared that will document the trade-offs remote clients are willing to make between many accommodation, fishing quality, and forest quality variables, as well as price.[2]

METHODS

Price and pricing-related information were obtained from advertising brochures published by each outpost operation. Most brochures were collected either at the various tourist information centres located throughout northern Ontario or at various travel trade shows, such as in Minneapolis, Toronto and Thunder Bay. All analyses were conducted using 1995 prices. Although several previous studies have relied on brochures as a data source for tourism and recreation research, these studies usually employed content analysis to describe basic information. For example, Eagles and Wind (1994) examined the Canadian ecotourism market through content analysis of brochures. From this study, it was shown that natural features are most prominently mentioned while cultural features were second in importance. Dilley (1986) also used a content analysis of the illustrations in international tourist brochures. In contrast, the present study attempts a more formal statistical analysis of brochure information by linking price to other salient attributes of outpost operations in northern Ontario.

The printed promotional material used by northern Ontario tourist operations typically consists of two parts: a glossy colour printed brochure, and a fact sheet containing information about price and the services associated with price.[3] The glossy section details the background information and attempts to sell the establishment on aesthetic appeal. The fact sheet is produced separately, and is usually printed on much cheaper paper to avoid the cost of reprinting the entire brochure every time aspects of the vacation package change. While content analyses frequently focus on pictures (e.g. Dilley 1986), our analysis of brochures focuses strictly on the text. Much of the text comprises colourful language while other text elements, especially those relating to price, are stated factually. The analyses below are based on the assumption that operators use brochures to position their operations favourably and to differentiate their product from competitors, and that the information provided is unlikely to be false or misleading.

The brochures collected for this study contain a wealth of information about the outpost, fly-in fishing product (Table 2). Besides the price, additional information relates to specifics of the flight component, characteristics of the accommodation, and the fishing experience. Attributes relating to price were collected to define similar packages based on duration of trip, group size, currency, and taxes. Flight-related variables provide information about flight distance from the airbase, and the airbases were grouped using the old administrative regions of the Ontario Ministry of Natural Resources (OMNR). The next two categories serve as indicators of the quality of the experience. The fish species category provides some insight into the resource availability of a fishing outpost and the operator's catch-and-release (CAR) policy, while the facility-related group provides a detailed description of the infrastructure provided at outposts. Finally, the other related variables provide the winter address and name of the operator and indicate whether hunting activities are pursued at the outpost. To answer concerns about whether brochures contain all the variables found in Table 2, the authors worked from the simple assumption that operators state the attributes that are relevant to the stated price in the brochure.

Table 2. Variables Collected from Brochures

Price Related (1995 quotes)	Species Related
Seven-day price	Walleye
Four-day price	Northern pike
Currency type	Lake trout
Attributes excluded from price	Brook trout
Guide cost	Bass
Group Size	Yellow perch
	Rainbow trout
Flight Related	Catch-and-release ethic
Flight distance (miles)	
Aircraft ownership	**Facility Related**
Airbase region	Sanitation amenities
	Lighting source
Other	Freezer availability
Winter address	Communications device
Hunting	Food provisions
Business name	Outpost capacity
Water body name	

This study is based on a sample of 418 fly-in, fishing outposts located throughout northern Ontario. However, this is an incomplete sample as, several operators only stated in their brochures that outposts were available. An attempt to collect this missing information currently is underway. Also, due to frequent missing data for some variables, the sample sizes in the various analyses are smaller than the total sample size. A future project will expand the information here to other aspects of a detailed synoptic analysis of resource-based tourism in northern Ontario. The analytical approach employed here also has the potential for temporal comparisons if prices can be collected systematically for several years. Efforts are underway to expand the database to include remote and road-accessible lodge data.

RESULTS

The first section of this paper provides a simple profile of the remote tourism outposts, in effect summarizing the information compiled from the brochures. Such a basic, yet systematic, overview has not been attempted before. The second section examines how price relates to other attributes associated with outposts. Next, the regional differences in outpost attributes are examined. Finally, a qualitative description of the effects of economies of scale is presented.

A profile of fly-in fishing outposts of northern Ontario

The information collected from the brochures is summarized in Table 3, which is organized into the same five groups as Table 2. Price-related information describes the various attributes that are essential to standardize price for the regression analysis. On average, an outpost operation charged $739.10 CDN and $634.47 CDN, respectively for 1995 seven- and four-day trips, with both federal and provincial sales taxes included in the prices as well as boat, motor and gas, but excluding fishing licenses. The variations around these means are large and suggest that the product is not homogeneous and various factors contribute to the price differences. Additionally, the high percentage of price quotations in U.S. funds demonstrates the importance of American clients to outpost operations.

The flight from a floatplane airbase to the camps is an integral element of the outpost experience. In most brochures, the fly-in cost is either integrated into the package price or is stated separately in the brochure. Most outpost operations in the sample also operate their own aircraft. The average flying distance is approximately 47 miles (71 km) with considerable variation ranging from five (8 km) to 240 miles (400 km). Outposts are located across northern Ontario, as indicated by their equal distribution over all four former OMNR regions. Most outpost operations have their own aircraft, offer hunting packages, and have owners with northern Ontario winter mailing addresses. Since almost 95 per cent of the sample offers hunting packages in the fall, a similar price analysis can be conducted in the future.

Information about the fish species available at the outposts provides insights into the type and quality of fishing available. Apparently, most outposts are located on warm-water lakes, as more than three-quarters of all operations report the availability of walleye. Fishing on cold-water lakes, as indicated by the presence of lake trout, is also important, albeit at only 19.7 per cent of lakes. Specialized fishing experiences, as indicated by fish species like brook trout and muskellunge, are important for a small segment of northern Ontario outposts. Interestingly, more than one-third of the operations advocate some form of conservation fishing in their brochures. A range of such voluntary restrictions exist that go beyond the locally applicable official regulations. Most frequently catch-and-release fishing (CAR) is simply encouraged (14 per cent of the entire

Table 3. A Profile of Outposts in Northern Ontario

Attribute	Specification	Frequency	Percentage	Average	Std. Dev.
PRICE RELATED					
Seven-day price*				739.10	250.48
Four-day price*				634.47	213.56
Currency	Canadian $	227	58.4		
	American $	162	41.6		
Attributes Excluded	none	4	1.0		
from Price	PST and GST**	1	0.3		
	licence (fishing)	23	5.9		
	licence, PST, and GST	336	86.4		
	{outboard motor fuel, licence, GST and PST}	4	1.0		
	licence and GST	15	3.9		
	licence and PST	6	1.5		
Guide Cost/day				139.45	28.83
FLIGHT RELATED					
Flight Distance (miles)				58.45	47.00
Aircraft Ownership	Operator	338	92.6		
	Other	27	7.4		
Airbase Region	Central	120	29.5		
	North-west	118	29.0		
	Northern	89	21.9		
	North-central	80	19.7		
SPECIES RELATED					
Walleye *	Present	244	76.3		
Northern Pike *	Present	280	87.2		
Lake Trout *	Present	63	19.7		
Brook Trout *	Present	41	12.8		
Bass *	Present	37	11.6		
Yellow Perch *	Present	19	4.5		
Muskellunge *	Present	7	2.2		
Rainbow Trout *	Present	4	1.0		
Catch-and-Release ethic	not mentioned	264	63.2		
	encouraged	60	14.4		
	discount offered	51	12.2		
	required	25	6.0		
	modified	18	4.3		
FACILITY RELATED					
Sanitation Amenities	no water	321	77.0		
	running coldwater (C)	8	1.9		

Table 3. continued

Attribute	Specification	Frequency	Percentage	Average	Std. Dev.
	running hot (H) and C and shower (S)	70	16.8		
	running H, C, S, and toilet	12	2.9		
	S only	5	1.2		
	gravity fed water	1	0.2		
Lighting Source	not mentioned	18	5.5		
	lantern	22	6.7		
	solar	34	10.4		
	propane	250	76.7		
	electric	2	0.6		
Freezer ***	Present	42	10.2		
Communications Device	Present	32	7.7		
	Available (extra cost)	33	8.0		
	Not Available	348	84.3		
Food ***	Provided	60	14.4		
Outpost Capacity	Insufficient Data				
OTHER					
Winter Address	northern Ontario	319	79.0		
	United States	54	13.4		
	other Canadian	31	7.7		
Hunting ***	present	396	94.7		

*   - price has been standardized to Canadian Funds, with PST and GST included
**   - PST refers to Ontario Provincial Sales Tax
           - GST refers to Canadian Goods and Services Tax
***   - refers to present/absent variables with only presence displayed
note   - sample sizes across attributes vary because of missing data
           - group size was constrained to four persons for price

sample); 12 per cent of all operations offer discounts for clients who practice some form of CAR fishing; six per cent of operations require CAR fishing; and four per cent of operations use a modification of CAR where a particular species is targeted for CAR fishing. Consequently, the precise definitions of catch-and-release vary slightly from operation to operation. Indications are that usually the CAR practice still allows clients to keep fish for shore lunches, and may also permit the taking of a trophy fish.

The facility-related variables list the infrastructure offered by the outposts and thus serve as indicators of quality. The vast majority of outposts belong to the basic category offering propane lights, but no running water, no freezer, no communications device, and no food (Table

3). However, several outpost operations offer higher standards with various combinations of the above variables. Given the diversity within outpost operations in northern Ontario, the focus now shifts to the more formal relationship between price variations and the characteristics of outpost camps.

Regression analysis

Exploring the relationship between the price charged by an outpost and other salient features of a given outpost is the primary goal of this study. Because of frequently missing data, for example, fish species not noted for a particular outpost, a concerted effort was made to reduce the model's complexity by collapsing categorical variables to a binary form. For example, for CAR, the single binary form simply indicates whether CAR was mentioned in some form or not. This enabled the researchers to place more confidence in the model of 418 outposts. Furthermore, since the flight distance variable violated multiple linear regression assumptions of linearity and homoscedasticity, this variable was transformed into the log of flight distance. Finally, the price variable was standardized to one common currency (Canadian funds with taxes) and one common form (no fishing license). Outposts for which no transportation charges were listed in the brochures were also deleted from the sample. The seven-day price variable was the most frequently and consistently quoted one.

The simplest model was produced by a stepwise linear regression describing the relationship between the seven-day outpost price and five other variables, accounting for an R^2 of 0.78. Table 4 displays the parameters, standardized parameters, and t-statistics for each variable and the intercept of this model. The parameters indicate the effect of a change of any one independent variable on the dependent price variable. For example, those outposts that provide a freezer are associated with an expected \$135.37 increase in the price of a seven-day trip. The standardized parameters indicate the relative importance for an attribute within the model and, thus, allow direct comparisons between significant variables. Finally, the t-value provides a measure for the significance of each dependent variable.

Table 4. Results of Multiple Regression Analysis (Dependent Variable = Seven-day Price for 1995)

Adjusted R^2 = 0.78, n = 294				
Variable	**Parameter**	**Standardized Parameter**	**T-value**	**Probability**
Airbase (region)	210.79	0.425	12.263	0.0000
Food	307.15	0.381	11.468	0.0000
Air miles (log)	151.97	0.179	5.905	0.0000
Freezer	135.37	0.163	4.357	0.0000
Shower	86.86	0.149	3.831	0.0002
Constant	353.42	NA	8.406	0.0000

The five statistically significant variables displayed in Table 4 provide an interesting description of how price is linked to other aspects of an outpost experience. The most significant price variation is not caused by any of the actual outpost characteristics, but rather depends on the location of the operation. The parameter estimate reveals that northwestern Ontario outposts, on average, charge $210.79 more for a seven-day package than northeastern Ontario outposts with all variables in the model held constant. Food is the second most important attribute associated with price and, as expected, the provision of a week's food leads to a large increase in price: food contributes to an increase of $301.15 in the outpost price. Flight distance, measured as the log of flight distance, follows in importance. The parameter estimate for this variable suggests that flying further distances raises the price of the experience although, as to be expected, the rate of increase diminishes with increasing distance. The final two significant variables, presence of a freezer and presence of a shower, relate directly to the quality of a camp. Of the five variables found significant, the regional variable emerged as the strongest, yet it is the most difficult to understand. To shed more light on the strong regional variations suggested by this model, the next section explores these differences in more detail.

Regional differences

This section examines whether regional differences exist among the variables collected in the brochures. The analyses were conducted via chi square tests and, where appropriate, t-tests. Only results that are statistically significant at a 95 per cent confidence level are reported.

Figure 2 compares those outpost characteristics that were included in the previous regression model. Given that all these variables were included in the regression model, the regional variable could not have acted as a surrogate for any of these variables. However, all of the amenities such as freezer, shower, and the provision of food are more frequently available for outposts in the northwest than in the northeast. As well, the flight distance is significantly greater for northwestern outposts. These observations suggest that the regional variable is related weakly to other attributes that determine price. However, tests for multicollinearity, such as the tolerance levels, did not reveal a problem with the parameter estimates.

To explore regional differences further, the analysis also examined variables that were not significant in the regression analysis. Figure 3 displays those variables that produced statistically significant differences between the two regions.

The northeast outposts are more likely to quote the price in Canadian currency than are northwestern outposts. This result is not unexpected since it is known that the northwestern clientele consists of a greater proportion of Americans (McKercher 1992). However, it is difficult to imagine that currency type alone would influence the setting of price. It merely reflects the dominance of the American market. Northwestern outposts were also more likely to promote the conservation practices discussed earlier. Although this difference is noteworthy and probably underlines some significant differences between the regions, the database here does not permit the examination of this difference in adequate detail. The presence of a communication device also is found more commonly in the northwestern outposts. Besides interpretations hinging on the quality of the establishments and clientele differences, another may conform with cost for safety precautions. Most outpost operations have either daily fly-overs or check flights during the week. Since northwestern outposts are, on average, located further away than northeastern outposts, the cost of this service will be slightly higher in the northwest. Therefore, the operators in the northwest may find cost efficiency by providing two-way radio communication with their outposts and negating the need for fly-overs. This premise has not yet been substantiated by detailed analysis.

Figure 2. Significant Regional Differences among Outposts for the Independent Significant Regression Variables 1995

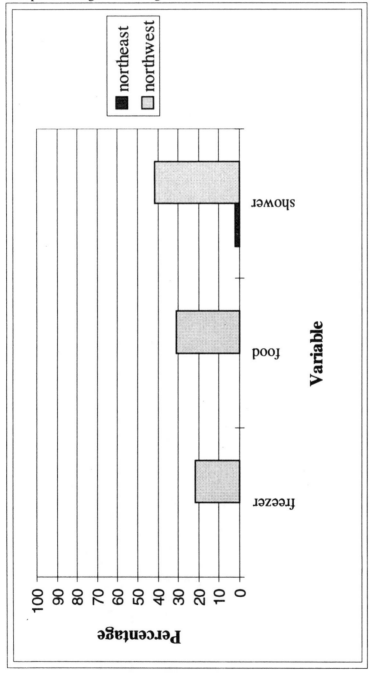

Figure 3. Significant Regional Differences among Outposts for Other Variables 1995

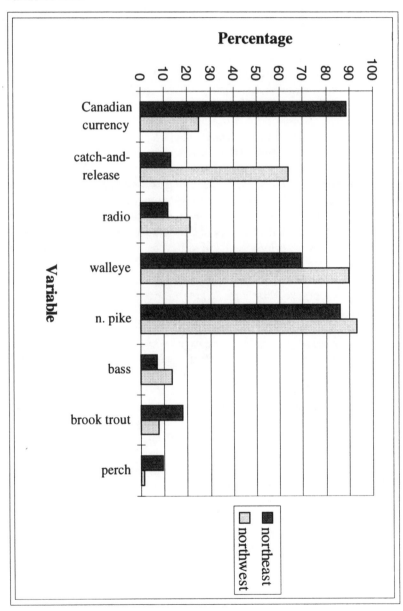

Significant differences between the regions were also observed for the fish species listed. Walleye, northern pike, and bass are available more often in northwestern outpost waters than in their northeastern counterparts. The northeastern outposts, in contrast, have greater concentrations of brook trout and yellow perch fishing opportunities than the northwest. Previous studies have revealed that walleye and northern pike are the most preferred fish species in Ontario for anglers as a whole (OMNR, n.d.) and, more specifically, for remote tourism clients (Haider & Carlucci 1994). Again, this difference suggests that the northwestern outposts offer an important attribute demanded by their clientele that northeastern outposts have in lesser quantity.

Many differences between the northwestern and northeastern outposts have been unearthed through this cursory analysis. The northwest outposts report more facilities, further flying distances, greater frequencies of the most preferred fish species, and a stronger catch-and-release ethic than outposts from the northeast. However, the discrepancy between reported and actual characteristics of the outposts may be considerable if clients in the two regions demand different items. For example, if northwestern and northeastern clients differ on the importance of shower availability, it would be misleading to conclude that northwestern outposts are superior because they have a greater proportion of showers than northeastern operations.

The spatial analysis can be refined further by segmenting the data set into the four previous administrative regions of the OMNR: the Western, Northcentral, Northern, and Central regions (see Figure 1). The statistically significant differences from chi square and ANOVA tests are highlighted in Table 5.

The data provide further refinement of the regional differences. Western outposts appear to have better facility-related attributes than outposts from the other regions. This is substantiated by the higher percentage of outposts in the western region that contain a freezer, a shower, or provide food. The northcentral outposts appear next in terms of facility quality, while the northern and central outposts equally lack these facility-related amenities. The general westward increase in important facility attributes is also reflected in the differences in average price for a seven-day outpost trip among the regions. On average the cost for the seven-day trip is $1,090.82 for western outposts, $823.22 for northcentral outposts, $605.57 for northern outposts, and $568.85 for central outposts. All differences in price are significant at 95 per cent for ANOVA tests with Bonferroni and Scheffe pairwise comparisons, except the price difference between the central and northern regions. The fishing quality varies less than the facility quality with only the central region having lower concentrations of the most preferred fish species, such as walleye and northern pike. The high abundance of brook trout in the central regions directly mimics the species' population differences in the regions.

Two further differences in Table 5 are worth emphasizing. First, the currency variable again emphasizes the importance of American clientele in the west. Over 98 per cent of western outposts list their prices in American currencies (1.9 per cent in Canadian funds). The support for catch-and-release regulations also shows a significant difference among regions. Somewhat surprisingly, the northcentral region contains the highest percentage of outposts mentioning some form of CAR fishing in the brochures. The reason for this is not easily explained, and the entire topic deserves a detailed exploration in a future study.

Economies of scale

Economies of scale provide an important opportunity for operators to reduce their average costs and, thus, offer lower prices at their outposts. The presence of economies of scale in the resource-based tourism industry of northern Ontario is documented by Tindale (1986) who found that the top one-third of resource-based establishments in northwestern Ontario accounted for 70 per cent of the sales. The brochure data also indicate the presence of economies of scale for outpost operations alone, which show up most prominently in the vertical integration between outpost operations and aircraft operations. For those operators using their own aircraft, significant economies of scale can be achieved by operating many outposts and, thus, reducing fixed and semi-fixed costs on planes like maintenance, loan payments, and insurance. This hypothesis is verified to some extent by the nonlinear relationship between flight distance and price. Check flight costs depend on the location of individual camps in relationship to each other and, thus, owning several outpost operations could lead to significant economies of scale. Another important economy of scale exists in advertising and marketing costs. Again, these costs can be reduced in proportion to sales by large scale operations. Finally, the external economy of scale known as agglomeration (localization) and, more specifically, product differentiation[4] is evident in northwestern Ontario. The regression and regional analyses suggest that consumers of outposts perceive the outposts of northwestern Ontario as better quality than those in northeastern Ontario and are willing to pay a premium for this location. Furthermore, northern Ontario outposts as a whole may enjoy a similar perception of superior quality over other destinations as evidenced by the strong loyalty of the

Table 5. Significant Regional Differences Among Outposts for Four Regions in 1995

% of outposts with	West	Northcentral	Northern	Central
a freezer present	29.2	11.3	1.1	0.0
food provided in whole or in part	53.1	0.0	0.0	0.0
a shower present	50.0	28.8	3.4	1.7
walleye present in fishing waters	87.2	93.0	85.5	56.6
northern pike present in fishing waters	93.6	93.0	96.1	77.8
lake trout present in fishing waters	24.4	21.1	7.9	23.2
brook trout present in fishing waters	2.6	14.0	11.8	22.2
Canadian currency	1.9	57.1	97.8	81.1
support for catch-and-release fishing	48.3	86.3	21.3	6.7
a radio telephone (communication)	17.7	26.3	18.0	6.7

clientele (Rushton/Shanahan & Associates Ltd. et al. 1979 and NOTO 1987). Although regional differences were identified on many fronts between outposts, it is highly probable that perceptual differences by clients account for some regional price disparity. Again this premise needs further research. Finally, an external diseconomy of scale also exists in northern Ontario. This is associated with the loss of familiarity or family-like atmosphere that is negatively related to the operation's size. It can only be hypothesized here that this diseconomy is more important for lodges than outposts which, by nature, are more secluded from operator-user contact.

SUMMARY

Five significant variables—shower, freezer, air miles, region, and food—account for 78 per cent of the variation of the seven-day price differences observed among outposts. Some variables, such as shower and freezer, appear to serve as good indicators for the overall quality of an outpost. Even the regional variable is a surrogate for many other differences between the northwestern and northeastern regions. Evidently, the region of the operation is very important in the industry in terms of pricing and stated facilities. Therefore, any study treating remote tourism as a homogeneous industry may be misleading.

A few caveats are worth discussing about the analyses completed above. First, the price charged by outposts may be affected by the existence of excess demand or supply. Baum and Mudambi (1995) demonstrated that the pricing of Bermuda's hotel industry was dependent on the level of excess demand. Since the study here examined a single point in time with no measures of occupancy rates, the existence of the excess supply or demand cannot be determined. Therefore, predicting future price levels from the significant parameters should be undertaken with caution. Furthermore, the analyses rely on a non-random sample of all northern Ontario outposts and, if systematic biases exist in the non-sampled population, the results can only be extrapolated to the population at large with caution. One such possible bias is that the brochure collection employed here could favour large operations, while small operations with one or two outpost camps may be under-represented since they would spend less in total on advertising.

As the data set becomes more refined and complete, removal of the regional variable will be possible by including other regional differences into the model such as fish species. Currently, this option is not available as the sample size and missing data on many variables would lead to serious questions about sample size adequacy if eight or nine binary variables were chosen.

NOTES

1. The only exception is the category 'outposts' under type of operation.

2. See Haider et al. in this volume for more information.

3. While this marketing strategy holds true for the majority of operations, some operations integrate price-related information directly into the glossy brochure, while others distribute a single colour leaflet with mostly factual information.

4. Although product differentiation does not reduce average costs, it still is considered an economy of scale because it creates a gain in efficiency for the operations (Berry, Conkling & Ray 1993: 215).

REFERENCES

Baum, T. & R. Mudambi. 1995. An empirical analysis of oligopolistic hotel pricing. *Annals of Tourism Research 22* (3), 501-516.

Berry, B.J.L., E.C. Conkling & M. Ray. 1993. *The global economy: Resource use, locational choice, and international trade.* Englewood Cliffs, N.J.: Prentice-Hall.

Dilley, R.S. 1986. Tourist brochures and tourist images. *The Canadian Geographer, 30* (1), 59-65.

Eagles, P. & E. Wind. 1994. Canadian ecotours in 1992: A content analysis of advertising. *Journal of Applied Recreation Research 19*(1), 67-87.

Econometric Research Limited and Ministry of Tourism and Recreation. 1990. *Economic impact of the remote tourism industry.* Ontario Ministry of Tourism and Recreation: Toronto, ON.

Environmental Assessment Board. 1994. Reasons for decision and decision - Class Environmental Assessment by the Ministry of Natural

Resources for timber management on crown lands in Ontario. Toronto.

Haider, W. & L. Carlucci. 1994. *Remote tourism in North Algoma (Visitor Survey 1991)*. Thunder Bay: Ontario Ministry of Natural Resources.

Hope, A.J. 1987. *Red Lake/Golden: Economic impact of tourism*. Ministry of Tourism and Recreation.

McKercher, B. 1992. Tourism as a conflicting land use: Northern Ontario's outfitting industry. *Annals of Tourism Research 19* (3), 467-481.

Northern Ontario Tourist Outfitters Association. 1987. *Northern Ontario tourism strategy: A white paper on the future of tourism in the North*. North Bay: Northern Ontario Tourist Outfitters Association.

Ontario Ministry of Natural Resources. (n.d.). *Recreational fishing in Ontario, 1990 (Fact Sheet)* North York: Ontario Ministry of Natural Resources.

Rushton/Shanahan & Associates Ltd., Hough, Stansbury and Associates Ltd., & Jack B. Ellis and Associates Ltd. 1979. *The fishing hunting lodge industry in Northern Ontario*. Ontario Ministry of Northern Affairs.

Smith, S.L.J. 1994. The tourism product. *Annals of Tourism Research 21* (3), 582-595.

Statistics Canada. 1994a. *Profile of census metropolitan areas and census agglomerations, Part B*. (Report 93-338). Ottawa: Minister of Supply and Services.

Statistics Canada. 1994b. *Profile of census divisions and subdivisions in Ontario, Part B*. (Report 95-338). Ottawa: Minister of Supply and Services.

Tindale, R. 1986. *Attributes for success: The tourist resort industry in Northwestern Ontario*. Thunder Bay: Ontario Ministry of Tourism and Recreation.

GREENING OF REMOTE TOURISM LODGES

Pamela A. Wight
Pam Wight & Associates

INTRODUCTION

The tourism industry, like other businesses whose operations affect the environment, is being held to close scrutiny and accountability for the effect of its activities on the environment. It is under tremendous pressure, both from the public and from regulatory agencies, to minimize its impact on the environment. Despite the fact that the tourism industry has for many years proclaimed awareness and sensitivity to the environment, actions have not always corresponded to those assertions. Tourism represents a potentially valuable instrument for sustainable development, and the industry has much to gain from promoting and applying this concept, which in this case means combining economic opportunities with environmental conservation and enhancement.

Internal and external environment

In tourism, and particularly in responsible tourism, many of the environmental concerns have dealt with the external environment, that is, conservation of natural, cultural, or urban environments. However, the internal environment of any tourism operation also plays a part in conservation (Wight 1994). This may be likened to the practice rather than the product, or the how of doing business. An establishment's organizational, managerial, and operational system should reflect a holistic approach to the environment and to sustainability. In doing so, the operator will respond to market demand.

Green practices in the hospitality industry

It is now well recognized that tourism businesses are beginning to build environmentally sensitive components into their facilities and operations. A prime example would be the leadership exhibited by Canadian Pacific Hotels & Resorts, with its *Green Partnership Guide*. Now, many hotel and resort properties are greening their operations. However, there are a number of concerns: many chain operations find that the implementation of green programs can only progress as far as the individual general manager is willing to support them; some quality standards of hotel and resort chains conflict with green practices (e.g. a specified minimum number of bars of soap per room, or disposable individual meal condiments); smaller properties tend to take an *ad hoc*, rather than a systematic approach to greening; others implement environmental measures as a form of individual problem-solving; and, the small, mom-pop type of operations which make up the bulk of the industry are not even beginning to think about implementing environmental initiatives.

MARKET DEMAND

Types of tourism accommodation preferred

Accommodation is a key component of the tourism industry: tourists need a place to stay. An accommodation may be a campsite or a fixed-roof accommodation, such as a cabin, lodge, bed and breakfast, ranch, motel, hotel, or resort. Apart from campsites, all accommodation is some form of fixed-roof facility. Whatever the specific type of accommodation markets prefer, there is growing interest in environmentally sensitive forms of accommodation. It is interesting to note the 64 per cent of U.S. travellers who are likely to patronize companies which support the environment are likely to take an ecotourism trip, and ecotourism travellers are often interested in remote, uncrowded, untouristic locations, such as the Canadian north (HLA Consultants & ARA Consulting 1994). While lodgings constitute a fundamental support service to experience a place, they usually are not the primary attraction.

Market preference: Accommodation type

In a recent Ecotourism Market Demand Assessment (HLA Consultants & ARA Consulting 1994), consumers were asked what kind of accommodation they preferred. Table 1 shows the range of preferences. The important finding is that ecotourists prefer a range of accommodations, and both general consumers and experienced ecotourist gave multiple responses. It is the experience which determines the accommodation, not vice versa.

Wight (1993b) has pointed out that a range or spectrum of accommodation types is appropriate for ecotourism, as shown on Figure 1. In practice, one may see greater emphasis on the ends of the spectrum (camping, and high quality fixed-roof such as hotels). However, in developed countries in particular, there is a dearth of mid-range fixed-roof accommodation for ecotourists.

Table 1. Accommodation Preferences of the North American Ecotourism Markets

Accommodation Type	General Consumer		Experienced Ecotourist	
	% Respondents	Number Responses	% Respondents	Number Responses
Cabin	14	194	66	280
Lodge/Inn	14	193	60	251
Tent/camping	17	229	58	246
Bed & breakfast	10	138	55	231
Hotel/motel	56	773	41	173
Ranch	1	16	40	170
Cruise ship	4	58	20	86
RV	5	68	2	8
Private home/friends	6	82	1	5
Condo, house, apartment	3	41	.4	2
Other	3	42	5	21
Total Responses		1837		1474
Total Respondents	1377		422	
Av. No. Responses per Person		1.3		3.5

Percentages do not total 100% due to multiple responses.

Source: HLA Consultants & ARA Consulting 1994.

In Britain, visitors to national parks may enjoy some alternative types of accommodation. These may be camping barns, which provide very simple accommodation in converted buildings for low cost; or bunkhouse barns, which are more elaborate than camping barns and have separate rooms; or, converted country houses. Demand has increased steadily, with demand for bunkhouse barns, for example, increasing 20 per cent over the last two years in the Peak District National Park (Countryside Commission et al. n.d.)

Other literature also indicates that a range of accommodation is desired, with considerable demand for smaller scale, rural and adventure-type accommodation, representing the middle range on Wight's spectrum (Figure 1). One market study divided Americans into five psychographic motivational groups. Nature-based travel, including ecotourism, was associated with a group called Get Away Active. Among other traits, the accommodations for this group tend toward the more rustic than lavish (Reingold 1993). Similarly, Nababan and Aliadi (1993: 50) point out for Indonesia that "appropriate accommodations for the [nature tourism] sites should be motels, cottages, and other small lodging types, instead of five-star hotels."

Figure 1. Ecotourism Accommodations Spectrum

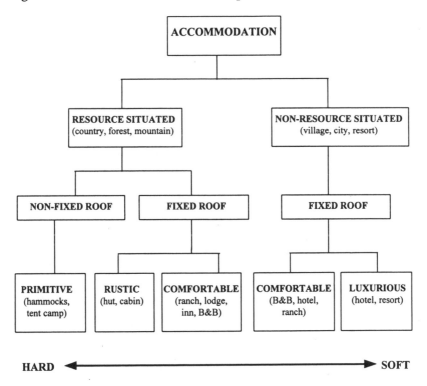

Source: Wight 1993b.

Backman and Potts (1993) indicate that southeast U.S. nature-based travellers stay in hotels or motels, while Silverberg, Backman, and Backman (1994), in their study of nature-based tourists to Southeastern U.S., found a range of accommodation preferences, from condominiums to campgrounds. Another study has found that there was relatively high use of rural and village-level accommodations by nature-oriented tour operation: 40 per cent rural/village; 27 per cent camping; 21 per cent luxury hotels; and, 33 per cent other hotels (Ingram & Durst 1989).

It has been said that "very few ecolodges exist in North America as the markets appear to favour independent camping, and/or comfortable recreational lodges" (ARA Consulting 1994: 1-3). However, the results of the market research do not indicate that this is due to market preference: markets are demanding a range of accommodation types, and experienced ecotourists, in particular, are expressing a preference for intimate, adventure-type accommodation.

The pertinent question may then become: What is the range of accommodation types that should be supplied by any destination area? In most cases, the supply is an abundance of the conventional hotels and motels, together with considerable opportunity for camping. The gap in many destinations appears to lie in the middle range of the spectrum, in the area of adventure-type, small scale, fixed roof accommodations. It is fortunate for Canada's north, that much of the accommodation is lodge and cabin type, that which appears to be preferred by ecotourists.

Demand for green travel opportunities

A number of surveys of travellers' opinions and behaviours have pointed to their desire to support environmentally sensitive business (Wight 1991; Cook et al. 1992; Wight 1995). For example, a survey asked U.S. travellers how important the recognition of the supplier as an environmentally responsible travel business was when selecting their travel suppliers (airline, hotel, restaurants, cruise ships, rental cars, attractions). One-half (50.4 per cent) indicated that this was an important or very important factor in their choice of supplier, and less than a quarter (22.5 per cent) said it was not a very important factor. This desire for environmental sensitivity is not a factor which is confined only to those who can afford to pick and choose. The highest importance rating of environmental sensitivity was found in the clerical/sales occupational groups, which shows how environmental interest has permeated many aspects of life.

In addition, when asked about their likelihood of supporting/ patronizing companies who promote/preserve the environment, 86.6 per cent indicated that this was likely or very likely. Virtually all of those who had said environmental sensitivity was an important factor to them indicated they were likely to patronize such companies. In addition, those who are likely to patronize companies who support the environment are equally likely to be hotel guests, or to stay at other kinds of accommodation (over 87 per cent of both types of guests are likely to patronize companies who support the environment).

Marketing environmentally sensitive facilities

An Australian guide called *Australia's Natural Holiday Guide* was designed for the general traveller (Australia Tourist Commission 1994). In it, Australian opportunities and experiences for resource based travel and tourism are described: parks, heritage areas, wilderness, outdoor activities, and cultural heritage. In addition, a range of accommodation businesses and other operators are featured. What is interesting, however, is the manner in which these are described. Each operation is featured on a matrix, along with whether or not it contains certain specified elements. Figure 2 shows the elements of the matrix, which clearly have a strong environmental focus.

Some elements of the matrix are examined in great detail, and one may wonder if, in fact, the travelling public is able to understand and evaluate the responses as presented. For example, would an average environmentally concerned traveller be able to say which of the seven Solid Waste Disposal Systems were environmentally more sensitive? Nevertheless, the matrix does present many of the detailed practices at a facility, highlighting environmental perspectives. This serves both to make the public more aware of environmental sensitivities and to demonstrate the Australian destinations as being environmentally concerned. Another example of a destination using environmental sensitivity as a marketing tool comes from Switzerland (*Welcome Swiss Hotels: Hotel Guide*). However, frequently this type of a marketing approach is implemented at the property level.

BENEFITS OF ENVIRONMENTALLY SENSITIVE PRACTICES AND SYSTEMS

Hospitality industry practices and systems

The hotel chain that initiated the first comprehensive green program was Canadian Pacific Hotels & Resorts. According to the company's research, the average guest generates one pound of solid waste a day and two pounds on check-out day. With 20,000 check-outs a day throughout Canada, the waste is considerable. Waste management has been found to be of direct economic benefit. For example, the purchase of bathroom amenities without elaborate packaging can reduce costs by up to 10 per cent.

Figure 2. Australia's Natural Holiday Guide
Accommodation Information Matrix Elements

ENVIRONMENT
DESCRIPTION OF
ACCOMMODATION
Camping
Wilderness lodge

ENVIRONMENT
DESCRIPTION OF
ACCOMMODATION
Camping
Wilderness lodge
Resort complex
Hotel
Caravan
Cottage
Farmhouse
Cabins
Motel
LANDSCAPED
Native plants
Exotic plants
GARDENS AND LAWNS
Pesticides
Herbicides
Fertilizers
WILDLIFE
Do you have a program to encourage native wildlife?
do you practice elimination of feral animals?
Do you have wildlife?
Do you have a wildlife breeding program?
Do you have plant or wildlife sanctuary areas?
Do you plant bird attracting plants?
Do you have accessible nature areas in excess of 20 hectares within walking distance from the complex?
SEWAGE TREATMENT
Primary
Secondary
Tertiary
CHEMICAL
Do you use phosphate-based detergent?
Do you offer dry-cleaning?
Do you use chlorine bleaches or cleaners?

WATER CONSERVATION
Program to minimize water use?
Guests to conserve water (e.g. for showering)?
Dual-flush toilets?
Low-flow shower heads?
RECYCLING:
USE OF NON-RECYCLED PRODUCTS
Polystyrene cups
Paper plates
Plastic plates
Plastic utensils
Recycled paper in promotional materials?
Unbleached paper for domestic use?
SOLID WASTE DISPOSAL SYSTEM
Shipped back to the mainland
Buried on property
Municipal recycle garbage system
Removed from the site
Burnt
Composting
ENERGY
SOLAR POWER SYSTEM
Hot water
Lighting
Heating
Heated swimming pool
Electricity
Energy key program
WASTE MINIMIZATION
SEWAGE DISPOSAL SYSTEM
Septic Composting
Free disposal
Town
Pit
Removed from site
Other

Australia Tourist Commission, 1994.

Many of the documented examples of benefits relate to urban-based accommodations. However, many of these practices and benefits may be applied to remote lodges. The *Australia Natural Holiday Guide* has shown that more remote and nature-based accommodations are tapping into the promotional benefits of credible green practices. Most companies that are committed to the principles of recycling and waste reduction have not paid higher prices simply to support public interest and demand. Rather, they have instituted new purchasing policies that offer additional business benefits. For example, the Westin's company policy is to use recycled paper products for its stationery, paper towels, and toilet paper. By using recycled paper for the Westin letterhead alone the company saved $10,000.

The Saunders Hotel Group's Boston Park Plaza is part of a property-wide conservation program. It has introduced a 24-ounce pump dispenser for liquid soap, mouth-wash, shampoo, and hair conditioner. These replace the more than two million individual packages annually which became garbage. Many hotels offer guests the option of having their towels and sheets changed every other day instead of every day, thus saving water and energy, cutting detergent use, reducing wear and tear, and reducing operating costs. Up to 40 per cent of guests accept this option in many locations.

In Ontario, Kenora's Inn of the Woods has achieved an annual $14,000 energy cost savings by converting 278 incandescent bulbs to compact fluorescent (Sennett 1992). The savings were exactly as originally projected, and the $11,000 conversion was paid back in about eight months. The planning of the retrofit involved Ontario Hydro, so the hotel qualified for a $4,200 rebate under their Energy Efficient Lighting Program. An additional advantage is that the new equipment needs far less maintenance.

In Boston, the Lenox Hotel was faced with stiff increases in water and sewer bills, so a retrofit took place. Showers were equipped with flow resistors and heads, reducing flow from six to seven gallons to three gallons per minute (g.p.m.). Water faucet aerators reduced flow from four to 1.5 g.p.m. and there was no noticeable flow difference to guests. Similarly, 1.6 gal/flush toilets replaced the six to seven gal/flush toilets. The results were dramatic: for the first quarter of 1989 the sewer and water use was 1.88 million gallons, down almost 75 per cent from the previous year. The retrofit paid for itself in less than two years (Marshall 1990). Benefits from conservation of hot water result in additional savings from less energy required to heat the water. Where there is no cost for water supply, lodges may still find a benefit in water conservation through less load on their septic tanks or other sewage management systems.

Remote lodge practices and systems

Alberta Economic Development and Tourism (1994) recently surveyed operators of Canadian remote lodges which use environmentally sensitive technologies in their facilities. Operators were asked to provide information on how the technologies were being used, their capabilities, advantages, disadvantages, and other information. The idea was to demonstrate that alternative technologies need not be viewed as experimental or with suspicion, rather, they have real value for the tourism industry in the north. The facilities surveyed, together with the category of environmental practice employed, are shown in Table 2.

Table 2. Alternative and Minimum Impact Technologies, by Facility

Remote Facilities	Site Development and Construction Technologies	Energy Technologies	Waste Management Technologies	Water Quality and Conservation Technologies
Wells Gray Park Backcountry Chalets, BC	X			
Sheep Mountain Visitor Information Centre, YK	X	X		
Sorcerer Lake Lodge, BC	X	X		
Tarryall Lodge	X	X		
Peterson's Point Lake Camp, NWT		X		
River Cove Campground, AB		X		
Mount Assiniboine Lodge, BC	X	X	X	
Selkirk Lodge, BC	X	X	X	
Boyne River Ecology Centre, ON	X	X	X	
North Knife Lake Lodge, MAN	X	X	X	
Arctic Watch Lodge, NWT	X	X	X	
Mistaya Lodge, BC	X	X	X	X
Purcell Lodge, BC	X	X	X	X
Alpine Huts, AB & BC			X	
Lake O'Hara Lodge, BC			X	X

Source: Alberta Economic Development and Tourism 1994.

Lodge operators were asked about the visitors' responses to the respective technologies employed. Specific comments related to quietness of certain power generation technologies; the curiosity and interest of younger visitors; and, the particular interest of Californians in low water volume toilets. An interesting observation was the "young people tend to respond to the environmental aspect of the technologies, whereas older people tend to respond to the money saving aspect" (Alberta Economic Development and Tourism 1994: 29). What is noteworthy is that virtually every respondent indicated that visitors were interested, impressed, and positive about the technologies.

At Tarryall Lodge in northwestern Ontario, power used to be provided by a diesel generator, which operated 24 hours a day. High cost prompted the owner to investigate alternative energy, and to install a photo voltaic (PV)—diesel hybrid system. During periods of low sunshine, the use of a diesel generator is reduced by drawing power from a bank of deep-cycle batteries. Now, the diesel is only operated once every three to four days in order to recharge the batteries. The capital cost of the system is high ($36,000). However, it is quieter, cleaner, and requires less maintenance and servicing. The total first year savings in fuel and maintenance charges amounted to $7,000.

Arctic Watch Lodge is located south of Resolute Bay on Somerset Island. Built in 1991, it was designed to incorporate new technologies for cost effectiveness and low environmental impact. These include energy efficient heating, low energy fluorescent lighting, and low water faucets and shower heads. PV solar energy is used to power the radio, repeaters, and water pump. An unaltered leach pit is used to dissipate human waste, through addition of pear moss, leaves, and insects to the pit. The maintenance and servicing of the systems is minimal, and the use of PV energy is cost effective because fuel and its air transport costs are not required. No disadvantages were noted by the lodge management.

ENVIRONMENTALLY SENSITIVE TECHNOLOGIES FOR REMOTE TOURISM FACILITIES

Whenever proposals for new tourism operations in remote and unserviced locations are under consideration, there is concern by the public, by agencies, and by the industry that developments be appropriate to the environment in which they are proposed, and that they reflect sensitivity for the environment in which they are located. The public, in particular, is concerned about the practices of such facilities, especially their consumption of energy and water, and systems of waste and sewage disposal. There is a range of environmentally responsible approaches to planning, design, construction, equipping, and operation of facilities.

A study was commissioned by Alberta Economic Development and Tourism to examine a range of environmentally sensitive systems and practices for remote tourism facilities (Nor'wester Energy Systems Ltd. et al. 1994). The technologies had to have relevant applications for two types of facilities: a stand alone lodge which would accommodate 25 people, including staff; and, a lodge with family unit cabins to accommodate a total of 60 to 70 people including staff.

The majority of the technologies or practices reviewed are applicable to both examples, the difference only being a matter of scale. All the systems presented are currently in use in remote tourism facilities or are feasible for such facilities. Technologies which were not yet commercially developed, or which were experimental, were not considered. In addition to information on the systems, lists of suppliers and sources of information were provided. Costs and applicability are very site specific, since the available resources and facility amenities vary widely. Figure 3 presents a number of technologies and practices which can improve resource conservation in remote tourism lodges.

Figure 3 lists renewable and other energy sources and a range of energy efficiency technologies and measures. Also listed are water sources, treatment, and water conservation technologies, including retrofit devices and management techniques. The figure outlines both conventional sewage treatment technologies aimed at the treatment of gray water and black water effluent generated by active-use facilities as well as emerging technologies such as rotating biological contactors, passive multi-component systems, and "living machines." Included are also six waste management strategies which address the four clear principles of waste management: reduction, reuse, recycling, and energy recovery.

A range of information was given for each system, since the intent was to provide a range of choices and information to the industry, not to stipulate the practices. The following categories were described for each technology:

- feasibility
- resource appropriateness/availability a) summer b) winter
- compatibility with other technologies/practices
- availability (including suppliers, services)
- reliability
- complexity
- conformance to applicable codes and regulations
- fuel/energy: a) requirements b) savings
- life span

- environmental consequences: a) aesthetics (visual and noise); b) human safety and comfort; c) biophysical; and, d) other
- benefits: a) economic b) non-economic
- disadvantages: a) economic b) non-economic
- order of magnitude costs: a) capital b) annual operating and maintenance
- payback period

Figure 3. Alternative and Low Impact Technologies

ENERGY SOURCES	
Renewable Energy	**Other Energy**
WIND	COGENERATION
• wind electric generation	WOOD HEAT
• wind powered pumping	• wood fuelled furnace
• wind powered aeration	• high efficiency wood stoves,
SOLAR	fireplaces
• solar electric generation (PV)	
• solar (PV) water pumping	
• solar water heating	
HYDRO	
STORAGE	
HYBRID SYSTEM	

ENERGY EFFICIENCY TECHNOLOGIES AND SYSTEMS	
WASTE ENERGY RECOVER	LOAD MANAGEMENT
• engine heat recovery	• energy management systems
• hot water pre-heat	• energy management practices
• hot water tank insulation	• power factor improvement
• hot tub cover	• energy efficient motors
• clothes dryer heat exchange	TRANSPORT
LIGHTING	• reduce motorized transport
• lighting control	requirements
• light fixtures	• reduces air transport requirements
• DC lighting	BUILDING EFFICIENCY
• day lighting	• air tightness
APPLIANCES	• air to air heat exchange
• efficient appliances	• windows
• gas ranges & dryers	• insulation/shutters
HEATING	• passive solar design
• temp setback	
• hot water temp setback	
• low flow shower head	
• heat pumps	
• efficient furnaces	

Figure 3. Continued

WATER SOURCES AND TREATMENT	SEWAGE TREATMENT SYSTEMS
SOURCES 1. Drilled wells 2. Surface streams/infiltration galleries 3. Rainwater collection 4. Freshwater hauling TREATMENT SYSTEMS 1. Pressure vessel filter systems 2. Package water treatment plants 3. Slow sand filters 4. Reverse osmosis & "nana" micro filters CONSERVATION TECHNOLOGIES 1. Retrofit devices for conventional toilets 2. Outhouse & portable outdoor toilet 3. Composting 4. Gray water recycling 5. Low flow toilets 6. Vacuum toilets 7. Low flow shower heads 8. In-line flow controls	<u>Conventional Techniques</u> 1. Effluent holding tanks 2. Septic tank & septic tile field 3. Effluent discharge to wetlands or by spray irrigation <u>Emerging Technologies</u> 4. Rotating biological contractors (RBCs) 5. Passive three component systems 6. Living machines

WASTE MANAGEMENT	
MANAGEMENT STRATEGIES 1. PURCHASING (GREEN PURCHASE POLICIES) - elimination & substitution (reduction) - bulk purchasing - packaging reduction - linking purchasing & recycling - purchasing durable/reusable/recycled goods 2. MATERIAL STORAGE & HANDLING - storage - spill prevention strategies 3.WASTE STORAGE & HANDLING - source separation of wastes - waste transportation - cooperative waste systems - waste disposal	4. EQUIPMENT MAINTENANCE & HANDLING - preventative maintenance - quality control 5. MINIMIZATION OF USE OF MATERIALS 6. CLIENT EDUCATION

Source: Nor'wester Energy Systems Ltd. et al. 1994.

Figure 4. Environmental Recommendations for Remote Tourism Lodges

---

ENERGY
Current Facilities
• reduce energy leaks to a minimum
• implement all measures which are both appropriate and cost effective
Proposed Facilities
• available and existing energy resources should be evaluated
• generating alternatives should be examined

WATER & SEWER MANAGEMENT
Proposed Facilities
• require detailed site specific analysis and assessment, including discussions with regulatory bodies
• simple, basic, and passive technologies should be considered first, even if initial capital costs seem higher
• unproven systems should not be used unless small scale pilot studies done
• natural systems (wetlands) should be used if possible

WASTE MANAGEMENT
Facility Planning Should Consider
• storage
• material handling
• a transport plan
Four Waste Management Planning Priorities
1. reduction in materials imported to the facility
2. reduction in amount of material generated at the facility
3. maintenance of the quality of used and residual materials
4. reduction in the weight and volume of materials which must be removed from the facility

Waste Minimization Recommendations
• client education
• reduced material importation
• use of local community programs and suppliers

Source: Nor'wester Energy Systems Ltd. et al. 1994.

CONCLUSION

Obviously, most operational aspects of remote lodges can be improved from an environmental perspective. Changes are possible with regard to the use of energy, water and sewage management, and waste management (Figure 4). Remote lodge operators should become more informed about the fact that in addition to delivering cost savings, environmentally sound practices can also be used for marketing purposes and might lead to competitive advantages.

REFERENCES

Alberta Economic Development and Tourism. 1994. *Environmentally sensitive facilities: Remote tourism case studies.* Report developed by Development Services Branch, Alberta Economic Development and Tourism, Edmonton, Alberta.

ARA Consulting Group. 1994. *Ecolodge survey: A supporting technical paper for the Government of Trinidad and Tobago tourism master plan.*

Australia Tourist Commission. 1994. *The natural holiday guide.*

Backman, K.F. & T.D. Potts. 1993. *Profiling nature-based travelers: Southeastern market segments.* South Carolina: Strom Thurmond Institute.

Cook, S.D., E. Stewart, K. Repass, & U.S. Travel Data Center. 1992. *Discover America: Tourism and the environment.* Washington, D.C.: Travel Industry Association of America.

Countryside Commission, Countryside Council for Wales, English Tourist Hoard, Rural Development Commission, and Wales Tourist Board. n.d. *Tourism in national parks: A guide to good practice.* Glasgow & Association: UK.

Husek, G. 1990. Hotels keeping watch on waste. *Hotel and Motel Management, 205,* September 10, 3, 81.

HLA Consultants & ARA Consulting. 1994. *Ecotourism - nature/ adventure/culture: Alberta and British Columbia market demand assessment.* Prepared for Canadian Heritage, Industry Canada, BC Small Business, Tourism and Culture, Alberta Economic Development and

Tourism, and the Outdoor Recreation Council of BC.

Ingram, C.D. & P.B. Durst. 1989. Nature-oriented tour operators: Travel to developing countries. *Journal of Travel Research*, 28(2) 11-15.

Marshall, A. 1990. Hotel discovers it pays to be stingy with water. *Hotel and Motel Management*, 205 September 24, 12.

Nababan, A. & A. Aliadi. 1993. Nature tourism profile: Indonesia, pp. 43-54. In *Nature tourism and Asia: Opportunities and constraints for conservation and economic development*. J. Nenon and P.B. Durest, eds. USDA, Forest Service, USAID, USDA, Office of International Cooperation and Development. Washington, D.C.

Nor'wester Energy Systems Ltd., MPE Engineering Ltd., and Willow Root Environmental Ltd. 1994. *Alternative and minimum impact technologies for remote tourism locations*. Prepared for Alberta Economic Development and Tourism: Edmonton, Alberta.

Reingold, L. 1993. Identifying the elusive ecotourist. In *Going Green*, a supplement to *Tour and Travel News*, October 25, 36-39.

Sennett, J. 1992. Envirowatch. *Canadian Hotel and Restaurant*, 70 (10):19.

Silverberg, K.E., S.J. Backman, & K.F. Backman. 1994. A preliminary investigation into the psychographics of nature-based travelers to the Southeastern United States. pp. 36-40. In *Tourism: The Economy's Silver Lining. TTRA Annual Conference Proceedings*. Bal Harbour, Florida, June 18-22.

U.S. Travel Data Centre. 1992. *Tourism and the environment study tables*. Conducted for the Travel Industry Association of America. May.

Wight, P. 1995. *Environmentally sensitive technologies/facilities: Responding to market demand for responsible travel and deriving economic benefit*. Paper presented at *Sharing Tomorrow: Exploring Responsible Tourism*, Interpretation Canada National Conference. Riding Mountain National Park, Manitoba. September 24-27.

Wight, P. 1994. The greening of the hospitality industry: Economic and environmental good sense, pp. 665-674. In *Tourism: The State of the Art*, A.V. Seaton, ed. John Wiley & Sons: Chichester.

Wight. P. 1993a. Improved business positioning: Environmentally responsible marketing of tourism. pp. 200-207. In *Expanding responsibilities: A blueprint for the travel industry, Proceedings of the 24th TTRA conference,* Whistler, BC June 13-16.

Wight, P. 1993b. Sustainable ecotourism: Balancing economic, environmental and social goals within an ethical framework. *Journal of Tourism Studies,* 4(2) 54-66.

Wright, W.J. 1991. The Angus Reid report: The environment and "green" products in recessionary times. In *The Canadian Green Marketing Alert,* 1(1) 4-7.

TOURISM NORTHWEST: A REGIONAL TOURISM DEVELOPMENT FRAMEWORK

R. Paul Maddock
Northwestern Ontario Development Network

Leslie Dickson
Superior North Community Development Corporation

This paper examines the development of Tourism Northwest, an informal tourism body that evolved from a partnership between the various chambers of commerce and economic development agencies from across northwestern Ontario. Since its formation, Tourism Northwest has focused its mandate on the establishment of partnerships and a framework for tourism development in the region. This paper will review the process which led to the development of several community fora on tourism development and will examine the outcome. Results indicate that the four most common concerns cited by those at the meetings include marketing, education and training, infrastructure and new trends in tourism. These four main issues formed the cornerstone for discussion at a regional forum attended by individuals from government, industry and the general public.

Following the regional forum, a series of five strategic ideas and action statements were generated. They included the formation of a regional tourism body, a promotional campaign for community tourism awareness, the development of a regional education and training committee, the development and implementation of community strategic tourism plans and the creation of a suitable accommodations grading system. Since the regional forum, Tourism Northwest has redefined its role regarding the implementation of the recommendations. Specifically, Tourism Northwest currently is concentrating its efforts on the introduction of hospitality training to communities throughout northwestern Ontario.

INTRODUCTION

During the past decade the tourism industry in Canada has been on a decline, and northwestern Ontario is no exception. This decline is reflected in a number of economic indicators. For instance, during the 1980s, Canada slipped from sixth to tenth place in the international tourism market. It has since dropped to fifteenth position. After adjustment for inflation, the value of Canada's tourism receipts fell between 1980 and 1988. American visits dropped in 1989.

The decline in the Canadian tourism industry coincides with the Canadian government's decision to reduce the tourism marketing budget by one-third. In comparison, countries such as the United States and Australia have increased their budgets for marketing. Provincially, the Ontario marketing budget remained stagnant for a decade and has since been reduced. Regionally, increased marketing effects are needed, but so is a clearly defined and developed product in order to see further growth in the tourism industry.

During the late 1980s and early 1990s, the resource-based industries on which the economy of northwestern Ontario is so highly dependent were reorganized and downsized to remain competitive in the international marketplace. The most highly affected sector was the forest product industry which registered a significant loss of jobs. As a result northwestern Ontario lost population. Faced with a downturn in their local economies and an uncertain future, communities began to turn to tourism as a means of diversification and economic survival. Unfortunately, in most of the resource-based communities, the public has not been highly supportive of the tourism industry.

However, there were individuals both inside and outside of the tourism industry that saw potential for growth and development in northwestern Ontario. They looked to the south at communities in northern Minnesota which survived the collapse of the mining industry in the early 1970s by building a thriving tourism industry that sustains a high quality of life. This gave an impetus to those in northwestern Ontario to build a strong, more vibrant tourism industry.

Northwestern Ontario's natural beauty and its vast wilderness put it in an ideal situation to respond to the upcoming tourism trends. According to the Ontario Government's tourism strategy *Ontario Tourism Industry: Opportunity-Progress-Innovation* (February 1994), trends in North America and global tourism demands are moving towards the more natural experience which northwestern Ontario can offer. With the tourism potential of northwestern Ontario evident and potential demand being identified, the challenge is to develop it. With deficit reduction a priority for all levels of government, the region's tourism industry could no longer look to the province or federal government for assistance. It had to become self-reliant. However, the industry in the region is primarily comprised of small, diverse operators spread throughout a vast geographical area. Something was needed to encourage all tourism players to collaborate for the growth of the industry to become a reality. This was the climate that sparked the creation of Tourism Northwest.

This paper examines the partnerships that led to the formation of Tourism Northwest and details the consultation process created to establish strategic priorities for tourism development in northwestern Ontario. It explains the series of community fora and the regional forum used to elicit input from all sectors of the tourism industry. The final component of the paper will analyze critically and reflect upon the accomplishments and drawbacks of the strategic planning process. In the conclusion, the paper briefly examines the present efforts of Tourism Northwest.

BACKGROUND

With downsizing in the resource industries, the business community began to search for alternatives to stabilize the economy of northwestern Ontario. Recognizing the problems as well as the great potential for the tourism industry in the region, the Northwestern Ontario Associated Chambers of Commerce (NOACC), representing 1,800 businesses in 14 communities, established a Tourism Committee in the spring of 1992. Its focus was to address issues facing the tourism businesses and to provide the provincial government with recommendations on solutions to the problems. In the fall of 1992, a meeting was arranged between the NOACC Tourism Committee and the provincial Minister of Tourism and Recreation. During the meeting, the Minister indicated strong support for an initiative which would bring together all tourism interests and establish a unified set of objectives.

A few years earlier, the Northwestern Ontario Development Network (the Network), representing the community economic development offices in the region, established a Tourism Committee to liaise with the provincial Ministry of Tourism regarding tourism development issues. Due to frustration as a result of the reductions in the provincial tourism budget and a lack of response from the ministry, the committee became inactive. In the fall of 1992, the Network established a new committee with a mandate to delve into problems stifling the tourism industry and to seek regional solutions.

Realizing that they both shared similar interests in tourism development, a partnership was formed between NOACC and the Network which resulted in the creation of Tourism Northwest. The first meeting was held in January 1993.

MANDATE OF TOURISM NORTHWEST

Tourism Northwest saw itself as a conduit to bring together all aspects of the tourism industry including the private sector tourist operators, economic developers, marketing specialists, and all tourism/recreation-related organizations. Never before had all these tourism stakeholders gathered to discuss common issues. To elicit input from other interests in the tourism industry, the membership of Tourism Northwest was expanded to include federal and provincial government representatives, tourism marketing associations, and representatives of First Nations. As a result, it became known affectionately as the 'cast of thousands.'

Despite the diverse interests within the membership, Tourism Northwest established itself as: "a forum to establish partnerships and a framework for tourism development in Northwestern Ontario" (Frood 1994, i). In pursuit of this mandate, Tourism Northwest planned a regional forum to bring together individuals from all aspects of the tourism industry. Forum participants would be given an opportunity to raise issues and establish a plan to address their concerns. Although the members of Tourism Northwest wanted to obtain input from all those involved in tourism in the region, they quickly recognized that it was unrealistic to expect small tourism operators to attend a meeting held hundreds of kilometres away from their operations. Therefore, plans snowballed to include a full round of community fora involving virtually every town, community, and district in northwestern Ontario.

Articles were published in regional and community newspapers promoting the community fora. The rationale for the effort was simple yet focused:

> Tourism affects and enriches the lives of all residents of Northwestern Ontario. It is a dynamic part of the regional and local economies. Strategic planning for tourism development will ensure that we are ready to meet the future with growing prosperity. Community-area workshops will guarantee broad-based consultation in the strategic planning process and provide a vital forum for information exchange (Frood 1994: 4).

COMMUNITY FORA

The community fora were the first genuine attempt at mass regional input on issues relevant to tourism development in northwestern Ontario. Over 300 people attended 14 community fora held in the fall and early winter of 1993-1994 in locations throughout the northwest region. Generally, members of Tourism Northwest acted as the local organizers of the community fora. For communities not represented on Tourism

Northwest, coordinators were recruited.

At each forum a facilitator and a recording secretary were employed to assure consistency among community fora. A standardized instructor's manual was created for each community facilitator. The kits included promotional flyers, background information on the tourism industry, questions and answer sheets, and a series of matrices to record the results of the discussions. Orientation notes were developed along with a series of questions to solicit participants' input. Following the community fora the data were compiled and synthesized. Four key issues were derived from the data and formed the basis for discussion at the regional forum.

Results of the community fora

A review of the information obtained from the community fora indicated a number of concerns and issues common to all areas and communities. The number one issue was marketing, referring to both promotion and packaging, as well as access to information and advice for product development. It was unanimous that marketing efforts had to be intensified and integrated. More effective and cooperative campaigns were needed at the local and regional levels.

The second most important issue was the need to improve awareness of the value of tourism among the local citizens, businesses and municipal governments. In most communities, tourism is at an early stage of development. Where the harvesting and utilization of the natural resources is the prime contributor to the local economy, local residents have shown little interest in tourism development. Another common concern was the attitude and lack of professional standards for staff and operators in the tourism industry. Improved training and greater access to training was identified as a high priority at most of the community fora. Improvement of the product base, in terms of developing more attractions and improving accommodations and facilities, was another common issue. A theme at almost every forum was that the variety and quality of local attractions had to be improved. Also, most participants felt that cultural attractions and events ranging from historic sites, museums, POW camps to local festivals and sporting events were key ingredients for diversification. At more than half of the fora there was special reference to the tourism potential of First Nations' art and culture.

The need to expand the tourism industry over all four seasons was also expressed. Winter recreation and festivals centring around activities such as snowmobiling, skiing, and ice climbing were suggested as the greatest opportunities for expansion of the winter tourism industry. Overall, four issues were identified as being paramount. They included marketing, infrastructure, education and training, and new trends in tourism. These issues were chosen as the main topics of discussion at the regional forum.

REGIONAL FORUM

Over 100 people attended the regional forum held April 27-28, 1994 in Thunder Bay. About 40 per cent were involved directly in the tourism industry (i.e. camp and lodge owners, hotel/resort operators, owners of tourism attractions and souvenir shops). The remaining 60 per cent were composed largely of community economic development officers, chambers of commerce members and government representatives throughout northwestern Ontario. The regional forum was unique in that it brought together the diverse interests of many different players involved in the tourism industry (both private and public sector) in an effort to discuss, develop, and synthesize a framework for tourism development in northwestern Ontario. Although the forum proved challenging from the aspect of workshop dynamics, the result was a working document used by Tourism Northwest to develop and shape the diverse components of the tourism industry throughout northwestern Ontario.

During the first day of the regional forum, a series of four workshops was held on marketing, infrastructure, education and training, and new trends in tourism. Individuals knowledgeable in each topic area acted as workshop facilitators. Facilitators led participants through a brief, yet focused discussion beginning with the development of a vision statement, followed by the identification of issues and opportunities, and concluding with the formation of strategic ideas and plans of action. The four workshops were held concurrently in both morning and afternoon sessions.

The following day, participants were divided into working groups to synthesized the ideas discussed in the previous day's session, and to formulate strategic goals and initiatives for future implementation. Based on the problems and issues identified at the community fora and regional session, the following action items were seen as priority for implementation by Tourism Northwest.

1. Maintenance/Creation of a Regional Tourism Organization

Due to the ineffectiveness of previous organizations in carrying out regional tourism initiatives, participants saw the need to establish and/or maintain a regional voice for tourism development in northwestern

Ontario. They suggested that "a system be created that improved the sharing of information, ideas and expertise" (Frood 1994: 26). Workshop participants also supported that the organization be a regionally-focused, credible, yet informal, body. Participants at the regional forum supported the idea that the Network and NOACC remain as main players in the organization of this informal body, but encouraged the inclusion of other key players including the Northern Ontario Municipal Association (NOMA), First Nations, and the Association of Northern Ontario Tourism Operators (NOTO).

In further discussion it was determined that the maintenance of an informal regional tourism organization would help to address many unresolved issues, such as tourism marketing and the training of staff regarding local tourism attractions and the value of tourism.

2. Promotional Campaign for Community Tourism Awareness

In all community fora and throughout the regional session, participants expressed the need to improve the community's awareness of the value of tourism. "There is a strong consensus that before [communities] can sell their region's tourist attractions, [communities] need to sell themselves. The need for internal development of tourism starting with local consciousness-raising is paramount" (Frood 1994: 27).

To increase the community's awareness of the value of tourism, participants suggested a three-pronged approach. First, a tourism promotional package would be created and sold to the communities and local civic leaders. This would be followed up by a series of organized trips to successful tourism-dependant communities to learn and understand how they were able to transform their economy successfully. The second approach would provide local information blitzes promoting the value of tourism. This would be accomplished through a series of media including town hall meetings, the publication of articles, and a designated week promoting tourism awareness. Finally, each community would create an inventory of local places, attractions, and facilities identified as having tourism potential. By promoting an awareness of tourism, a change of attitude towards tourism takes place and with it comes a willingness to create tourism infrastructure in the community.

3. Community Strategic Tourism Plans

Throughout the regional forum, participants noted that, with the obvious exception of Thunder Bay, most communities throughout northwestern Ontario did not have a strategic tourism plan. Therefore, they encouraged communities to establish their own tourism plan, preferably one that was tied into the overall vision outlined in the community's strategic plan. Delegates agreed to the importance of creating a strategic plan in that it "formalized the will of the community in regards to the type and extent of tourism desired, and prepared a clear blueprint from which local and outside interests (could) work" (Frood 1994: 28). Apart from being a good document to guide communities in future tourism development, the strategic plan is an essential component in the process of securing federal, provincial, or municipal funding.

4. Accommodations Grading System

Despite previously unsuccessful efforts, participants recommended the creation of a credible accommodations grading system for northwestern Ontario. Many tourism operators, critical of the criteria used in grading systems, refuse to participate in them. They are also afraid that if they participate, they may receive a grade that is not representative of their establishment. However, by having no standardized grading system across northwestern Ontario, the consumer is at a disadvantage, having no accurate means to compare one establishment to another.

5. Regional Education and Training Committee

The improvement of general skills and awareness of workers and proprietors in the tourism industry was judged a top priority by participants in the regional and community fora. "There is a clear need for a better skilled and informed tourism workforce and large improvements in the consistency, availability, and affordability of training throughout the region" (Frood 1994: 27). Participants suggested that a sub-committee be formed within Tourism Northwest to address this issue. The first action of the training and education committee would be to create a list identifying providers of training and what kind of tourism training is available.

ADMINISTRATION AND BUDGET

Of the two founding organizations, only the Northwestern Ontario Development Network had sufficient staff to provide administrative services for Tourism Northwest. Without their considerable efforts, Tourism Northwest could not have coordinated and organized the 14 community fora and the regional forum. A co-op economic development student seconded from the Ministry of Northern Development and Mines assisted by compiling the data collected from the community fora.

Although there was an enormous amount of volunteer time involved in the planning and organization of the fora, the consultation process was not without expense. To conduct the regional strategic planning initiative, Tourism Northwest was funded jointly by Employment and Immigration Canada (now known as Human Resources Development Canada) and the provincial Jobs Ontario Community Action (JOCA) program. Other revenue sources included the founding organizations, NOACC and the Network, and the travel associations.

Although the community fora were each given a budget of $1,025.00, most came in under budget, averaging approximately $870.00 for a total cost of $12,187.26. The expenses for the regional forum were $28,465.43. In total, the Tourism Northwest process cost $40,625.69 (see Table 1 for the budget details).

REFLECTIONS

Tourism Northwest's greatest success was the consultative process undertaken. Never before had any organization approached so many people in the communities for input in establishing regional priorities in any sector, let alone from the tourism sector. When the partnership was established, a list of tourism-related organizations in northwestern Ontario was not available. However with the help of members within Tourism Northwest, a list of tourism operators was compiled and was included as part of the final document *Tourism Northwest, Partners in Progress* (Frood 1994).

At both the community fora and the regional session, various groups participated. Many of them had previously not been recognized as being related to the tourism sector. Some examples included recreation groups, such as snowmobile clubs and ski clubs. In addition to the two founding partners, there were many individuals who volunteered their time to sit on the steering committee. There were those at the community level organizing and promoting the community fora, and federal and provincial funding partners, who also sat at the planning table. It was a true partnership in the fact that no one group controlled or dominated the steering committee.

Although there was representation of First Nations organizations on Tourism Northwest, very few aboriginal people participated in the fora. More efforts are needed to encourage First Nations communities and aboriginal tourist operators to participate in the decision-making process.

Table 1. Tourism Northwest Budget Summary 1993-1994

REVENUE:	ACTUAL
Human Resources Development Canada (HRDC)	$11,881.75
Jobs Ontario Community Action	20,000.00
Northwestern Ontario Associated Chambers of Commerce	1,000.00
Northwestern Ontario Development Network	1,425.57
Regional Forum Registrations	6,407.72
North of Superior Travel Association	300.00
Sunset Country Travel Association	150.00
Dryden EDO & Dryden Chamber of Commerce	300.00
Sale of Regional Reports	187.65
TOTAL REVENUE	**$41,652.69**
EXPENSES:	
LOCAL FORUM EXPENSES	
Community Forum Expenses	$11,552.25
Meeting/Miscellaneous Expenses	1,331.21
Printing/Mailing Expenses	303.80
TOTAL LOCAL FORUM EXPENSES	**$13,187.26**
REGIONAL TOURISM FORUM EXPENSES	
Forum Expenses	$22,372.36
Post-forum Expenses	6,093.07
TOTAL REGIONAL FORUM EXPENSES	**$28,465.43**
TOTAL EXPENSES	**$41,652.69**

In the midst of the planning, the provincial government conducted its own consultative process and developed a provincial strategy for tourism development. While provincial representatives were holding consultation meetings in regional centres throughout the province, members of Tourism Northwest deliberated about cancelling their plans to prevent any duplication. However, it was soon realized that the continued efforts of Tourism Northwest were needed because the province would not solicit input from the small rural communities. Hence, the group persevered.

As a result of the consultative process, there was a greater awareness of the impact and potential of tourism among the tourism operators and the residents of the region. In some communities, it was the first time the owner/operators of tourism business ever came together to discuss mutual concerns. Tourism Northwest was the catalyst for the development of several new tourism-related initiatives.   New partnerships were established, such as the Lakes of Legend, a tourism marketing association covering the area surrounding the communities of Geraldton, Longlac, Nakina, and Beardmore.

The steering committee had not planned for a follow-up to the regional forum and there was no sense of assurance that the recommendations would be acted upon.   The considerable length of time between the regional forum and the release and circulation of the final document created a loss of momentum and enthusiasm.   Although the regional forum recommended that a regional tourism organization be established, there was some confusion about its mandate.   Following the regional forum, several individuals of the Tourism Northwest Steering Committee felt that they had accomplished their goal and stepped down from their duties.   Those who remained wanted to ensure that there was some action taken on the recommendations from the fora.

Following the release of the Tourism Northwest report in August 1994, the steering committee held a series of meetings as a follow-up to the regional forum.   In November 1994, an information session was held for committee members.   Three key speakers were invited to address the five strategic initiatives identified at the regional forum.   Several months later, a strategic planning session was held for members of the steering committee to refine further the strategic initiatives.   The key to the discussion was to identify initiatives that Tourism Northwest could immediately act upon without duplicating the efforts of other organizations.   As a result, Tourism Northwest established the SuperHost program in northwestern Ontario.   SuperHost is an internationally recognized program designed to raise the standards of service and hospitality for visitors and local customers.   In cooperation with Tourism Northwest, the Network applied and received approval to implement the program throughout the region (excluding Thunder Bay).   Programs like these will provide Tourism Northwest with the desire and the means to continue promoting tourism development throughout northwestern Ontario.

CONCLUSION

The efforts of Tourism Northwest illustrated in this paper have been quite unique.   Through the community and regional fora, Tourism Northwest brought together an eclectic group of tourism players.   The result has been the formulation of a strategic direction for tourism development in northwestern Ontario.   In the report, Tourism Northwest received a mandate for future tourism development, namely the formation of a permanent regional tourism advisory and information-sharing organization, a campaign for promoting community tourism awareness, the creation of a regional tourism education and training committee, assisting and encouraging communities to develop their own strategic tourism plan, and the implementation of a credible mandatory accommodations grading system.

Not only was the process a first of its kind in northwestern Ontario, but more importantly, it also was driven by the communities through grass-roots participation. Although its success was due to the efforts of the Network and NOACC, Tourism Northwest grew to involve other partners, including aboriginal organizations and government agencies. It is the desire of Tourism Northwest to have these partnerships expand further to include other players.

As a follow-up to the regional forum, Tourism Northwest has addressed two of the strategic directions. It has assumed the role of a regional tourism advisory and information-sharing organization and it has begun to coordinate the delivery of a service and hospitality training program. Through these and other proposed initiatives, Tourism Northwest is helping communities to capture the growing opportunities for tourism development throughout northwestern Ontario.

REFERENCES

Frood, D. 1994. *Tourism Northwest: Partners in Progress*. Final Report of Tourism Northwest Regional Forum. Northwestern Ontario Development Network and Northwestern Ontario Associated Chambers of Commerce.

FORESTS AND CHANGING VALUE SYSTEMS: IDENTIFYING RECREATION AND TOURISM USES AND VALUES IN A CANADIAN MODEL FOREST

Alex Hawley
University of Northern British Columbia

Dave Robinson
University of Northern British Columbia

Mark Robson
University of Northern British Columbia

INTRODUCTION

Debate among the public, interest groups, forest managers, and scientists suggests that it is no longer acceptable for forest management to have a narrow focus or to be based only on decisions made by forest managers, planners, and scientists (Brooks & Grant 1992). As Eidsvik (1990) reported in a speech to foresters of the Ontario Ministry of Natural Resources:

> It is becoming clear that Canadian resource management agencies are no longer seen to be the guardians of the future. A lack of public trust in the political process combined with the growth of the Environmental non-governmental organizations is changing established practices (p. 11).

At the heart of the forest management controversy lies a conflict within society over the values and uses of forests. Forest values and uses are products of socio-cultural appraisal, and they change over time and space. In Canada, the traditional industrialized view of forests having primarily economic value through fibre production is expanding to include other values and uses. These changes reflect a change in the nature of the relationship between society and forests, and demand a re-definition of what comprises appropriate forest management.

In British Columbia, public interest in forest management issues has increased dramatically since the 1960s (Commission on Resources and Environment 1994). Outdoor tourism became a rapidly growing industry that was largely dependent upon the appearance of untouched natural landscapes. Interest in outdoor recreation flourished and fish and wildlife protection became a major public concern. A recent Council of Forest Industries study of northern forestry issues indicated that, while timber jobs were still foremost to interviewees, other aspects of quality of life, such as outdoor recreation, were becoming more important as communities matured (Bonderud 1994). A recent telephone survey in the Prince George area disclosed that spokespersons for various recreational groups were generally satisfied with how resource management issues were managed (Ministry of Forests 1995). However, concerns were expressed by the hiking and river-boating communities concerning issues such as clearcutting and slash burning (the burning of timber waste and other vegetation following clearcutting). In a related study involving a random telephone survey of guide outfitters, respondents acknowledged the importance of the forestry industry, but identified problems associated with increased access (Ministry of Forests 1989).

While these studies indicate that society values forests for their timber, it is clear that outdoor recreation and tourism values have gained in importance. Forest managers need to know what these values are and which forest management issues are important to the public in order to be able to design management strategies that protect outdoor recreation and tourism values.

Canada's model forests

Canada's Model Forest Program was announced in 1990, and had as its purpose the development of new approaches to sustainable forest management through the development of 10 model forests across the country. These model forests were to serve as regional models for fully integrated, sustainable forest management (Robson et al. 1995). The McGregor Model Forest (MMF) is one of these 10 sites.

The role of the MMF Association, a partnership of public and private interests which provides direction for the MMF, is "to facilitate achieving the goals of social, economic and ecological sustainability" (MMF Association 1994: 1) in the management of the forest. The Association aims to do this through the "use of appropriate partnerships, application of systems, technologies, and an increased knowledge and information base" (MMF Association 1994: 2).

The MMF is located 30 kilometres northeast of Prince George in British Columbia (Figure 1) and covers 181,000 hectares of mostly Crown or public land that approaches the western slopes of the Rocky Mountains. The MMF is a largely forested area dotted with rock, lakes, rivers, swamps, and meadows, and is used for a wide range of forestry-related, trapping, guide outfitting, recreational, and subsistence activities.

Figure 1. Location of the city of Prince George, B.C. and the McGregor Model Forest (T.F.L. 30)

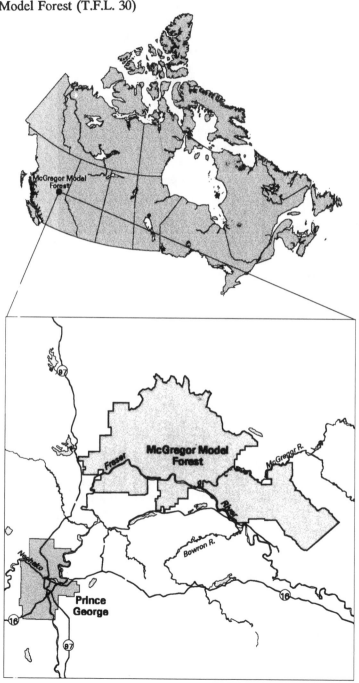

The MMF is contiguous with the boundaries of Tree Farm License 30 (T.F.L. 30) which is assigned to and managed by Northwood Pulp and Timber Limited for the purpose of commercial timber production. This production has been a major source of softwood lumber and market pulp in the economy of the surrounding region (Forestry Canada n.d.).

Central to the MMF program is the development of a decision support system (DSS) that will facilitate the sustainable integration of social, ecological, and economic factors in the development of forest management plans. As part of the development of a DSS, a social analysis research program was undertaken to determine the issues and values of the public regarding forests and forest management, using T.F.L. 30 as a model of a working forest.

The first phase of the social analysis program, the results of which are reported herein, involved identifying the community of interests namely, those who care about the McGregor Model Forest and what they care about (Robson et al. 1995). This information was used to formulate specific questions in a forest values mail survey of local, provincial, and national publics. The results of this survey will be used in the development of social indicators for use in the DSS. The purpose of the present study was to appraise local public use of and orientation towards T.F.L. 30, and to obtain public input that would be the basis of questions included in the broader public survey on forest values and uses.

METHODS

Data collection

Public input was obtained using two approaches. The first involved a request for information (RFI) procedure which solicited written or verbal input from the general public. The second approach comprised interviews with known users of the MMF. The intent was to maximize the breadth and diversity of uses and values identified through this process. Therefore, data collected from individuals were not limited to their uses and values, but included direct knowledge they had of uses and values held by others. For example, an individual who provided information on their own use of T.F.L. 30 might know of a different forest use by a family member. Respondents' views on potential uses were also included.

Request for Information. The RFI process encompassed people in the Prince George and surrounding area and involved the following approaches to obtaining public input.

a. One hundred and ninety-nine specific individuals or special interest organizations were contacted (Table 1). These contacts were identified through a snowball sampling process in which each contact led to several others, until the process stopped revealing new contacts.

b. News releases or interviews in three regional newspapers and local radio and television stations were used to solicit input from the local and regional public.

c. Letters requesting input were sent to the Lheidli T'enneh Band (formerly the Lheit-Lit'en Nation), whose traditional territory included T.F.L. 30.

d. Members of, and visitors to, the University of Northern British Columbia were solicited for their input through notices on an electronic bulletin board and at an information booth at a university open house event.

e. Request for information sheets that identified the nature of the project and invited anyone who was interested in the MMF to contact the authors (mailing and e-mail addresses and phone and fax numbers were provided) were posted on public bulletin boards, in post offices and at other public sites in each of the 50 rural communities in the region.

Interviews. Forty-five individuals were interviewed about their use of, and values for, T.F.L. 30. These individuals were identified through contact with individuals and special interest groups as outlined in part (a.) above. Semi-structured interviews lasting two to three hours were conducted with each individual and involved the identification of specific values the individual held for the area and the identification and mapping of specific activities and uses of the forest. Mapping involved the interviewer marking on 1:50,000 topographic maps of T.F.L. 30 and surrounding area the nature and sites of activities as identified by the interviewee. This was accompanied by a geographically linked information base that provided characteristics of the use (e.g. season of use, number of participants). Values associated with geographic areas were also identified. For example, a respondent might identify a strong aesthetic or spiritual value that is held for a specific location or vista. Each response was coded as to whether the response applied to the respondent personally, whether the respondent knew the item applied to other people, or whether the respondent was identifying a potential use or value in the area.

Data collation and analysis

The RFI approach generated responses from 37 people. Of the 45 people interviewed, 43 had actually visited T.F.L. 30 and five had already

Table 1. Types of individuals and organizations specifically contacted as part of the request for information process.

Group	Number contacted
community associations	22
guide outfitters	41
logging contractors	11
McGregor Model Forest Association partners	20
Ministers of the Legislative Assembly	2
recreation commission presidents	22
recreation-related organizations	36
regional district Directors and their alternates	15
silviculture contractors	9
trappers	21

responded through the RFI process (only the interview data from these individuals were used in this study because these data largely encompassed the information in the RFI responses). Thus, a total of 77 people from the local region provided data on the uses of, and values for, T.F.L. 30.

Data collation and analysis comprised three stages. First, interviews were summarized by the interviewers and the information pooled with information from the RFI process to produce a single data set encompassing all input from all respondents. Second, all spatial use data obtained during the interviews were transcribed by the MMF into a geographic information system and compiled into a single recreation and other non-timber use map of T.F.L. 30 (values associated with specific sites were spatially coded but are not included in this analysis). Third, a comprehensive review of all data was conducted to identify specific values and uses identified by the participating public.

Public values and uses were identified in the following manner. One author (Robson) reviewed all public input and developed for each respondent a list of words or statements reflecting the items and issues of importance to the respondent. Respondents were not directed with respect to the identification of important items. Thus, the diversity of these comments was great and ranged from individual species associated with specific uses such as "Mink for trapping" or "Fishing dolly varden" to general comments about values and uses such as "Enjoy skiing" or "Logging taking place too close to areas with recreational potential." Items of importance were coded by a numeric code for the respondent, so that different items from the same respondent could be associated.

The items of importance identified above were assigned to key topic areas. Five key topic areas (harvest practices, access, clearcutting, partial cutting, and vegetation management) were identified by the Forest Practices Team (FPT) of the MMF, a group of forestry professionals advising the MMF on issues relating to timber harvesting and forest renewal. These topics were identified by the FPT as those which were used to characterize their own discussions about forest management issues. By using these topics in the present study, public input could be most readily related to forest practices and planning. No effort was made to force public input into any of these topic areas. Such association was only made if input from respondents clearly and specifically matched with one or more of these five topic areas as evaluated by the authors. The remaining, unassigned statements of important items were assigned to additional key topic areas that were derived directly from the respondents' comments to represent the minimum list of topics that the authors felt encompassed all items or issues of importance.

Related items of importance were aggregated into categories within each key topic. For example, the topic area "Species use" related to specific plants and animals removed from T.F.L. 30 and had the categories hunting, fishing, trapping, and flora. Using this approach, some items of importance identified by an individual respondent might be phrased in such a way as to appear in more than one key topic area. For example, the comments of interviewee number three regarding moose hunting activities in T.F.L. 30 appeared as "Moose" under the topic "Species use" and as "Has severely [negatively] impacted moose" under the topic "Access." It is important to note that all categories were identified *a posteriori* from the input made by respondents.

RESULTS

Respondent socio-demographic characteristics

Most of the 77 respondents resided in the city of Prince George (n = 58 respondents). Other respondents were from the smaller outlying communities of Summit Lake, Willow River, McBride, Miworth, Manson Creek, Kamloops, Dome Creek, and Hixon. The Lheidli T'enneh Band did not participate in the RFI or interview processes. Most respondents were male (n = 66) and ranged in age from 29 to 77 years, with an average age of 47.6 years. The highest level of education most interviewees had attained was high school (n = 32). This was followed by college or undergraduate university (n = 29), graduate degrees (i.e. Masters or PhD, n = 10) and primary school education (n = 5).

The greatest number of respondents was either employed in the forest products industry (n = 24) or in an industry entirely dependent on the forest products industry (n = 5). Other forms of employment of respondents included commercial recreation (n = 7), other industries entirely dependent on outdoor recreation (n = 2), ranching (n = 4), trapping (n = 4), fiddlehead fern harvesting (n = 2), fish and wildlife management (n = 5), park management (n = 2), transportation services (n = 5), medical services (n = 4), communication services (n = 4), other service industries (n = 12), and retirement (n = 4). Some interviewees worked in more than one occupation and were represented more than once in the above.

Statements of importance

A total of 1549 separate use or value statements were identified in input from the 77 respondents. These statements were identified as being expressions of 371 separate comments or statements of importance, which ranged from expressions of interest or concern over a specific species (e.g. "moose," respondent #3, 15 and others) to rather lengthy comments on use or value (e.g. "Areas logged using methods common in the 1960s that left the right amount of cover and did not disturb the soil now exhibit good berry picking conditions," respondent #2). These statements of importance were in turn identified as comprising 76 categories within 18 key topic areas (Robson et al. 1995). On average, individual respondents made comments that fell into five of the 18 categories (range = 0 to 10). Thirteen of the key topic areas involved explicit statements related to recreation or tourism and are reported herein (Table 2). The remaining key topic areas (i.e. forest regeneration, vegetation management, management process, range use, and other development) considered topics that were indirectly related to recreation or tourism, but that did not involve explicit statements in this regard (Robson et al. 1995).

Economic use. Twenty-seven of the 77 respondents (35 per cent) made economic use of T.F.L. 30 (Table 2). This use included activities related to timber (e.g., harvesting, reforestation, site preparation, fire fighting), plant and animal products (e.g., fiddlehead fern picking, trapping, ranching, fish and wildlife management), recreation (e.g., guide outfitting, outdoor recreation equipment sales), and other forest services (e.g., machinery and equipment sales). Approximately one-half of all respondents who commented on economic use of T.F.L. 30 derived income from a timber-related activity, one-third from the collection of other plant or animal products and 26 per cent from recreation (Table 2).

Table 2. Number of distinct items of importance, number of comments, and number of different respondents for key topic areas and categories identified in responses from 77 respondents.

Key topic	Category[a]	Items[b]	Comments	Respondents
Economic use	timber-related	7	16	14
	recreation-related	4	7	7
	plant and animal products	4	9	9
	other service industry	2	3	3
	Total			27
Non-economic use	consumptive/extractive	7	91	50
	educational/research	6	20	15
	motorized recreation	6	50	34
	non-motorized recreation	23	208	57
	Total			62
Species use	hunting	5	35	20
	fishing	6	32	20
	trapping	13	26	4
	flora	5	16	14
	Total			38
Importance values	ease of access	2	9	9
	economic	3	29	27
	education/research	4	6	6
	lifestyle/subsistence	5	21	18
	experience nature	11	52	28
	recreation/relaxation	12	33	25
	history	1	1	1
	Total			48
Non-commercial recreation	general	5	13	10
	motorized	2	2	2
	non-motorized	7	15	11
	aesthetics	2	3	3
	opportunity	7	8	8
	environmental impact	5	8	7
	regulation/conflict	5	23	16
	Total			31
Commercial rec/ tourism	conflict	1	1	1
	promotion and development	3	3	2
	negative impacts on commercial	4	4	3
	Total			4
Harvest practices/ general	education/research	3	3	3
	environmental impacts	12	12	11
	mechanization	1	1	1
	overharvest	1	2	2
	future outlook	3	3	2
	positive recreation impact	1	1	1

Table 2. continued

Key topic	Category[a]	Items[b]	Comments	Respondents
	negative recreation impact	3	3	3
	good corporate citizenry	9	10	9
	Total			26
Clearcutting	positive aesthetics	1	1	1
	negative aesthetics	7	23	19
	excessive wood waste	2	5	5
	efficient harvest method	2	3	3
	negative environmental impact	20	57	19
	overcutting	6	8	6
	positive recreation impact	1	1	1
	negative recreation impact	3	3	2
	Total			30
Partial cutting	general	3	14	12
	Total			12
Access	don't like it	3	3	3
	negative environmental impact	10	21	15
	like it	11	23	13
	public relations	2	2	1
	road building practices	2	2	2
	vandalism	2	2	2
	Total			24
Ecosystem	education/research	4	5	5
	availability	2	2	2
	habitat protection	4	17	16
	negative human impact	3	4	2
	pest management	2	2	2
	regulation	5	7	6
	integrity/biodiversity/ old growth	4	10	9
	uniqueness	4	4	3
	Total			28
Management process	criticism	3	4	3
	support	9	26	23
	overemphasis on timber	7	10	8
	public input	12	22	17
	accountability/regulation	6	6	6
	Total			35
Site manipulation	negative impact of burning	3	3	2
	Total			2

[a] Details of categories are available in Robson et al. (1995).
[b] Number of distinct expressions of important items or values within the category.

Non-economic use. Forty-two distinct statements related to non-economic uses of, or values for, T.F.L. 30 were identified in respondents' comments (Table 2). Non-motorized recreation was the most commonly identified non-economic activity, identified by 74 per cent of all respondents. This was followed by consumptive/extractive activities, motorized recreation, and educational/research activities. Specific activities that were identified most often were hiking (n = 44 respondents), fishing (n = 44), camping (n = 36), hunting (n = 34), backcountry skiing (n = 28), snowmobiling (n = 24), wildlife viewing (n = 18), canoeing (n = 16), and caving (n = 15). Other, less frequently identified uses included educational activities such as heritage and nature interpretation and research, motorized recreation uses such as waterskiing, ATV use, four-wheel driving, and boating, and non-motorized recreation activities such as rock climbing, watching timber harvesting, mountain biking, mountaineering, whitewater rafting, snowshoeing, picnicking, ice climbing, cabin use, snowboarding, horseback riding, caving, salmon viewing, whitewater kayaking, swimming, heli-skiing, paragliding, and photography.

Species use. Thirty-eight respondents identified a total of 24 animal species and five types of plants that they used in T.F.L. 30. Twenty of these respondents identified hunting and fishing as consumptive activities (Table 2). Fourteen of these 20 respondents identified both hunting and fishing as activities. The most commonly pursued species were trout, moose, bear, berries, dolly varden, and grouse. Other consumptive uses included the collection of mushrooms, grasses, fiddlehead ferns, and firewood, and trapping and panning for gold.

Importance values. Forty-eight of the 77 respondents made specific comments on values (Table 2). The majority of expressions of value surrounding T.F.L. 30 involved outdoor recreation in the form of experiencing nature (n = 28 respondents) or pursuing specific recreational activities (n = 25). Seventeen respondents identified both of these values. Twenty-seven of the 48 respondents identified economic values for T.F.L. 30, but 18 of these also identified outdoor recreation values. One respondent commented on the historical importance of T.F.L. 30 (part of the Giscome Portage Trail, a critical link during the fur trade between Arctic and Pacific watersheds, passes through a northwest portion of the T.F.L.).

Non-commercial recreation. Thirty-one respondents made specific reference to non-commercial recreation (Table 2). Existing recreational opportunities that were identified included the existence of good berry picking in areas that had been logged sensitively in the 1960s, good opportunities for big game hunting, the existence of internationally important caving systems, excellent snowmobile opportunities, and hiking in alpine areas.

Generally, T.F.L. 30 was seen as having huge potential for non-commercial recreation opportunities that to date had been under-developed. The perspective was clearly presented that user groups should be willing to pay for development and up-keep of recreation services. Respondents also indicated that local people would be willing to volunteer for recreation facility development. The area also was believed to be large enough to support both commercial and non-commercial recreational use.

The promotion of motorized recreation opportunities was restricted to the development of a wilderness circle automobile tour and the opportunity for snowmobile touring. Non-motorized, low-impact recreation opportunities were regarded as offering the greatest potential for local user groups. Provision of services and recreational opportunities included the identification of regulated fishing opportunities, and the development of an alpine hut system for non-motorized use. Need was also identified for both primitive and developed campsite facilities near rivers, lakes, and alpine areas, and trails for hiking, mountain biking, and skiing.

Respondents identified the need to maintain the natural beauty of areas where the main focus of users was recreational enjoyment. Maintaining visual attractiveness of trails was emphasized and the suggestion was made that cedar stands should be left along trail areas. Comments on the need to manage recreational use to reduce environmental impacts were numerous. Emphasis was given to the need to promote non-motorized use, as well as the need to regulate motorized use to prevent the disturbance of waterfowl in lake and river systems, and the restriction of snowmobilers in areas, such as the alpine elevations, where soils and trails are likely to be degraded.

Over half of the 31 respondents commented on conflicts among recreational uses and the need for regulation. For example, heli-skiing was seen as an activity that would fit well into the alpine areas of T.F.L. 30, but concern was expressed that this may conflict with other recreation user groups if all use was not regulated carefully. Concern was also expressed that any commercial activity should be regulated carefully in guiding areas to negate potential impacts on wildlife activity. The potential for conflict between user groups was seen as high, especially between skiers and snowmobilers in winter. Hunting was regarded as having dominated almost all other recreational interests in T.F.L. 30 to date. A management vision for the area was stressed that would provide for a variety of recreational opportunities while regulating use to prevent crowding and to maintain the recreational experience.

Commercial recreation and tourism. In addition to the comments above that related to commercial recreation, four respondents commented specifically on commercial recreation and tourism in T.F.L. 30 (Table 2). Respondents suggested that the potential for commercial recreation in T.F.L. 30 was large. The area was considered to be a potentially prime area for commercial outfitters, with special opportunities existing in alpine areas.

It was felt that promotion of the area, and northern British Columbia in general, by tourism agencies in British Columbia had been poorly done, due to a focus on tourism opportunities in southern British Columbia. It was also stated that the world had a poor image of northern British Columbia as a tourism destination due to the failure of marketing to overcome the misperceptions of many people regarding logging practices. It was believed that more local accommodation was necessary to serve better the commercial outfitters of the area.

It was suggested that international clientele who have visited the area are often shocked by past logging practices. It was stressed that management of the forest should seek to reduce the noise associated with logging and motorized activity if the commercial recreation industry were to be supported.

Overall, responses suggested that socially acceptable management options for commercial recreation and tourism should be similar to those of non-commercial recreation activity. Effective, integrated forest planning and management that allows for the development and promotion of commercial recreation and tourism opportunities was seen as essential in the model forest.

Timber harvesting practices: general. Comments on timber harvesting and related practices embraced six aspects: general comments about logging practices (e.g. environmental impacts), clearcutting and partial cutting (e.g. the relative merits of each), access (e.g. the benefits and detriments of increased access associated with logging), site preparation (e.g. slash burning), regeneration (e.g. aesthetics of planted areas), and vegetation management (e.g. application of herbicides). Of these, only the topics of vegetation management and regeneration did not include specific comments regarding recreation or tourism, and are not included herein.

In general, recreation or tourism comments made in relation to harvesting practices were directed at aesthetic and opportunity values. Past timber harvesting practices were considered to have compromised current and potential recreational and tourism activities (e.g. logging was considered to be taking place too close to areas with recreational potential, potential existed for serious accidents between logging and recreational traffic). Timber harvesting was also considered to have impacted wildlife negatively, particularly moose and fish populations, in T.F.L. 30. Slash burning was felt by one respondent to impact recreation negatively.

Clearcutting and partial cutting. Thirty respondents commented on clearcutting, with the majority of these respondents having commented on the negative aesthetics and negative environmental impact of clearcutting (Table 2). Comments concerning the negative environmental impacts of clearcutting outnumbered all other clearcutting comments combined. These comments focused on habitat fragmentation and its impact on wildlife, the effects of clearcutting riparian areas, and clearcut-caused erosion resulting in stream sedimentation and the destruction of fish stocks. Comments also centred around drastic fluctuations in river levels caused by increased water runoff from clearcut areas, the reduction of shading of rivers causing water temperatures to rise and thereby threatening the spawning of salmon, the destruction of berry picking areas, and increased wind in clearcut areas. Other comments included concerns that caribou and moose would not enter a clearcut area or a tight, immature forest; cutting to the edge of lakes has caused moose to disappear; higher elevation cutting has resulted in fewer caribou; and, clearcutting has resulted in the drying of soils and increased water run-off, leading to a rise in river levels. One respondent suggested that recreation areas be logged selectively as opposed to being clearcut.

Access. The greatest number of positive comments with respect to timber harvesting and recreation related to access. Over half of the 24 respondents commenting on access viewed the increase in access related to forestry to be positive (Table 2). However, five of these respondents also expressed concern about the negative environmental impacts of increased access.

Logging road construction was considered to have created easier and increased access to areas for hiking, skiing, fishing (lakes), wildlife-viewing, and caving. Disadvantages included the potential for crowding by user groups, increased conflicts of trappers and guide-outfitters with recreationists, degradation of the area's natural beauty for scenic driving, negative impacts on wildlife (especially grizzly bear) populations, negative impacts on sensitive soils and plants in alpine areas, and increased vandalism of facilities within the T.F.L.

A number of potential access management practices were identified, including reducing motorized access in order to reduce over-exploitation of fish and wildlife resources, limiting winter access to protect wildlife populations, restricting motorized access to the alpine areas, increased winter ploughing of the roads, more parking areas for user groups, and road deactivation. Some respondents viewed road deactivation as a negative management option.

Ecosystem. Twenty-eight of the 77 respondents made comments related to ecosystem integrity and maintenance (Table 2). Sixteen respondents commented on the need for habitat protection (Table 2). None of these comments made specific reference to recreation or tourism, but many were related indirectly because of the importance of ecosystem integrity to the recreational experience.

The sustainable management of the forest was considered essential. To this end, research studies were considered necessary to inventory habitat types within the model forest and to better understand the impacts of human activity on wildlife populations. A number of regulatory options were identified for wildlife protection, including the presence of fish and game wardens to enforce consumptive activities within the forest, the closure of moose hunting to allow for population recovery, a closure on marten trapping to allow for population recovery, and a resource agency-driven effort to curb poaching, which was seen as a serious problem in the area.

Forest management processes. Thirty-five of the 77 respondents made comments regarding forest management practices (Table 2). These were related to recreation and tourism in three major ways. First, there was strong support for the concept of integrated resource management as exemplified by the MMF. Second, there was strong support for public involvement in the forest management process. Finally, there was strong support for a balancing of uses and values, which would see the forest managed for both timber and recreation-related uses and values.

Some comments were critical of what was seen as an overemphasis on timber values in the MMF program and forest management planning in the region. Several statements also discussed the need for greater accountability and regulation of forest products companies (e.g. the need for a forest practices code).

Spatial distribution of non-timber uses

Twenty-seven non-timber uses, plus nine types of uses, were identified spatially for T.F.L. 30. The locations associated with these uses are not highly precise, partly because interviewees were sometimes reluctant to disclose the specific locations of what they considered to be special areas. Although every effort was made to include as much known and potential use as possible, these data cannot be construed as representing all types and locations of activities in T.F.L. 30. However, the data are representative of the types and distributions of uses in the T.F.L. Hunting covered the largest cumulative area identified for T.F.L. 30, followed by snowmobiling, backcountry skiing, hiking, guiding, fishing, trapping, and a variety of other recreational activities (Figure 2). Access roads also covered a relatively large area of the T.F.L.

Major recreational activities were dispersed very differently within the T.F.L. (Figure 3). There were two primary focus areas of recreational use, one in the west-central part of T.F.L. 30 that involved primarily hunting and snowmobiling, and one in the southeast corner of the T.F.L. that involved primarily backcountry skiing and hiking (Figure 3). Examination of topographic and anthropogenic feature maps disclosed that the west-central recreation focus area was associated with the highest density of access roads in the T.F.L. (Figure 3) and a high density of recent clearcuts (MMF, unpublished data). The southeast recreational focus area was associated with major topographic relief and the presence of alpine areas (MMF, unpublished data). Fishing was concentrated outside of these areas, along the major rivers that flow through the T.F.L., and in two areas with an abundance of lakes.

DISCUSSION

Respondent socio-demographic characteristics

The socio-demographics of respondents reflected a preponderance of males and high involvement in forest-based resource sectors. The high proportion of respondents involved in natural resource-related occupations and related activities is in agreement with the results of the survey by Robinson et al. (1997) and reflects the predominance of these types of occupations and activities in northern forest regions of British Columbia. The very high proportion of male respondents (85.7 per cent) in the present study may be the result of several factors. The methods selected for those individuals who had an interest in, were somehow involved with, or cared about T.F.L. 30. Many of the region's economic and non-economic uses of the forest (i.e. the forest industry, fishing, hunting, and trapping) are also traditionally associated with males. In addition, males may be more likely to participate in, and be identified by, this type of information gathering.

Figure 2. Areal extents of non-timber-related activities in T.F.L. 30

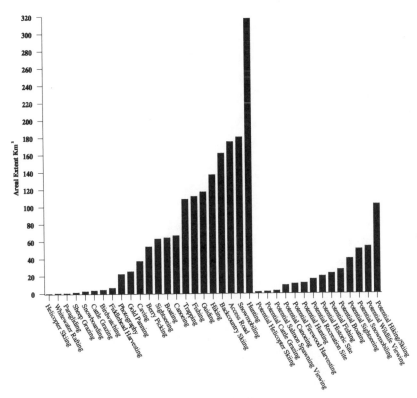

Non-Timber Activities

Figure 3. Spatial distribution of selected recreation-related activities and roads in T.F.L. 30

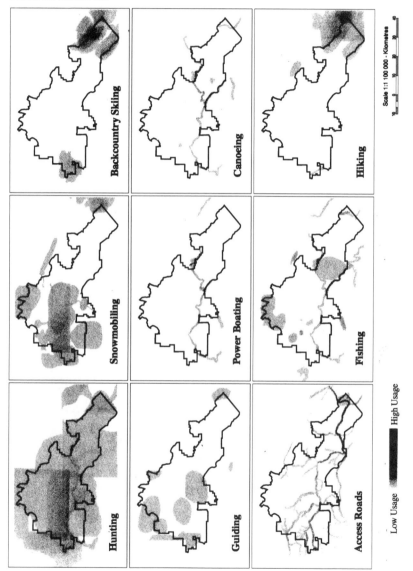

The large number of respondents who lived in the city of Prince George (75.3 per cent) was expected, given that Prince George is the largest population centre in the region, the city lies in close proximity to T.F.L. 30 (see Figure 1), and the city received the request for information message more often than other communities.

Statements of importance

The methods employed in this study specifically selected for those individuals who had an interest in T.F.L. 30. Thus, respondents were not representative of the general public. As a consequence, uses and values identified for T.F.L. 30 may not be complete, and priorities identified by respondents may not represent those of the general public. Nevertheless, the process provided much information on uses and values held by the public for T.F.L. 30. The data indicated that, although a few individuals had narrowly defined interests, most respondents had a great breadth of interests and concerns regarding T.F.L. 30. Expressions of interest and concerns regarding recreation-related issues were paramount among this group. This emphasis was present even among respondents who derived economic benefit from T.F.L. 30. The recreational importance of T.F.L. 30 involved a variety of uses and values, most of which were dependent upon the maintenance of the natural conditions and ecological integrity of the area.

Economic and non-economic uses. The high representation of people who derive economic benefit from forestry-related occupations reflects the overwhelming economic importance of forestry-based industries in T.F.L. 30 and the surrounding region. However, other uses of T.F.L. 30 were clearly identified. Indeed, the high number of responses related to non-economic uses of T.F.L. 30 indicates that a majority of respondents considered non-economic uses to be important. Therefore, management in the model forest should recognize other forms of benefit derived from the forest. The large number of non-economic use responses, in particular the overwhelming frequency with which respondents engaged in and mentioned non-motorized activities, clearly highlights the need for managers to consider this type of recreation in forest management plans. The need to restrict timber harvesting to maintain other values was considered in Northwood Pulp and Timber Limited's management plan for the area (Northwood Pulp and Timber Limited 1994a).

Species use. The variety of flora and fauna pursued in T.F.L. 30 underlines the natural diversity of the area and the diversity of its use.

The three species most commonly pursued by respondents in this study (trout, moose, bear) were also identified as important in Northwood's recreation analysis (Northwood Pulp and Timber Limited 1994b). These results suggest that management in the model forest should ensure the preservation not only of these species, but also of opportunities to pursue these species recreationally, economically, or for subsistence.

Importance Values. Tree Farm Licence 30 was important to respondents primarily for the opportunity it provided to experience nature, derive economic benefit, or recreate. The vast majority of respondents identified various non-economic importance values. The view that natural resources are important non-economically as well as economically coincides with previous studies of Canadian and northern British Columbia residents (Bonderud 1994; Forestry Canada 1992; Energy, Mines and Petroleum Resources Canada [EMPRC] 1993). These results support the contention that while jobs are important, other aspects of quality of life are important too, and recreation is among the foremost.

Non-commercial and commercial recreation and tourism. The large number of specific comments relating to non-commercial and commercial recreation and tourism probably reflects the familiarity of a high proportion of respondents with these aspects of use, and their concerns regarding the impacts of forest management on recreational and tourism opportunities. The existing level of non-commercial recreation in T.F.L. 30 is high, with considerable potential for commercial recreation. However, respondents' comments pointed to the issue of conflicts of use, not only between timber and non-timber-related activities, but also among recreational user groups. These conflicts are intertwined with issues related to access and motorized versus non-motorized use. This points to the need of forest managers to anticipate and prevent conflicts among forest uses. Managing conflict between motorized and non-motorized uses, and between timber harvest and recreation priorities, may require a change in decision criteria relating to access road development and maintenance. Including a recreational focus in the process of road development would allow managers to relate the flow and distribution of people and recreation to types of timber harvest practices. For example, partial cutting techniques could be used in areas where access roads are maintained and lead to non-motorized recreation sites.

General Timber Harvesting Practices. The negative environmental impacts of the timber harvesting process, and the need for responsible harvesting to accommodate other non-timber uses in the model forest, were the two major concerns of respondents. Similar concerns were expressed in an EMPRC (1993) survey of Canadians on various resource sectors, Northwood's management plan (Northwood Pulp and Timber Limited 1994a) and recent interviews of community leaders in northern British Columbia regarding timber harvesting (Bonderud 1994). In the EMPRC (1993) survey, respondents believed the forest industry was causing significant environmental damage in Canada. Northwood Pulp and Timber Limited (1994a) stated that moose may be affected by the harvesting of residual stands, that caribou require mature forests, and that trapping and guide outfitting operations may be impacted negatively by the rate of cut. Interviewees in the Bonderud (1994) study appreciated the timber industry for the jobs it provided, but were concerned about the falldown (acute decline in timber production) that would result if the timber industry maintained current cutting levels. Interviewees were also concerned about the environmental cost of present timber harvesting practices on their communities.

Whether it be at the landscape, local, provincial, or national level, there is much agreement on these issues. If timber harvesting practices are to be developed that are socially acceptable to Canadians, British Columbians, residents of local timber dependent communities, and people who work in the timber industry, then forest managers must address public concerns of negative environmental impacts and the need for more responsible timber harvest practices.

Clearcutting and partial cutting. The vast majority of comments regarding clearcutting were negative. In the results of a telephone survey conducted by Northwood Pulp and Paper Limited (1994b), clearcutting was one of the most pressing environmental issues that Prince George residents wanted the company to address. Among European corporate buyers of forest products (Natural Resources Canada 1993) and Canadians (Forestry Canada 1991), clearcutting is considered to have negative environmental impacts. Large clearcuts are a particular concern among residents of northern British Columbia (Bonderud 1994). Spokespersons for hiking groups in the Prince George area felt that a limit should be placed on timber harvesting above 4500 feet to protect habitat for caribou. They felt that visual quality should be considered in harvest planning, that cutblocks should conform to the lay of the land and that islands of forest should be left within large cutblocks (Ministry of Forests 1995).

These studies indicate that the negative environmental impacts of clearcutting are a concern which many segments of the public share. Since clearcutting is the dominant harvesting method in Canada, this may reflect a public perception that timber harvest practices are one and the same as clearcutting practices. Thus, the negative public perception of clearcutting may extend to a negative view of timber practices in general by association. In contrast to comments on clearcutting, all comments on partial cutting were positive. Since the vast majority of harvesting takes place using clearcutting techniques, the lower number of comments on partial cutting may reflect a lower level of familiarity of respondents with this technique. The positive orientation towards partial cutting may reveal a lack of experience with the technique or a genuine satisfaction with its results.

Access. There were a substantial number of comments related to access. These generally fell within one of two categories: support of access for recreation reasons; and, concern that access resulted in negative environmental impacts such as habitat fragmentation, destruction to streams, over-hunting, and over-fishing.

The data highlight the paradox regarding access in relation to recreation, tourism, and timber extraction. Road development associated with timber extraction processes as presently employed in T.F.L. 30 results in the creation of vehicular access to areas of the forest that were previously inaccessible by car or truck. This greatly increases the accessibility and use of remote areas for recreational and other uses, but also has significant impacts on maintenance of the ecological integrity of these areas. Comments by the public in this and other studies (e.g. Ministry of Forests 1989) disclose the public's recognition of this problem. Northwood considered the detrimental impacts of access on caribou in a recreation and landscape analysis report for T.F.L. 30 (Northwood Pulp and Timber Limited 1994b) and on grizzly bears, trapping, and guide outfitting operations in its management plan for T.F.L. 30 (Northwood Pulp and Timber Limited 1994a).

The issue is complicated further by the relationship between non-motorized recreation and access, and the conflict between non-motorized and motorized recreation. Although certain activities themselves may be non-motorized, the remoteness of T.F.L. 30 suggests that some motorized access is required to reach and depart from specific activity sites. Thus, access is still a key issue related to non-motorized recreation, and many of the people who commented on non-motorized recreation also commented on access. Conflicts between non-motorized and motorized use were identified by respondents and were anticipated in a 1994 analysis of Recreation Opportunity Spectrum classes within the model forest (Northwood Pulp and Timber Limited 1994b). Despite the report's prediction that demand for non-motorized backcountry opportunities will increase over the next 20 years, the land available for semi-primitive non-motorized opportunities is expected to decrease from 22 per cent in 1994 to 2.7 per cent in 2014 due to anticipated road developments. Some areas may need to have access restricted in order to maintain or improve fish and wildlife populations, while other areas may require access development for recreational use. Indeed, the development of access is a management tool that can be used to regulate the distribution of people, in addition to controlling the harvesting of trees.

Ecosystem. Respondents' concerns over the maintenance of ecological integrity were high. This related indirectly to recreation and tourism since the flora and fauna thereby maintained are important components to much of the recreation and tourism uses and values identified for T.F.L. 30. Public concern extended to recommending the use of regulations to protect fish and wildlife from recreational use. In addition, more research should be conducted to ensure effective forest management. The need to protect fish and wildlife using regulations was suggested in both Northwood Pulp and Timber Limited's recreation and landscape analysis report (1994b) and the management plan for T.F.L. 30 (1994a). These documents proposed using Ministry of Forests and Ministry of Environment lands and parks legislation to manage snowmobile and hiking access in areas of important caribou habitat, and to regulate ATV access in grizzly bear areas. Management options should emphasize the preservation of habitat for both non-game and game species.

Forest Management Processes. A large number of responses focused on the forest management process. Comments were overwhelmingly in support of multiple use, the MMF program, and incorporating the broad array of public values and knowledge into forest management planning. Ensuring local control over local resources and recognizing the importance of other non-economic values in management decisions were themes that were also reflected in Bonderud's (1994) report on northern forestry issues. Comments critical of the MMF program forest management planning in the region, and statements regarding the need for greater accountability and regulation of forest products companies (eg. the need for a forest practices code) were consistent with the general distrust of big industry among community leaders identified by Bonderud (1994). Forest management options should emphasize effective integrated forest planning to provide for the provision and maintenance of a variety of recreational opportunities, regulation of recreation user groups, and the promotion of non-motorized and environmentally sensitive recreational opportunities. Concerns over public perceptions and misinformation indicate that a two-way flow of information between the public and forest managers is required.

Spatial distribution of non-timber-related activities

The distribution of non-timber uses reflected the geography and the infrastructure of the site. Hunting and snowmobiling were both concentrated in an area which had experienced considerable logging, resulting in a relatively dense network of roads and clearcuts. Access roads and open spaces in the forest are of benefit to both of these types of recreation. Backcountry skiing and hiking were concentrated in a mountainous alpine area. Although respondents who engaged in these latter types of recreation generally viewed clearcuts negatively, access roads are essential for them to pursue these recreations, even though the activities themselves are non-motorized. Recognition of these associations and the availability of spatial data to relate them to timber harvest plans are essential tools for the DSS of the model forest.

Implications for management of the model forest

Forest values reflect the relative importance society attaches to various elements of the forest. In the past, forest valuations have been expressed primarily through economic and political means. This provides an inadequate means of incorporating a wide range of social values, including recreation and tourism, in forest management. Development of a more inclusive operational model is precisely the intent of the model forest approach. Social analysis offers an approach to measuring societal values and an effective means of facilitating society's demands for a sustainable, multi-value approach to forest management. Respondents in this and other studies clearly support public involvement in forest management. Studies such as the present one and the survey conducted by Robinson et al. (1997) are the beginnings of efforts designed specifically to involve the public in a meaningful way in all levels of forest management.

The results of the present study demonstrate that individuals hold diverse interests in, and uses for, the forest. Although non-users do not have as direct a relationship with a specific forest area as the people who use it, non-users' social values are extremely important. The social values of non-users along with those of users underlie most laws, policies, and institutional arrangements (Forests for Tomorrow 1990). Though it is clear that there are general values that can be derived from the broader Canadian public, it is also necessary to pay special attention to local uses and values.

The public is the obvious source of information on public interests and concerns regarding forest management, and on the specific uses that individuals make of the forest. However, the public is also an excellent source of information on regional characteristics of the forest and site-specific uses and attributes. This was demonstrated clearly by the spatial data in the present study. In addition, the public is a source of specific and possibly innovative ideas on alternative management practices.

Management of the model forest must recognize the public's emphasis on both economic and non-economic uses, and the importance of recreation and tourism in integrated resource management. Two over-riding concerns in this regard are the maintenance of ecological integrity, and management to prevent or reduce conflict among users.

Maintenance of ecological integrity is fundamental to sustaining all economic and non-economic uses and values of the forest. Thus, an erosion of ecological integrity affects the sustainability of all forest uses and values. It is apparent that many aspects of forestry practices are considered to be at odds with the maintenance of ecological integrity and recreational and tourism uses. But the relationships are not simple, even with a forestry practice as contentious as clearcutting. Even if we limit the discussion to recreational uses alone, the impact of clearcutting is dichotomous. For example, clearcutting is considered by some to have very negative impacts on recreation (e.g. aesthetics), but can also have positive recreational impacts (e.g. hunting, snowmobiling). Indeed, forestry practices, such as the development of access roads, are fundamental to providing certain types of recreational and tourism opportunities. But excessive or conflicting uses of an area as a result of improved vehicular access can denigrate some recreational experiences. This is the conundrum surrounding access and its regulation. It is worth pointing out that it is very often not roads themselves, but their uses that produces problems. Thus, the management of access really means the management of people and their activities.

Management of the model forest must incorporate public input and involvement. This will not make management decisions easier. In fact, inclusion of information on public uses and values will increase greatly the complexity of the management decision process. However, such inclusion is necessary. The most suitable mechanisms to do that are yet to be developed. Spatial representation of use and value data will be an important tool for relating spatial and temporal plans for timber extraction to recreational and other uses. Social science techniques will be important tools for gathering and focusing public input. Data on public values and uses must be integrated with data on biological and ecological conditions in the forest. Public values that are illegal or impossible to satisfy may have to be discounted, but public forest managers may then need to communicate to the public why public preferences or values cannot or should not be met. Economic and other forces impacting on commercial forestry decisions and practices still remain. The creation of a management system to integrate these multiple types of information (i.e. the DSS) is the challenge presently facing the MMF.

ACKNOWLEDGEMENTS

This research was funded by the McGregor Model Forest Association. The McGregor Model Forest Association also processed the spatial use data and prepared the figures for this report. We thank all the individuals who participated in the gathering of information and invested so much time and effort in helping us come to an understanding of the issues involved in socially sustainable forest management. We especially thank people of the McGregor Model Forest Association for their support and commitment to this process. Finally, we thank a variety of graduate students and others who provided invaluable technical assistance to this project and without whom the project would not have been possible.

REFERENCES

Bonderud, R.M. 1994. *A communications needs assessment of communities in the northern interior lumber sector of COFI*. Prepared by Bonderud Public Relations.

Brooks, D.J. & G.E. Grant. 1992. New approaches to forest management. Background, science issues, and research agenda. *Journal of Forestry* 90 (1): 25-28.

Commission on Resources and Environment. 1994. *A sustainability act for British Columbia*. The Provincial Land Use Strategy Volume 1. Victoria: Queen's Printer.

Eidsvik, H.K. 1990. *Policy formulation and communication in changing times*. Notes from an address to the OMNR, Sault Ste. Marie, Ontario.

Energy, Mines and Petroleum Resources Canada. 1993. *1993 National public opinion survey on natural resources: Final report.* Prepared by Corporate Research Associates Inc.

Forestry Canada. n.d. *Canada's Model Forest Program- An initiative for sustainable development.* Petawawa National Forestry Institute.

Forestry Canada. 1991. *Survey of professional foresters in Canada.* Conducted by Omnifacts Research Limited, Environics Research Group Limited and CROP Inc.

Forestry Canada. 1992. *1991 National survey of Canadian public opinion on forestry issues.* Conducted by Environics Research Group Limited, Corporate Research Associates Inc. and CROP Inc.

Forests for Tomorrow. 1990. *Witness statement no. 4 the forest or the trees: Non-timber values and forest management in Ontario.* Toronto, Ontario.

McGregor Model Forest Association. 1994. *The McGregor Model Forest Association concept paper.* Prince George, B.C.

Ministry of Forests. 1989. *Guide outfitters of British Columbia: Opportunity analysis.* Prepared by The DPA Consulting Group, Vancouver, B.C.

Ministry of Forests. 1995. *Prince George timber supply area socio-economic analysis.* Prepared by the ARA Consulting Group Inc., Vancouver, B.C.

Natural Resources Canada. 1993. *The state of Canada's forests 1993: Forests, a global resource.* Fourth Report to Parliament, Canadian Forest Service.

Northwood Pulp and Timber Limited. 1994a. *Recreation and landscape analysis report TFL 30.* Prepared by Timberline Forest Inventory Consultants.

Northwood Pulp and Timber Limited. 1994b. *Statement of management objectives, options and procedures TFL 30 Management Plan 8.*

Robinson, D., A.W.L. Hawley & M. Robson. 1997. *Social valuation of the McGregor Model Forest: Assessing Canadian public opinion on forest values and forest management. Results of the 1996 Canadian forest survey.*

Prepared for The McGregor Model Forest Association, Prince George, B.C.

Robson, M., D. Robinson & A.W.L. Hawley. 1995. *The community of interests and the social values related to the McGregor Model Forest. Volumes 1-3.* Prepared for The McGregor Model Forest Association, Prince George, B.C.

COGNITIVE LENSES EMPLOYED BY DIFFERENT TYPES OF VISITORS IN EVALUATING THE ATTRACTIVENESS OF A NATIONAL PARK LANDSCAPE

Bart Richardson
Minnesota Department of
Natural Resources

David W. Lime
University of Minnesota,
Minneapolis

David G. Pitt
University of Minnesota,
Minneapolis

Ross Martin
Landscape Ecology Consultant
New York, NY

INTRODUCTION

The aesthetic expectations of Anglo-Americans visiting natural settings in North America are rooted in the eighteenth century English philosophy of aesthetics known as the picturesque theory. As such, the expectations of modern day tourists for the appearance of natural areas are not unlike those of their eighteenth and nineteenth century counterparts in England. In North America, the picturesque ideal was codified as an aesthetic framework for designing and managing park environments by enabling legislation that created federal and provincial/state parks, and it remains today an important source of expectation in apprehending the aesthetic dimensions of human-environment transactions in natural settings. After tracing some of the origins of the picturesque theory, defining idealized qualities of landscape from a picturesque perspective, and describing its relationship to the pursuit of outdoor recreation activities, this paper presents findings from a study conducted with 315 visitors to the Pictured Rocks National Lakeshore in Michigan's Upper Peninsula. The findings are derived from perceptual responses to digital image simulations developed using picturesque principles of roadway design to portray the appearance of a proposed parkway in the lakeshore. The findings of the study demonstrate: that different dimensions of the picturesque theory are alive and well in the mind's eye of lakeshore visitors; that different sectors of the lakeshore's visiting clientele focus on different dimensions of picturesque theory in framing their perceptual response to roadway scenes; and, that management action with respect to the parkway needs to be sensitive to differences in the picturesque lenses which different segments of their visiting clientele employ.

DEFINITION AND DEVELOPMENT OF THE PICTURESQUE THEORY

The picturesque is an aesthetic theory that affected the arts of painting, poetry, architecture and garden design and combined all the fine arts into a single art of landscape (Hussey 1967). The etymology of the word picturesque has connections with the early seventeenth century Dutch *schilderachtig* which means picture-like (Hipple 1957). While the word is most closely linked to landscape painting, in the beginning of the eighteenth century, the picturesque was also applied to literary styles that were especially vivid or graphic or, in other words, capable of painting a picture in the reader's mind. By the end of the eighteenth century some theoreticians of landscape aesthetics argued that the picturesque should be simply defined as qualities that were suitable for painting.

The transformation of the word picturesque from that meaning anything suitable for painting into the English picturesque aesthetic was expedited by the writings of Edmund Burke on the philosophy of association, a general premise of which is that specific objects or landscapes are capable of triggering specific emotions. Burke popularized the associational theory in his 1757 essay entitled *A Philosophical Inquiry Into the Origin of Our Ideas of the Sublime and the Beautiful*. His most noteworthy contribution to aesthetic theory held that the beautiful and the sublime were both pleasurable. While the beautiful obviously elicits pleasure, the sublime causes a sensation of abstracted pain or anxiety which elicits pleasure by virtue of aesthetic (and actual) distance from the source of the anxiety.

The picturesque can be defined as an emotional reaction which combines elements of both the beautiful and the sublime. To identify a picturesque landscape and its associated objects, one must first identify a beautiful landscape and a sublime landscape. The paintings of Claude Lorrain and Salvator Rosa serve as prime examples of beautiful and sublime landscapes in the eighteenth century. While Claude's painting typically triggers the associated beautiful response to the repose of the scene, Salvator's work represents the antithesis and is associated with the sublime.

The sublime

Burke succinctly defines the sublime as "an idea belonging to self-preservation; that it is therefore one of the most affecting we have; that its strongest emotion is an emotion of distress; and that no pleasure from a positive cause belongs to it" (Burke 1757: 124). This is not to say that the sublime does not bring a sense of pleasure, perhaps somewhat warped at times, but that the source of sublime pleasure is solely from negative, dangerous, and life threatening causes. The emotion most commonly associated with the sublime "is astonishment; and astonishment is that state of the soul, in which all its motions are suspended, with some degree of horror" (Burke 1757: 98). Emotional reactions to the possibility of death are made pleasurable by one's psychological or physical distance from life-threatening circumstances. Several dimensions of the sublime are associated with specific conditions in the landscape.

Terror is caused by a perceived danger. It is the foundation of the sublime and can be caused by many elements in nature from a hostile ocean or a wind-whipped lake to a high precipice.

Obscurity leads to apprehension and fear of the unknown. In the landscape, atmospheric affects like fog or smoke can play a large role. Darkness or a poorly marked trail can also create obscurity.

Power can easily inflict pain and suffering, thus having the ability to stimulate terror and thoughts of death. A great cataract epitomizes power in nature. Power can also be experienced through contemplation, such as imagining the great glacial forces required to carve the Canadian Rockies.

Privation is associated with vacuity, darkness, solitude and silence. The thought of being alone on a vast ocean or in the wilderness, or in today's terms, being lost in outer space, are the physical examples of privation.

Vastness is associated with greatness of dimensions. Huge perpendicular faces with rough textures are given as examples.

Infinity fills the mind with a "delightful horror." Burke argues that nothing in nature is truly infinite (the ocean eventually meets land), but the eye is unable to see the bounds and thus perceives many things to be infinite.

Light and its absence are sublime, and the quick transition from light to dark is very powerful. Darkness is more sublime than lightness partly because of the obscurity it creates. Places with great contrasts in light can be sublime, such as an old growth conifer forest next to a clearing, or a canyon with one side bathed in blinding light while the other side is pitch black.

Colours that are sublime are "sad and fuscous colours, as black, or brown, or deep purple, and the like" (Burke 1757: 121). Exposed bedrock, mountain summits, decaying forest litter and storm clouds may possess such colours.

Sound and loudness such as the noise of huge cataracts, thunder storms or artillery "awakes a great and awful sensation in the mind" (Burke 1757: 122).

Suddenness creates a feeling of the unexpected and the idea of danger. Thunder or a falling tree are good examples.

Intermittent events or sounds create feelings of the unexpected. This is similar to obscurity in that not knowing what will happen can be terrifying. An unexplainable sound in the woods near by could be quite sublime.

Smells and taste that are pungent or bitter can be sublime. A smell may implant on one's memory a painful event, and thus become a sublime association.

Feeling pain, the "idea of bodily pain, in all the modes and degrees of labor, pain, anguish, torment" (Burke 1757: 124) creates a sublime passion. An arduous hike, a rain soaked canoe trip, bitter cold while winter camping or a day with insidious black flies can all be sublime experiences.

The beautiful

Burke defined the beautiful as "that quality or those qualities in bodies, by which they cause love, or some passion similar to it" (Burke 1757: 127). Burke defined love as "that satisfaction which arises to the mind upon contemplating anything beautiful, of whatsoever nature it may be, from desire or lust." He argued that there is a great difference between the lust of a man for a beautiful woman and the appreciation of beautiful features in animals. While both elicit love, only the man's lust for the woman causes desire. He thus separated the passion of the beautiful, which he calls love, from the passion of desire or lust. Burke argued that the "violent and tempestuous passions" of love are caused more by desire than by beauty (Burke 1757: 128).

The causes of beauty are "some quality in bodies acting mechanically upon the human mind by the intervention of the senses" (Burke 1757: 148). Burke's associational qualities of the beautiful are outlined below:

Smallness is measured in relationship to the great dimensions that cause sublime emotions. Burke observed that objects of love are typically given diminutive epithets. Small things are controllable and produce pleasure. "We submit to what we admire, but we love what submits to us" (Burke 1757: 149).

Smoothness was viewed as so essential to beauty that Burke could not think of anything beautiful that is not smooth. Smooth leaves, smooth slopes of earth in gardens, and smooth streams in the landscape find their antithesis in roughness or ruggedness.

Gradual variation of smooth objects brings delight and pleasure to the eye because it is difficult to find either a beginning or end of the object. Rolling prairie hills or a smoothly meandering path are superlative examples of smooth gradual variations.

Delicacy in appearance is important to the beautiful. Burke extolled the orange tree, the almond, and the jasmine vine for their beauty because of their delicate nature. Flowers were beautiful because of their "weakness and momentary duration."

Colours must be clean, fair, and variegated, yet not dusky or muddy. They must also be mild in nature; light greens, soft blues, weak whites, pink reds and violets. Variegated flowers are beautiful. Gradual variation of the colours is desired.

The picturesque: Elements of the sublime and the beautiful

Burke clearly mapped the boundaries of the sublime and the beautiful. Landscapes, or the elements that made up the landscape, could be classified as being either sublime or beautiful. A smooth rolling lawn with clumps of trees was obviously beautiful while a frightening precipice was sublime. Problems arose, however, when the landscape did not fall clearly into either classification. What if the smooth rolling lawn abruptly ended at the end of a dark, wild forest? How did one classify the landscape with a beautiful lake at the base of a sublime cliff? The changeability and relativity of the landscape defied exact classification.

The latter half of the eighteenth century brought a recognition that not all landscapes or features could be classified as strictly sublime or beautiful. A third aesthetic evolved to more easily identify landscapes that possessed both sublime and beautiful elements; the aesthetic of the picturesque. Several late eighteenth century English philosophical dilettantes, most notably Richard Payne Knight and Uvedale Price, used the associational theory to identify beautiful, sublime and picturesque landscapes. Picturesque landscape elements were defined as being the tincture of the sublime (Price 1794). The development of the picturesque paralleled a growing acceptance of the sublime; and, the picturesque in some cases was seen merely as a habitable cousin of the sublime. The Reverend William Gilpin (1792), on the other hand, viewed the picturesque as a subset of the beautiful. He wrote extensively about picturesque beauty, a quality which allowed the sublime and the beautiful to exist in the same landscape depending on one's position or the time of day.

In his Essay on the Picturesque, Price (1794) presented the picturesque as a category distinct from the beautiful and the sublime. Price understood that landscapes possessed inherent changeability over time which endowed them with picturesque association. The passage of time brought ruin to the landscape and marked it with age. The once beautiful temple, of classic proportion and symmetry, became picturesque in ruins. In the English landscape, the gothic ruin and the shattered tree became emblematic of the antiquity, and therefore, because of the association with mortality, the sublimity, of the scene. Immanent or seasonal effects—fog, shifts in light, weather—could add incidental obscurity or variety and heighten association. These subliminal elements of the actual landscape expanded for Price the dynamic possibilities of a picturesque associational realm beyond the composed, and, ultimately static, realm of the pictorial.

An openness toward unknown or ungovernable elements of nature combined with the comforting presence of God permitted the appreciation of raw and wild nature. In this same vein the picturesque was transformed from a narrow range of effects governed by the classical ideals in painting to the appreciation of the wild, rough, rugged and varied landscapes. Gilpin understood the viewing of landscape to be a religious experience, perhaps triggering the same type of emotion one would feel while in church. Gilpin viewed the landscape as a place for religious inspiration, and he felt it should be able to inspire moral consciousness and virtuous deeds from the people. He saw little difference between admiring picturesque beauty and the beauty of virtue, for they are both the product of God. A good summation of the period's attitude toward nature was stated simply by Gilpin (1792: 47) "Nature is but a name for an affect, Whose cause is God."

Transformation of beautiful landscape into the picturesque

By the middle of the eighteenth century, the landscape tastes of the English gentry had largely abandoned the classical symmetrical garden designs of the continent and embraced a natural style. This natural style of gardens and landscape was championed by William Kent and Lancelot "Capability" Brown, landscape gardeners in England. Popular gardens created an artificial pastoral setting, emphasizing smooth lawns, human-made lakes and random clumpings of trees, all cast in the idiom of the beautiful. After several decades, these seemingly natural designs began to be viewed as sterile, dry and artificial. The late eighteenth century classification of the picturesque into Burkian terms had also shed an entirely different light on these landscaped estates. The development of a multi-layered picturesque aesthetic postulated that the old natural gardens were in fact shallow, simple and sometimes insipid. The ideas of Gilpin, Knight and Price embraced a more wild landscape. This view marked the transition between the pastoral picturesque (of Brown) and the wild and emotional picturesque (of Gilpin, Knight and Price). Gilpin and others felt that unmolested nature was one of the most pure and beautiful things in the world. Nature was now appreciated for its infinite number of variations and contrasts, and Knight wrote extensively about the need to practice accident and neglect in the making of the garden. He thought that the landscape could be improved if it was left to go wild; dead branches left on the trees, shrubs permitted to become entangled at the base of the trees, and water left to take its natural course. Knight noted that for the garden to have a constant picturesque appearance one must judiciously profit by the accidental occurrences of nature. The goal was to give the garden qualities of roughness while maintaining the delicacy of the design (Knight 1796: 48). The manipulated pastoral landscapes, especially those created by Brown, could not stand up in beauty, variety and contrasts when compared to wild nature.

By the end of the eighteenth century a few gardens had evolved with the picturesque, changing from a smooth Brownian lawn to rough and wild estates. The inclusion of wildness in the garden went hand-in-hand with the developing appreciation of the wildness in the countryside.

PICTURESQUE TRAVEL: TOURING THE ENGLISH LANDSCAPE

Travelling or touring in the eighteenth century English landscape epitomized the way to experience the picturesque. Travel added another aspect of the dimension of time to the picturesque. To the traveller the journey became as important as attaining the destination, weaving picturesque aesthetics and the romanticizing of bucolic settings into all aspects of the tour (Hipple 1957).

The recreational qualities of travelling were divided between identifying an interesting object and the amusement and pleasure one receives from pursuing that object. The pursuit of the object frequently led the traveller to new and unexplored landscapes in which the changing scenery kept the traveller in constant suspense (Gilpin 1792: 47). The reward of travelling is realized when the object is found. "After the pursuit we are gratified with the attainment of the object. Our amusement, on this head, arises from the employment of the mind in examining the beautiful scenes we have found" (Gilpin 1792: 48).

The desire to experience the picturesque *in situ* resulted in the development of organized and printed picturesque tours. By the 1760s several destinations had become popular tourist spots: the Lake District, the River Wye, Mount Snowdon, the Highlands in Scotland and the Peak District in northern England, for example. Gilpin was the favourite author of tour guides to many of these popular destinations. His guides acted as both a road map and an aesthetic education of the region. He has been credited with popularizing the idea of travelling about the countryside in search of specific picturesque landscape elements for recreational pleasure.

Gilpin advocated the capturing of a pastoral representation of landscape as a memento or token of picturesque tourism, commenting as follows: "[walking] a few miles into the Country; at which Times I always take my Paper and black-lead Pencil with me, and never fail to bring Home something or other, which together with the Pleasure and Benefit of the Walk makes me think my Time not ill spent" (Barbier 1963: 17). For Gilpin, sketching memorable objects was one of the amusements of picturesque travel (Gilpin 1792). Like a hunter, Gilpin stalked his game, and the sketch provided proof of a successful encounter with the quarry (Jackle 1985).

Upon reaching a specified place of picturesque virtue, tourists following Gilpin's tourbooks had several options for capturing their impressions of the landscape. One could paint or sketch the vistas while taking liberties with its composition and objects, or one could imagine the vista compositionally as a painting. For those tourists who could not draw or paint well, several mechanical aids were available to help travellers see the world in two dimensions. The camera obscura, a crude box and lens apparatus, permitted the traveller to sketch the landscape from a projection within the box. The box was arranged in a manner similar to a view camera with the image being projected onto a ground glass on which one could lay a piece of tracing paper and copy the image of the landscape. The Claude glass was a concave oval mirror that created the illusion of a landscape painting from the chosen vista reflected in the mirror. The glass came in different coloured tints, each colour giving the landscape a different mood or feeling, with the most popular colours being blue and yellow. Tourists would turn their back on the landscape, hold the mirror up and view the landscape from over their shoulder. The reflected vista gave a quality similar to a warm and delicate Claude painting.

THE PICTURESQUE MIGRATES TO NORTH AMERICA

At the beginning of the nineteenth century in North America, several factors prepared the way for the free adoption of the picturesque as both an intellectual and a popular vocabulary about the landscape: a developing upper middle class had the time and the resources to pursue landscape aesthetics; the landscape was wild and unsettled; and, Canada and America had maintained intellectual ties with England. By the early part of the nineteenth century the British principles of the picturesque had been transformed to fit the North American culture and countryside. Burkian ideals which related the sublime to terror, and the beautiful to pleasure remained the same but took on slightly varied definitions in the face of such spectacles as Niagara Falls, the Grand Canyon and the frozen ice of Hudson Bay in January.

The North American picturesque evolved to include the associations of the sublime (a spectacle, infinity, privation, the sky, and silence) and the associations of the beautiful (smooth to rugged, and moralistically pure). The Transcendental Movement of the mid-nineteenth century embued the beautiful and the sublime with greater religious and moralistic overtones, and it allowed Anglo-American culture to continue the tradition of deifying nature which had begun in the eighteenth century with the picturesque movement in England. The unspoiled quality of the New World helped create the impression that it was free from corruption from the Old World. It was as if Western civilization had been granted a clean slate with the New World. North America was the promised land, the new arcadia, the land of God. Anglo-American culture embraced these ideas and made a strong connection between God and nature. In many publications in the nineteenth century the word nature was frequently capitalized, placing it on equal footing with God. To be one with nature was to communicate with God. Partly because God was seen as part of the landscape, the nineteenth century spawned the beginnings of wilderness conservation.

The national parks movement evolved directly within and as a product of this culture, and it was with the intention of protecting yet making accessible to the touring public the great picturesque icons of the North American landscape that national parks in Canada and the U.S. were created and are maintained (Fairfax & Dana 1981). While events leading to the creation of the picturesque theory are more than two hundred years old, and while the transformation of the English picturesque into a North American picturesque occurred in the last century, pursuit of the picturesque ideal remains an important motivation for late twentieth century tourism in natural settings. Many vacation goals and outdoor recreation activities are dependent on the visual appeal of the landscape. The 1990 U.S. President's Commission on America's Outdoors found that the number one reason vacationers chose to visit a national park was for its natural beauty. To many tourists visiting national parks, experiencing the picturesque or scenic landscape is the primary goal of their trip.

The parallel between the eighteenth century picturesque tourist and the late twentieth century vacationer is evident in tourists' reactions to the landscape. As society in the eighteenth century sought out picturesque landscapes with a sketchbook, camera obscura or Claude glass in hand, the twentieth century vacationer is on a quest for scenic wonders to record with a point-and-shoot camera and a video cassette recorder. Rather than following tourbooks written by the Reverend William Gilpin, today's North American tourists are instructed on the picturesque ideal through the tour guides of Fodor's, Mobil, the American Automobile Association or the Canadian Automobile Association, or the interpretative programming of Parks Canada and the U.S. National Park Service. Specific landscape types that were appreciated in the eighteenth and nineteenth centuries for their picturesque attributes have been passed down and are influencing our perceptions and understanding of aesthetic value in the twentieth century landscape.

The inheritance of landscape aesthetics from eighteenth century England is the fundamental reason why the picturesque must be studied to understand fully the aesthetic appreciation of natural landscapes in the twentieth century. The subtle variations of the pastoral construction of the picturesque with its more explicit use of qualities drawn from the beautiful and the sublimity of the wild and emotional picturesque represent divergent, yet related, cognitive lenses employed by late twentieth century tourists in their pursuit of the picturesque ideal. The choice of which of the two picturesque cognitive lenses (i.e. the pastoral lens or the wild and emotional lens) a tourist will employ in a particular visit to a natural area is likely to vary with several dimensions of the human-environment transaction (Pitt 1989). Childhood experiences, for example, are likely to establish a frame of reference within which visitors learn to adapt to the use of one or the other of the cognitive lenses (Yoesting & Christensen 1978). The individuality of personality produces personal styles of transaction both in the sense of what a recreationist chooses to do in a given environment and in the way an individual identifies and attends to salient attributes of the environment (Knopf 1987; McKechnie 1974). Perceptions of experiential qualities of the transaction are also apt to be associated with motivation and purpose for visiting the natural area (Ditton et al. 1983; Schreyer & Roggenbuck 1978), experience level (Schreyer et al. 1984), familiarity with the physical setting of the transaction (Knopf 1987), the package of expected benefits to be derived from the transaction (Brown 1984), the peer group with whom one interacts during the transaction (Manning 1986) and the mode of travel a recreationist uses during a transaction (Graefe et al. 1984).

EXAMINING PICTURESQUE VALUES AMONG VISITORS TO
THE PICTURED ROCKS NATIONAL LAKESHORE

The Pictured Rocks National Lakeshore is a unit of the U.S. National Park System. Designated in 1963, the lakeshore contains a core area consisting of the Lake Superior shoreline from Munising to Grand Sable, Michigan. The core area is owned in fee simple by the U.S. National Park Service (NPS), and the NPS regulates land use on privately owned land within a peripheral area along the boundary of the core area.

The lakeshore contains many elements that directly invoke picturesque associations, including: the sublimity of the shoreline's Late Cambrian sandstone bluffs that have been severely eroded by weather and wave action; the vastness of the lake horizon; the tranquillity of the lakeside environment during calm periods; the tempestuousness of the lake during storms and the rapidity with which such meteorological transformations occur; the antiquity of nineteenth century mining and ore processing ruins; ruins of a slide used during the logging era to bring logs down to the shoreline; an abandoned light station; and, the presence of a diverse flora that includes soft and rounded qualities of the beautiful stands of maple and beech as well as the more pointed and jagged qualities of the sublime stands of red and jack pine and northern white cedar. Thus, the lakeshore is an especially appropriate location to examine the presence and use of picturesque filters by visitors in their perceptions of scenic beauty.

The 1981 General Management Plan for the Pictured Rocks National Lakeshore proposed development of a scenic drive through a corridor of the lakeshore located in the shoreline zone along the bluffs of Beaver Basin, adjacent to Lake Superior. The proposed drive (Beaver Basin Rim Road) would provide a more direct connection of activity areas in the southwest section of the lakeshore (e.g. Munising Falls Interpretative Center and Miners Castle Overlook) with the Au Sable Light Station, the Twelvemile Beach and Hurricane River campgrounds, and Grand Sable Dunes in the northeast section of the lakeshore.

Pursuant to the National Environmental Policy Act of 1969, the National Park Service was required to prepare an Environmental Impact Statement before proceeding with the development of specific scenic drive road alignment and design proposals. As part of the impact assessment process, the Department of Landscape Architecture in cooperation with the Cooperative Parks Studies Unit of the University of Minnesota undertook a survey of visitor perceptions of the attractiveness of 72 video simulations of alternative roadway environments.

Characteristics of visitors surveyed

Types of Visitors Surveyed. Visitors to the lakeshore tend to fall into three categories: backpackers who drive to the lakeshore, park their cars and take overnight hikes through backcountry areas in the lakeshore; day hikers who drive to the lakeshore, park their cars and take hikes that are less than one day in length; and, non-hikers who generally stay close to their automobiles taking walks of less than a two hour duration. A total of 315 visitors participated in the survey of roadway environments, including 59 backpackers, 193 day hikers and 63 non-hikers.

Experience Level. Whereas one-third of the backpackers report they had never previously visited the lakeshore, 42 per cent of the day hikers and 53 per cent of the non-hikers are first-time visitors. More than half of the non-hikers spend two or fewer nights in the lakeshore, while more than two-thirds of backpackers and day hikers are likely to stay between two and five nights.

Existing Automobile Use. Non-hikers and day hikers are more likely than backpackers to use their automobile as an integral part of their lakeshore experience. Over two-thirds of the day hikers and three-fourths of the non-hikers report driving for pleasure as an activity during their visit, while one-third of the backpackers report driving for pleasure. Over half of the day hikers but less than one-fourth of the backpackers also report car camping.

Hypotheses on Picturesque Value System. By virtue of the facts that backcountry visitors tend to be repeat visitors to the lakeshore, tend to spend longer periods of time in the lakeshore on each visit, tend not to rely on their automobile as a major component of their visit, are intensive users of the wilder parts of the lakeshore, and took the opportunity in a free response portion of the survey used to gather roadway perceptions to express their attraction to the backcountry, it is hypothesized that:

H1: The constructs of landscape aesthetics used by backcountry visitors are more likely to be associated with the wild and emotional perspective of the picturesque. As such, their aesthetic preferences will tend toward sublime aspects of the roadway environment in the lakeshore's landscape.

H2: The non-hikers and the day hikers, on the other hand, are hypothesized to hold aesthetic values driven by the pastoral perspective of the picturesque. Lacking the knowledge, skills and experience for living in, appreciating and revering the wildness of the backcountry, non-hikers and day-hikers will espouse aesthetic preferences for roadway environments containing more explicit references to the beautiful in the lakeshore's landscape.

Visitor perceptions of alternative roadway environments

Gathering Visitor Perceptions of Roadway Attractiveness.   In an attempt to understand potential visitor perception of the Beaver Basin Rim Road, visitors were shown a videotape containing colour video simulations of 72 roadway environments that could be created when a road having a 40 miles per hour design speed is constructed. The simulations illustrate roadways:

a) in three forest vegetation communities (jack pine, red pine, maple-beech);
b) with two road widths (20 feet and 26 feet);
c) having two horizontal alignments (continuous curve, straight-away with curve at the end); and,
d) with three roadside ditch vegetation management strategies in place (grass on ditch foreslope and backslope, grass on foreslope and woody shrub vegetation on the backslope, woody shrubs on both foreslope and backslope).

The simulations reflect picturesque associations in three ways. First, the roadway alignment variation (i.e. continuous horizontal curve contrasted with a tangent and curve) tests the overall strength of the picturesque ideal among visitors to Pictured Rocks.   Regardless of whether visitors defined the picturesque from a pastoral perspective or a wild and emotional perspective, the tenets of picturesque theory would have them preferring the arcing alignment over the arc and tangent alignment. Beholders of the pastoral perspective are hypothesized to possess stronger positive affect toward roadway scenes depicting the softer, rounded, more delicate forms and lighter colours of the maple-beech vegetation. Preference for the pastoral representation of the picturesque also should be associated with roadside ditches containing the soft, fine textures and lighter colours of grass and the more rounded forms of the topographic contours of the ditch that are revealed only when the ditch contains grass on foreslope and backslope. The smooth grassy ditch vegetation in combination with the maple-beech forest vegetation also provides greater visual penetration into the forest, giving the entire scene a stronger sense of airiness and lightness. Beholders of the wild and emotional perspective of the picturesque, on the other hand, would be more receptive of the darker colour and more jagged form of the red pine and jack pine. Similarly, the wildness of the roadside ditch filled with shrub vegetation would be more preferred by holders of the wild and emotional perspective.

Twelve versions of a roadway environment (two road widths times two road alignments times three ditch vegetation treatments) were developed for two sites containing jack pine vegetation, one site containing red pine, and three sites containing maple-beech vegetation. The simulations presented the roadway as seen from the centre line looking as far down the travelled way as was visible. As each video image was presented, visitors were asked to assume they were driving on the roadway depicted in the video and to rate the attractiveness of the roadway on a seven point scale. Visitors were instructed to a record a value of one on this scale for those roadways they considered to be extremely unattractive, a value of seven for those roadways they considered to be extremely attractive, and values between one and seven to record their perceptions for roadways whose attractiveness fell somewhere between the two extremes. Values recorded by visitors were subsequently converted to standard normal z-scores by normalizing each visitor's scores across the 72 simulations. Each simulation remained present on a 19-inch colour monitor for eight seconds. Visitors viewed 10 randomly selected roadways to gain a sense of the variation in what they would see before beginning to record their attractiveness perceptions. The total viewing time per subject, including the 10 trial simulations, was approximately 16 minutes and 30 seconds.

While the validity of using slide and photographic representations of landscape as surrogates for *in situ* presentation in aesthetic evaluation studies is well documented (see Zube et al. 1987 for a discussion of this work), the validity of video representations remains essentially untested. Similarly, there is a need to document the validity of digital image simulation technology as a surrogate for *in situ* presentation (Perkins 1992; Daniel 1992). Studies conducted to date suggest that simulated slide representations generated from digital image technology elicit perceptual responses similar to slides of the same scenes (Vining & Orland 1989; Bishop and Leahy 1989). Responses elicited from slide representations of landscape simulations do not vary significantly from responses elicited to videotape representations of the simulated scene, and responses elicited from either slide or videotape representations of simulated images do not vary from responses to slides of the actual scene (Pitt et al. n.d.).

Analysis of Visitor Response Patterns. The responses of the visitors to the 72 roadway simulations were analyzed for each group of visitors using one-way analysis of variance and correlation analyses. The analyses were conducted separately for each of the four main effects in the survey (i.e. forest vegetation type, road width, roadway alignment, and roadside vegetation). For each visitor group, these analyses examined the following hypotheses:

H3: The mean standardized attractiveness values of roadways in red pine vegetation are not different than the mean standardized attractiveness values of roadways in jack pine or maple-beech vegetation.

H4: The mean standardized attractiveness values of roadways having a roadway width of 26 feet are not different than the mean standardized attractiveness values of roadways having a width of 20 feet.

H5: The mean standardized attractiveness values of roadways having an arcing alignment are not different than the mean standardized attractiveness values of roadways having an arc and tangent alignment.

H6: The mean standardized attractiveness values of roadways having grass on both the foreslope and backslope of the roadside ditch are not different than the mean standardized attractiveness values of roadways having grass on the foreslope and woody shrub vegetation on the backslope of the roadside ditch or roadways having woody vegetation throughout the roadside ditch.

Correlation analyses were also conducted on each visitor group wherein standardized attractiveness values were correlated with levels of the four main effects. The correlation coefficients (r) reveal the strength of any significant main effects. Finally, each visitor group's respective standardized attractiveness values were entered into a factorial analysis of variance with four main effects. These analyses reveal the same information as the one-way analyses of variance but they also permit examination of interactions among main effects. They also permit an examination of the overall strength of any main or interaction effects in explaining total variance in the response patterns, as revealed by the magnitude of the Coefficient of Determination (R^2).

Effects of Forest Vegetation on Perceived Attractiveness of Roadways. Backpackers are indifferent to the type of forest vegetation through which the roadway will pass. The attractiveness perceptions of non-hikers and day hikers, on the other hand, are sensitive to corridor vegetation. Both groups view the roadways containing maple-beech vegetation as significantly more attractive than roadways containing jack pine, and day hikers also discriminate significantly between red pine and jack pine.

Effects of Roadway Alignment and Width on Perceived Attractiveness. All three visitor groups see roadways having an arc alignment as significantly more attractive than the roadways with a tangent alignment, but none of the groups differentiates the attractiveness of 20-foot roadway widths from the attractiveness of 26-foot widths.

Effects of Roadside Ditch Vegetation on Perceived Attractiveness. Day hikers are indifferent to the presence of different vegetation management strategies in roadside ditches. Non-hikers, on the other hand, perceive ditches containing mown grass on backslopes and foreslopes to be significantly more attractive than ditches containing woody shrub vegetation on backslope and foreslope. Backpackers perceive ditches containing only woody vegetation to be significantly more attractive than ditches containing any amount of mown grass.

Combined Effects of Roadway Design Criteria on Perceived Attractiveness of Roadways. The results of the factorial analysis of variance reveals that the roadway attractiveness perceptions of all 315 visitors participating in the video simulation study can be explained with a 76 per cent accuracy rate by knowledge of the forest vegetation through which the roadway travels, the type of alignment present in the roadway, and the type of vegetation maintained in the roadside ditches (Table 1). Among visitor groups, the accuracy rate ranges from 38 per cent for the non-hikers to 81 per cent for the day hikers.

Similar factorial analyses of variance conducted on the responses of the three visitor groups yield significant interactions among the main effects for only the backcountry visitors. Table 2 reveals that four per cent of the total variance explained in the analysis of backcountry visitor responses (R^2 = .48) is attributable to two-way interactions between roadside ditch vegetation and corridor vegetation and between ditch vegetation and roadway alignment. The tendency for backcountry visitors to highly rate simulations containing woody roadside ditch vegetation is greater in maple-beech corridor vegetation. High ratings assigned by backcountry visitors to simulations containing woody roadside vegetation are also accentuated by the presence of an arcing roadway alignment.

Discussion of visitor perceptions of roadway attractiveness

The findings suggest that the picturesque is alive and well among visitors to the Pictured Rocks National Lakeshore. It is also clear that the backcountry visitors view the picturesque from its emotional and wild perspective while the day-hiking visitors and the non-hikers view the picturesque from its pastoral perspective.

Evidence for the use of the picturesque is found in the universal appeal of the arcing roadway alignment over the arc and tangent alignment. The curvilinear undulation of the arcing alignment is a classic representation of the role of the beautiful in establishing aesthetic appeal of the picturesque.

Table 1. Effects of Roadway Design Parameters on Attractiveness Perceptions of All Visitors (N=315).

Source of Variance	F-value	Adjusted R-square
Main effects		
Vegetation type	173.2**	0.6
Alignment type	43.7**	0.15
Pavement width	0.1	
Ditch vegetation type	0.5	
Two-way interactions		
Vegetation x alignment	0.01	
Vegetation x pavement width	0.1	
Vegetation x ditch vegetation	7.2*	
Alignment x pavement width	0.2	
Alignment x ditch vegetation	1.2	
Pavement width x ditch vegetation	0.2	

Total Adjusted R-square = .76

* F-values are statistically significant (p < .05).
** F-values are statistically significant (p < .01).

Table 2. Effects of Roadway Design Parameters on Attractiveness Perceptions of Backcountry users (N=59).

Source of Variance	F-value	Adjusted R-square
Main effects		
Vegetation type	0.2	
Alignment type	70.9**	0.2
Pavement width	0.2	
Ditch vegetation type	49.7**	0.24
Two-way interactions		
Vegetation x alignment	0.1	
Vegetation x pavement width	0.3	
Vegetation x ditch vegetation	59.3**	0.04
Alignment x pavement width	0.1	
Alignment x ditch vegetation	3.7*	
Pavement width x ditch vegetation	1.0	
Total Adjusted R-square = .48		

* F-values are statistically significant (p < .05).
** F-values are statistically significant (p < .01).

The patterns of response for the day hikers and especially for the non-hikers reveal an inclination toward use of the pastoral definition of the picturesque in assessing aesthetic values of potential roadway environments within the lakeshore. Both groups of visitors, but especially the non-hikers, exhibit strong preferences for the roadway when it travels through maple-beech vegetation. The non-hikers also exhibit preference for roadside ditches maintained with mown grass vegetation. As noted earlier, the presence of maple-beech vegetation and mown grass ditches are associated with the pastoral picturesque. They convey the smooth and rounded forms, delicate and fine textures, light colours and high levels of illumination typical of a Lancelot Brown landscape.

In contrast, the responses of the backcountry visitors respond to elements of the landscape more closely associated with the emotional and wild picturesque. The presence of the dark, dense, gnarled and scraggly looking jack pine vegetation has no negative effect on the backcountry visitor's evaluation of the potential roadway environments, being evaluated as no more nor no less attractive than red pine or maple-beech vegetation. The backcountry visitor also exhibits strong preference for woody vegetation in the roadside ditches, especially if the vegetation covers the entire ditch. The apparent wildness of the ditches under these conditions reflects the predilection of backcountry visitors toward the wilder parts of the lakeshore. Given that the backcountry visitors' trips are motivated by a desire for a first-hand experience of the backcountry, it is understandable that their perceptions of the simulations would employ the emotional and wild picturesque in evaluating the scenery of the lakeshore.

CONCLUSIONS

The purposes of this paper were to document various traditions of landscape aesthetics as defined by the eighteenth century picturesque theory and to demonstrate the pervasiveness of this theory in framing perceptions of attractiveness in the late twentieth century landscape. The paper traced the evolution of the beautiful and the sublime as definitions of attractiveness, and it explored the fusion of these opposing constructs in the creation of two renditions of picturesqueness, the pastoral and the emotional and wild. These concepts of landscape aesthetics were shown to permeate tourists' expectations for pursuit of scenic beauty in eighteenth century England and nineteenth century North America. The examination of visitor perceptions of roadway attractiveness in the Pictured Rocks National Lakeshore finds these constructs of landscape aesthetics still driving the definition of scenic beauty in the late twentieth century.

These findings are both gratifying and troublesome. They are gratifying because they provide yet another example that, while beauty may be in the eye of the beholder, our eyes are trained to see from a somewhat common perspective. It is also gratifying to see a perspective that can begin to fill the theoretical vacuum in which much of the landscape aesthetics work over the last 20 years has been conducted. While the theoretical constructs of the picturesque have been in existence for over two hundred years, very little of the empirical investigation of its tenets as a basis for evaluating twentieth century landscape has been attempted.

The fact that a visitor can hold either of two perspectives on the picturesque (i.e. the pastoral and the emotional and wild) and the finding that visitors to Pictured Rocks tend to align themselves with one or the other of these perspectives is troublesome to designers and managers responsible for orchestrating visitor experiences. At Pictured Rocks, backcountry visitors tend to use the emotional and wild perspective, while day-hikers and non-hikers tend to see the landscape from a pastoral perspective. To the extent that the use patterns of these visitor groups segregate themselves in time or space, the dilemma of which perspective to use in managing the landscape is clear. But in areas where use patterns overlap, such as in road systems or interpretive areas, the perspectives conflict with one another and an additional logic for management must be defined. For example in evaluating the alignment of the proposed Beaver Basin Rim Road, a curvilinear alignment should be located in maple-beech vegetation. Two out of three visitor groups perceive the roadways in maple-beech vegetation as more attractive than the pine vegetation, and the third group is indifferent to the type of vegetation present in the roadway corridor. The history of logging on the sandy plains of the lakeshore suggests that the pine communities are less resilient than the maple-beech stands to disturbances associated with roadway construction. The positive effect of the presence of maple-beech vegetation on the perception of roadway attractiveness coupled with the low resiliency of pine vegetation to disturbance argues for selection of a roadway alignment that is dominated by maple-beech vegetation.

The conflicting values perspective between the pastoral and the emotional and wild picturesque with respect to roadside ditch vegetation has two potential resolutions. Day hikers comprise at least half of all visitors to the lakeshore, and they are indifferent to the type of strategy used in managing ditch vegetation. Thus, a strategy of maintaining ditch foreslopes in mown grass vegetation and woody vegetation on the backslopes will be received favourably by at least half of the lakeshore's visitors. The presence of both grass and woody vegetation in the ditches will provide ditch vegetation patterns comprised of components acceptable to all three visitor groups.

An alternative strategy would involve mowing the entire ditch vegetation community. If current use patterns are any guide to future use patterns after development of the road, backcountry visitors are not likely to be frequent users of the Beaver Basin Rim Road. Their current patterns of use involve hiking from parking lots at either the Chapel Beach trailhead or the Grand Sable Visitor Center. Non-hikers perceive the mown ditches as more attractive than ditches containing any woody vegetation, and day hikers are indifferent to ditch vegetation management strategies. Thus, mowing the ditches would be perceived as appropriate by those groups of visitors most likely to drive on the Rim Road.

If the lakeshore were to adopt the strategy of mowing the roadside ditches to provide the pastoral experience desired by the non-hikers, one has to wonder about the sustainability of the policy choice. Mowing the ditches several times a season to maintain them in a grassland condition consumes fossil fuel energy. Given the droughty soils that characterize much of the lakeshore, a fertilization regime will also likely have to be maintained. Maintenance of a roadside ditch in grassland conditions will also amplify edge conditions in the adjacent forest. In short, maintenance of the pastoral picturesque landscape has many implications for the sustainability of the larger landscape through which the road will pass. This is a larger social issue as it questions the sustainability of landscapes created under picturesque conventions of aesthetics and requires exploration of landscape design theory that responds to ecological as well as aesthetic processes.

ACKNOWLEDGEMENT

The authors are indebted to Lance Neckar, Department of Landscape Architecture, University of Minnesota for his invaluable assistance with this paper. The research described in this paper was supported by the Midwest Regional Office and the Denver Service Center of the National Park Service through a cooperative agreement with the Cooperative Park Studies Unit at the University of Minnesota. The authors also wish to acknowledge the valued involvement and advice of park personnel at the Pictured Rocks National Lakeshore and professional staff at the Denver Service Center.

REFERENCES

Barbier, C.P. 1963. *William Gilpin: His drawings, teaching, and theory of the picturesque*. Oxford: Clarendon Press.

Bishop, I.D. & P.N.A. Leahy. 1989. Assessing the visual impact of development proposals: The validity of computer simulations. *Landscape Journal*, 8(2): 92-100.

Brown, P.J. 1984. Benefits of outdoor recreation and some ideas for valuing recreation opportunities. In G.L. Peterson and A. Randall (ed.) *Valuation of wildland resource benefits*. pp. 209-220. Boulder, CO: Westview Press.

Burke, E. 1757. *A philosophical inquiry into the origins of our ideas of the sublime and the beautiful.* London, England: R. and J. Dodsley.

Daniel, T. 1992. Data visualization for decision support in environmental management. *Landscape and Urban Planning,* 21: 261-263.

Ditton, R.B., A.J. Fedler & A.R. Graefe. 1983. Factors contributing to the perception of recreational crowding. *Leisure Sciences,* 5: 273-288.

Fairfax, S. & S.T. Dana. 1981. *Forest and range policy.* New York: J. Wiley and Sons, Inc.

Gilpin, W. 1792. *Three essays on picturesque beauty on picturesque travel; and on sketching landscape: to which is added a poem on landscape painting.* London, England: R. Blamire.

Graefe, A.R., J.J. Vaske & F.R. Kuss. 1984. Social carrying capacity: An integration and synthesis of twenty years of research. *Leisure Sciences,* 6: 395-431.

Hipple, W.J. 1957. *The beautiful, the sublime and the picturesque in eighteen century British aesthetic theory.* Carbondale, IL: Southern Illinois University Press.

Hussey, C. 1967. *English gardens and landscapes, 1700 - 1750.* London, England: Country Life.

Jackle, J.A. 1985. *The tourist: Travel in 20th century North America.* Lincoln, NE: University of Nebraska Press.

Knight, R.P. 1796. *Landscape: A didactic poem.* London, England: W. Bulmer & Co.

Knopf, R.C. 1987. Human behaviour, cognition and affect in the natural environment. In D. Stokols and I. Altman (ed.) *Handbook of environmental psychology.* pp. 783-825. Wiley: New York.

Manning, R.E. 1986. *Studies in outdoor recreation.* Corvallis, OR: Oregon State University Press.

McKechnie, G.E. 1974. The psychological structure of leisure: Past behavior. *Journal of Leisure Research,* 6: 27-45.

Perkins, N., 1992. Three questions on the use of photo-realistic simulations as real world surrogates. *Landscape and Urban Planning*, 21: 265-267.

Pitt, D.G. 1989. The attractiveness and use of aquatic environments as outdoor recreation places. In I. Altman and E.H. Zube (ed.) *Public spaces and places. Human behaviour and environment: Advances in theory and research.* pp. 217-254. Volume 10. New York: Plenum Press.

Pitt, D.G., J.I. Nassauer, D.W. Lime & D.J. Snyder. n.d. *The validity of video imaging presentation media as compared with photographic slides.* Unpublished manuscript. Minneapolis, MN: Dept. of Landscape Architecture, University of Minnesota.

Price, U. 1794. *An essay on the picturesque as compared with the sublime and the beautiful; and, on the use of studying pictures, for the purpose of improving real landscape.* London: J. Robson.

Schreyer, R. & J.W. Roggenbuck. 1978. The influence of experience expectation on crowding perceptions and social-psychological carrying capacities. *Leisure Sciences*, 4: 373-394.

Schreyer, R., D.W. Lime & D.R. Williams. 1984. Characterizing the influence of past recreational experience on recreation behavior. *Journal of Leisure Research*, 16(1): 34-50.

Vining, J. & B. Orland. 1989. The video advantage: A comparison of two environmental representation techniques. *Journal of Environmental Management*, 29: 275-283.

Yoesting, D.R. & J.E. Christensen. 1978. Reexamining the significance of childhood recreation patterns on adult leisure behavior. *Leisure Sciences*, 1: 219-229.

Zube, E.H., D.E. Simcox & C.S. Law. 1987. Perceptual landscape simulations: History and prospect. *Landscape Journal*, 6(1): 62-82.

BENEFITS-BASED RECREATION-TOURISM PARADIGM SHIFTS

Don Bruns
Bureau of Land Management
Colorado State Office

A new approach to leisure services has developed as a result of renewed interest in the value recreation adds to people's lives. When this conceptual framework is used to guide policy and management, it has been referred to as the Benefits Approach to Leisure (BAL). When the concept is applied to on-the-ground recreation-tourism service delivery systems, it has come to be known as Benefits-Based Management (BBM).

The expanded BBM model is advancing significantly traditional recreation-tourism management paradigms. It builds on existing activity- and experience-based frameworks, but does not require them. Its treatment of outputs goes beyond activity- and experience-based management by addressing the value which recreation adds to the lives of individuals (both participants and non-participants), households and communities, economies, and the environment. BBM stops assuming that any form of recreation is good, *per se*, and requires providers to explicitly identify the value to be added to the lives of customers through the recreation and leisure services supplied by the respective recreation opportunities.

The notion of benefits is rooted in the recreation movement of a century ago. Its founders maintained that recreation added value to people's lives, improved the human condition, and was therefore good in itself (Godbey 1995). Since then, practitioners, managers, policy makers, and academics alike have lost that clear focus. Instead they have focused on rearranging elements of the recreational setting, building facilities and programmes, and delivering services, but never questioning whether this kind of management indeed produced the desired results. BBM recognizes that recreation is not inherently good and, therefore, requires explicitly targeting those specific improved conditions that people want to achieve in any given recreation area through the respective facility development (Allen 1996). BBM thereby restores this essential value-added focus to the recreation profession.

In this regard, BBM represents no new thinking. New is the degree to which it makes explicit what was heretofore only assumed. Thus, BBM is, at one and the same time, both simple and complex.

The Experience-Based Management (EBM) framework first established the notion of managing for outputs. For several years, a set of recreation experience preference scales has been available for managers to expand their conceptual management framework (Driver, Tinsley & Manfredo 1991). In EBM, experiences were defined as psychological outcomes realized by individuals on-site, during recreation engagements.

Although we have substantial anecdotal evidence of how parks and recreation areas and programmes are improving the human condition (Parks and Recreation Federation of Ontario 1992; Sefton 1994), our publics still tend to regard parks and recreation areas as discretionary rather than essential services. Publicly supported services require greater responsiveness to community and social needs; the mere provision of recreation services is insufficient to satisfy public expectations (Allen 1996). A major weakness of the parks and recreation profession has been its assumption that the development and use of recreation areas and programmes automatically adds value to people's lives; by now it is known that this is not necessarily true (Allen 1996). BBM therefore targets specific value-added conditions by developing explicit BBM objectives. These benefits are subsequently translated into other beneficial consequences to individuals, society, and other entities.

The following definition of benefits adds clarification:

- changes that are viewed to be advantageous or improvements in condition (gains) to individuals (psychological and physiological), to groups, to society, or even to another entity such as an endangered species;
- the prevention of worse condition; and,
- realization of desired and satisfying on-site psychological experiences (Driver & Bruns 1997).

Figure 1 summarizes different stages of benefit production. In addition to the familiar on-site psychological outcomes, the framework distinguishes between other on-site benefits and off-site benefits along one dimension, and acknowledges that beyond the on-site psychological outcomes realized by individual participants (Bruns et al. 1994), these benefits also accrue to aggregate social structures such as households and communities, local and regional economies and the bio-physical and cultural landscapes. These additional benefits can be summarized as follows.

The other on-site benefits are the improved psychological and physiological conditions realized by visitors and residents alike. Examples include improved physical and mental health, restored mind from unwanted stress, improved self-image, restored body from persistent fatigue, and renewed human spirit.

Figure 1. Different Stages of Recreation Benefits

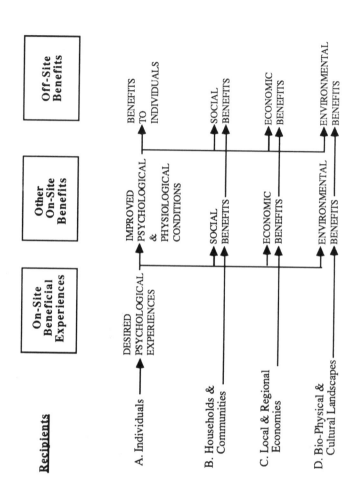

Off-site benefits to individual recreation users are the improved psychological and physiological conditions realized by customers off-site, and also include on-site benefits that endure off-site and off-site improved conditions that flow from on-site benefits through a "benefit chain of causality" (Lee & Driver 1992). These include an improved sense of control over one's life, increased adaptability, improved physical and mental health, improved self-image, and enhanced respect for traditional cultures.

On- and off-site benefits to groups of individuals also include improved conditions to society and culture, both on the household and community level. They include such things as improved functioning of individuals in family and community, reduced numbers of at-risk youth, heightened sense of community satisfaction, and better community integration.

On- and off-site benefits to local and regional economies include decreased job turnover, positive contributions to local-regional economic stability, reduced health costs, and well-equipped customers.

Lastly, on- and off-site benefits to the environment are the improvements to both natural and cultural aspects of the environment. They include such aspects as an improved relationship with the natural world, greater community involvement in environmental issues, and increased stewardship of the community's distinctive architecture.

WHAT BBM DOES

BBM expands the recreation-tourism manager's conceptual framework beyond a traditional preoccupation with activities and programmes. It does this by addressing explicitly the physical, social, and managerial setting inputs, and the consequent outputs that add value to people's lives as a result of theirs and others' leisure engagements. This expansion is achieved by (1) conceptualizing recreation and tourism services as inputs to the benefits production process, and (2) applying the integrated benefits-based framework to management, marketing, and monitoring/ evaluations.

The recreation production process: Wider understanding and application needed

BBM is a major catalyst in helping resolve two long-standing problems in the amenity disciplines (Driver 1994). The first is that recreation is not perceived widely enough as a production process (Figure

Figure 2. The Recreation Production Process

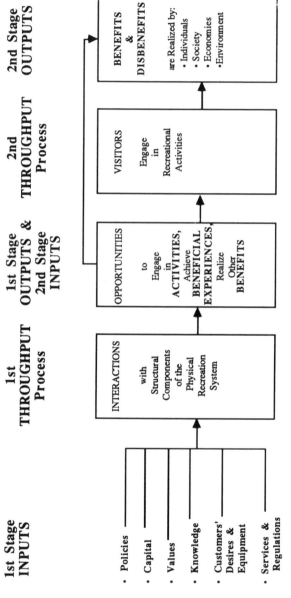

Adapted from B.L. Driver, The Recreation Production Process: The Benefits-Based Approach to Amenity Resource Policy Analysis & Management, In *Friluftsliv: Effeker og goder*, Dn-notat 1994-7, Direktoratet for Naturforvaltning Tungasletta 2, 7005 Trondheim, Norway, pp. 12-30

2) by recreation practitioners, managers, and policy analysts. The process begins with users and their paraphernalia, institutional policies, public and private capital, labour and entrepreneurial knowledge, and cultural values. Even our understanding of the production of first-stage outputs is not widely shared. It is the provision of opportunities for visitors to engage in certain highly-valued recreation activities (i.e., activity opportunities), to achieve certain satisfying experiences (i.e., experience opportunities), and to realize other value-added improved conditions and prevent worse conditions from occurring (i.e., benefit opportunities). An understanding of the production of second-stage outputs is perhaps the least widely-shared aspect of the production process. This stage includes the realization of benefits and disbenefits by both visiting and affected resident customers. Participants use these first-stage outputs as second stage inputs to produce benefits for themselves and others, affected communities, their economies, and even the environment. BBM's expanded conceptual framework embraces the entire production process. We are in this business to provide desirable settings wherein both visitors and residents can engage in desired leisure activities to improve their own condition and that of other individuals, their households and communities, their economies, and the environment.

The second problem BBM is helping overcome is that many recreation managers and policy analysts do not adequately apply and use the knowledge they already have. It has been known for nearly two decades that, within a hierarchy of recreation demands, people exhibit varying preferences for activities, for the settings within which they occur, and for resulting experiences those settings provide as a direct result of leisure participation (Driver & Brown 1978). Nonetheless, most managers are still working within the context of an activity-based management framework; the notion of managing settings as inputs to the production of explicitly-stated benefit outputs is still foreign to many recreation managers. BBM plays a key role in actually pushing managers out of traditional models of thinking about recreation and tourism by providing them with a working understanding of the recreation demand hierarchy. That is the subject of this paper.

Thinking and acting within a benefits-based conceptual framework

BBM shifts the almost exclusive setting and activity focus of parks and recreation management from means to ends. One can no longer afford to focus on-site management solely on the tangible elements of the product such as special designations, facilities, brochures and interpretive exhibits, visitor controls, and programmes. The results of those actions in people's lives deserve equal attention. What are we doing to ensure that the recreation-tourism service delivery system actually contributes something of value to our customers' lives? Do our actions lead to improved conditions and prevent worse conditions from occurring? Or, has the absence of a clear focus on outputs or outcomes at times degraded quality of life of our customers, caused a loss of value, and led to disbeneficial consequences?

BBM'S ROLE IN SHIFTING PARADIGMS

The limited understanding of the positive as well as the negative impact of recreation and tourism on society at a variety of scales is of growing concern. For example, the threats to the authentic early American character of small-town rural communities posed by business and industry's over-promotion of recreation and tourism use (Bruns & Stokowski 1995) is usually not addressed adequately in tourism and recreation planning. The failure of some community recreation directors to consider the impact of programme supervisor behaviour on outcome achievement can also make otherwise value-added recreation programmes distasteful and undesirable (Allen 1995). Driver explains the role of BBM in the following analogy:

Understanding activities only would be like a medical doctor only understanding that people come in limping, people come in with bloody noses and. . .without having any understanding of how he or she might somehow impact that client. I operate under the position that we in leisure need to gain the same level of understanding of specificity of what we are doing to and for people as a medical doctor does. I believe that very strongly. We have just as much social importance in the welfare and quality of people's lives as medicine, education, and other public services. But unless we get some Einsteins and Pasteurs in recreation who can help us articulate these benefits, we are still going to operate primarily in the intuitive realm and in the realm of quackery (Driver 1995).

BBM is playing a significant role in helping managers to shift their recreation-tourism paradigms. Wherever BBM is adopted and fully applied, recreation paradigms are being shifted in at least four broad areas: building collaborative management partnerships; managing to add value to customers' lives; providing definitive marketing, information, and education; and, sustaining improved conditions (Bruns 1995). These four areas coincide with four principal phases of BBM implementation.

Prior to completing a meaningful benefits-based customer assessment, partnerships must be built involving all recreation-tourism providers who will affect ultimately the character and availability of benefit opportunities. Such partnerships engage each provider in the assessment of customer desires, and each will benefit in direct proportion to the degree to which all providers are involved. So collaborating partnerships must first be initiated.

Next, under a BBM model, customer assessments are completed and results are applied, ideally at three levels: developing benefits-based management objectives; writing benefits-based plans for definitive marketing, visitor information, and education; and, formulating long-term, benefits-based monitoring and evaluation strategies to sustain delivery of targeted benefits. BBM is shifting recreation-tourism management paradigms at each of these four stages of implementation. The main body of this paper is therefore structured around these four components.

Building collaborative management partnerships

BBM is playing a significant role in stimulating community-based collaborative management partnerships (National Recreation and Park Association 1994) (cf., BBM implementation efforts on the Bureau of Land Management's Ruby Canyon-Black Ridge implementation pilot in Colorado). BBM is shifting managers' attitudes towards greater collaboration with other recreation-tourism providers in three significant ways.

First, in the area of collaborative management partnerships, BBM is shifting recreation-tourism paradigms by *recognizing* the necessity of involving all affected recreation-tourism providers in benefit opportunity delivery. In any community, each provider is, at least to some degree, dependent upon other providers who also contribute to the delivery of benefits and disbenefits to their clients.

At least three key sectors are inextricably involved in the delivery of recreation-tourism benefits: local communities and their governments, adjoining public land managing agencies, and private-sector support service providers. Local communities are hosts both to public land managing agencies and private-sector service providers. They host the customers of adjoining public land managing agencies and those of private sector business clients (including tour operators, outfitters and guides, recreational equipment, and retail sales customers) through their support service infrastructure, including park and recreation programmes. In terms of benefit opportunity delivery, neither public agencies nor private industry businesses can function apart from their community hosts.

The converse is also true. Public lands and support services contribute significantly to outdoor-oriented lifestyles, quality of life, and economic livelihood of rural communities. Service businesses make similar, no less significant contributions to the quality of life of local residents. It is this mix of all three sectors that gives rural tourism destinations their distinctive character and synergistically either contributes to or detracts from their desirability as places to live and work as well as visit.

Providers within all three sectors are inextricably involved in the recreation-tourism service delivery system. For example, customers shopping for mountain bikes are not just buying gears and gear frames. They are buying potential benefits. Biking for improved family bonding requires one kind of area and equipment while biking for improved fitness requires another. Good bike shop operators, canoe outfitters, and other equipment suppliers already know the differences and their implications for outing choices and benefit achievement. Wise land managers and tourism businesses will engage them as service partners in order to determine which customer segments want to develop improved relationships with the natural world; which ones want to acquire greater outdoor skills; and, which ones are looking for fitness or escape. Each requires different kinds of equipment and often a different destination. Even gas stations, restaurants, and lodging businesses must be considered as service partners and indispensable information sources about where customers can go to realize desired benefits. Each should know how to provide customers definitive information on the location and character of available benefit opportunities.

Mere recognition of the need for collaboration across all three sectors will neither establish a willingness to involve others, nor secure mutual commitments for collaborative management. While partnership is a "buzzword" of the 1990s, few partnerships are truly collaborative. A clear definition of genuine collaboration, embraced by all, is needed. Although most natural resource agencies have moved beyond autocratic modes wherein individual managers function as the decision-maker, most partnerships still function more interactively than collaboratively. Some managers, fearful of losing control of any decisions, keep themselves in the "driver's seat" (Bruns & Stokowski 1995).

By way of contrast, true collaboration "emerges from the community, honors a full spectrum of values and assumes that everyone is responsible for the community's success. There's no one leader, and no one is excluded from the table" (USDA Forest Service 1993). In genuine collaborative partnerships, all three key sectors empower each other and their stakeholders as equal partners to develop jointly a management plan, foreclosing all independent and advance decision-making. Within this model, each manager consciously shifts from "controller" to "facilitator," proactively enlisting the involvement of other providers as equals in a self-determining process, envisaging and managing to achieve a shared, desired future. Collaboration of this nature encourages partners to remain open to collectively identify issues and formulate a vision, management objectives, and implementing management actions (Bruns, Richardson & Sullivan 1995) (Figure 3).

Second, BBM is also shifting recreation-tourism paradigms in the area of collaborative management partnerships by *recasting* the notion of customer to include local host community residents as well as visiting guests. This shift in emphasis is required by the expansiveness of BBM's five dimensions—taking it beyond mere management for desired and satisfying psychological experiences—and by the translation of benefits through the benefit chain of causality. The off-site impact of recreation and tourism is limited neither to individuals nor to participants.

For example, from the Ruby Canyon-Black Ridge BBM Implementation Pilot in Colorado, "Meeting desired challenges/Enjoying risk-taking adventure" is an on-site beneficial experience which may be processed cognitively into the on-site benefit of "Improved outdoor knowledge, skills and self-confidence." This on-site individual benefit may subsequently survive off-site as well as be transformed into the "Greater cultivation of an outdoor-oriented lifestyle" and "Increased work productivity." While these later benefits continue to be realized by participants, they may also be realized by non-participants within the community. In the same way, the beneficial experience of "Enjoying learning about human's influence on the natural world" chains to "Improved understanding of the rural-urban interface" and "Improved understanding of how involvement in natural resource settings builds character." Each of these, in turn, is linked to significant environmental and social benefits off-site: "Improved understanding of human dependency on the land" and "Reduced numbers of at-risk youth" (Figure 4).

In this regard, BBM is turning out to be a major catalyst in helping dispel a popular myth among recreation's antagonists: that recreation and leisure provide something of value only as long as the activities last. BBM has moved the leisure profession forward a quantum leap by its explanation of how value continues to be added to people's lives following their on-site recreation engagements.

Figure 3. Collaborative Community-Based Planning

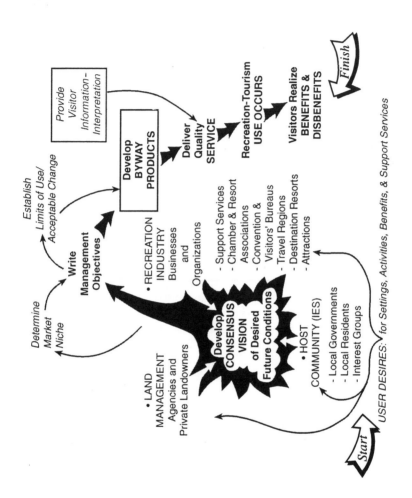

Figure 4. Significant Beneficial Experiences and Other Benefits: Black Ridge East-Pollock Canyon Complex

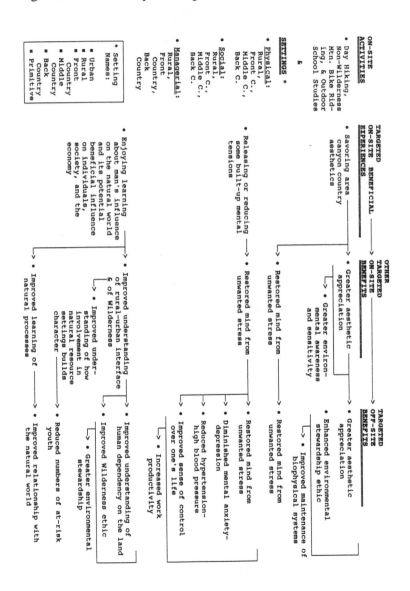

Thirdly, BBM is shifting recreation-tourism paradigms in the area of collaborative management partnerships by *redirecting* land managers and recreation-tourism businesses to hold themselves accountable to local host communities and their governments. Both public agencies and private sector businesses serve as guests within host communities where they work. In the past, each has too often functioned without this sense of local accountability. Federal land management agencies in the United States were once seen as more integral to their local communities than they are today, largely because they seem to have lost a sense of accountability to those communities over the past several decades (Chapman 1993). In the 1960s and 1970s, national environmental legislation and effective national interest groups turned heads towards Washington D.C. and away from the local scene. Yet real accountability still exists to local as well as national and regional publics. On the positive side, some of this is being regained as public agencies and local governments attempt to pool their resources in the face of dwindling budgets, and there is growing evidence of a genuine desire for community-based partnerships that involve collaborating public and private, federal and local providers as equals (National Recreation and Park Association 1994; USDA Forest Service 1993).

Activities provided by private sector recreation-tourism support services also can impact local communities substantially. Like public institutions, private sector providers depend upon and benefit from local community infrastructure and services, and their clients benefit from amenity resources within the community and on public lands. Though private sector business decisions are made within the free enterprise system, the impacts of those decisions are felt and shouldered by local, state, and national public agencies and especially by local host community residents. Recreation-tourism industry businesses are, · therefore, increasingly pressured to change the way they do business and own up to this impact. Managing to deliver desired benefits provokes both public and private providers to build and sustain mutual accountability relationships with local communities and their governments.

Managing to add value to customer's lives

Recreation-tourism providers too often have been preoccupied with resource, visitor, and programme inputs to the physical recreation system. Yet managing only on the basis of system inputs does not address behavioural impacts to our customers. BBM expands this perspective by explicitly considering the degree to which actions yield benefits as well as disbenefits.

BBM's enlarged conceptual framework relates the way park and recreation areas and programmes are managed—addressing their physical, social, and managerial attributes—to benefit opportunity availability. It helps managers to define the improved conditions desired by different market segments, specify with greater precision the opportunities provided to realize those desired improved conditions, and explain where those opportunities will be provided. Where economic issues have historically overshadowed other values, as in tourism-dependent communities, BBM helps bring greater parity to non-economic values; it helps to quantify the psychological and physiological value recreation adds to individuals' lives and the social and environmental value it adds to households and communities. It, therefore, helps to guide important recreation-tourism planning decisions and subsequent implementation actions. For monitoring and evaluation, BBM helps managers to measure the degree to which conditions are improved for different beneficiaries. BBM technology helps to determine who ends up achieving the improved conditions targeted. When used as a framework for marketing, BBM also enhances consumer sovereignty; it enables visitors to match up their own benefit preferences with the recreation areas, facilities, and programmes that can best satisfy their desires. In summary, BBM advances the recreation-tourism profession (Driver, Brown, Peterson & Bruns 1991).

First, in the area of value-added management, BBM is shifting recreation-tourism management paradigms by *requiring* identification of all customers' expectations, both of visiting and resident customers. BBM brings an entirely new meaning to the term market analysis. For BBM practitioners, customer analyses no longer centre on profit margins and the identification of new markets for increased sales. Currently, the commercial dimension of tourism is so dominant that some recreation professionals have actually defined tourism as the commercial side of recreation (Lennon 1992). The BBM model captures non-economic values of recreation and tourism. Whereas more traditional recreation-tourism market analyses focus on the identification of traveller profiles and reaching new markets, BBM expands this focus to target improved conditions which both visitors and participating host communities seek from recreation and tourism (Allen 1996).

The most definitive BBM assessments of recreation-tourism visitors completed at the time of this writing are correlating expressed customer benefit opportunity desires and their perceived benefit achievement with specific geographic or administrative units within individual recreation-tourism attractions and areas and with the activities and settings through which they are realized. Substantial variation in benefit preferences has been shown to occur among users of adjoining areas that offer different attractions within different physical, social, and managerial settings and that provide different opportunities for recreation activity engagement. Moreover, individual benefit opportunity preferences may also vary by trip characteristics, social profiles, and social units of participation. BBM implementation pilots are finding both qualitative and quantitative analyses useful. Qualitative assessments (e.g., who, what, when, where, and why) are useful in narrowing the list of potential benefit opportunities to be quantitatively assessed through actual surveys (e.g., how much).

The point is not to draw a sharp distinction between the two types of assessments (e.g., some have falsely maintained that focus groups do not involve interviews; yet all qualitative assessments, by their very nature, must involve at least some degree of quantification if their results are to be useful), but to point out that some very valuable information on customers' expectations may be obtained through qualitative methods without having to rely solely on structured surveys. In the Ruby Canyon-Black Ridge effort, for example, both community influentials and recreation providers were interviewed through focus groups to ensure that quantitative assessments of expectations were geared to the kinds of improved conditions of greatest concern to different groups. Quantitative instruments were designed to link visitors' desires for satisfying activities to both the desirability and attainment of specific benefits—and their preferences for associated physical, social, and managerial setting attributes—all within the context of well-defined geographic zones.

If the Ruby Canyon customer assessment were to be completed with our current understanding of benefits, it would look very different. With each new BBM implementation effort, our knowledge of how to design instruments to effectively quantify and differentiate among different customers' expectations is improving (Appendix A).

Secondly, BBM is shifting recreation-tourism paradigms in the area of value-added management by *redefining* recreation-tourism products. These are primarily not highly-valued physical, social, and managerial setting inputs of important attractions and destinations but are rather the explicitly-stated benefit opportunity outputs. Heretofore, recreation-tourism management objectives dealt almost exclusively with the nature of resource and cultural attractions, facilities, the nature of support services, and programmes. Having identified who the customers are and their desires, BBM asks the question "What are the value-added conditions that you will target for realization by your various customers?"

Managers' abilities to deliver confidently desired benefit opportunities by specifying the exact, determinative setting inputs is improving. These relationships are not yet as well defined as most managers would like, but BBM implementation efforts presently underway are demonstrating that enough is known to proceed. Additional research is needed to establish a more precise relationship between social and managerial inputs to the physical recreation system—including the land and facilities, visitors, and the administrative/programme environment—and resulting benefit opportunity availability (Allen 1996).

Certainly, the recreation-tourism service delivery system does require building and maintaining facilities, caring for the land, managing programmes, informing visitors, and interpreting attractions. Support service businesses surely cannot survive without reasonable profit margins, and both providers and consumers understand recreation activity opportunities more readily than they do beneficial experiences and other resulting benefit opportunities. However, BBM reveals that management focused on areas, programmes, and activities alone provides an insufficient basis for meeting customer desires. The need is urgent for both public and private sector recreation and tourism services to identify the value-added conditions in greatest demand, explicitly target them in their management plans, clearly communicate them to their customers, and continuously monitor and evaluate them to ensure their long-term delivery (Allen 1996).

Even if recreation-tourism managers were only to think about their day-to-day management activities in terms of benefits provided—to different individuals, affected households and communities, their economies, and the environment—it would revolutionize their jobs, and their customers' satisfaction. Some may object that BBM is nothing new, that they have always had in mind the good of their clients and customers; however, at the time of this writing only a few recreation-tourism management plans are being written with explicitly-targeted benefits-based management objectives. But more than a mindset, BBM leads to the development of explicitly-stated benefits-based objectives; these address both determinative setting inputs and desired activity and benefit opportunity outputs. Explicitly-stated, time-bound, and quantifiable objectives foster public accountability, promote mutual understanding, and serve as standards of control for delivering real customer value.

Thirdly, BBM is shifting recreation-tourism paradigms in the area of value-added management by *repositioning* the service delivery system. Except for economic benefits, most policy makers and governing bodies continue to view recreation and tourism services as discretionary rather than essential. This is no less a problem for the tourism industry than it is for other leisure service providers. Some public policy-makers may find it difficult to view the tourism industry, which is primarily occupied with economic gain—sometimes at the expense of host communities where it operates as a guest—as providing anything essential. Related public recreation and tourism agencies thus tend to compete rather poorly for public funding against other more well-documented social service providers (Allen 1996).

Against this tradition, BBM actually pushes recreation-tourism managers to take a longer view of their organization's contribution to the public good. BBM's conceptual structure does this by prompting managers to address all categories of benefits—individual, societal, economic, and environmental. Recreation providers are finding a pressing need to reposition their services to ease significant community problems and proactively capture opportunities to meet the essential human needs of its citizens, community influentials, and decision makers (Crompton 1993).

BBM drives recreation and tourism managers to demonstrate how recreation and tourism contribute real value to local communities and to society at large. To do so, providers collectively must shift their service delivery systems away from discretionary services and "Beyond Fun and Games" (National Recreation and Park Association 1994) to meet their customers' desires for improved individual, societal, economic, and environmental conditions.

Providing definitive marketing, information, and education

To communicate clearly which benefit opportunities are being targeted, BBM requires a greater emphasis on educating our people, at all levels of our organization and informing an increasingly discriminating clientele consisting of both resident hosts and visiting guests. Even if collaborating managers do a good job targeting and providing customers' desired benefit opportunities, without a firm commitment among recreation-tourism providers to help both resident and visiting customers understand the nature of benefits—including exactly which ones are provided, where, and how to obtain them—actual benefits will not be realized.

Before addressing the specific role which BBM is playing in shifting marketing paradigms, we first will look at how BBM is changing the perspective of communities where recreation-tourism providers from each of the three key providing sectors are developing a better understanding of their impact on local communities and visitors in terms of benefits or disbenefits. Plog (1991) explains that, given enough promotion, a natural progression occurs which steadily moves recreation-tourism attractions up the scale from being unknown, uncharted areas to well-developed and well-known destination resorts. With that progression comes a loss of authenticity and a more synthetic recreation-tourism experience. This spells bad news for any community whose customers desire benefits that are determined by its distinctively authentic setting characteristics.

Plog is right; well financed but indiscriminate tourism promotion and development is changing natural and cultural landscape features. Often an accompanying push to expand and modernize the supporting infrastructure completely transforms attractions. The challenge is to arrest this progression at the point desired by the community, before things get out of hand. To do that requires a vision for the future and a plan to achieve it.

All of this underscores the importance of completing management plans and developing products before any marketing occurs. First, in the area of marketing, information, and education, BBM is shifting recreation-tourism paradigms by *reordering* the way of doing business. First comes visioning, then the development of a management plan containing explicitly-stated benefits-based management objectives, visitor service/marketing plans, and a long-term evaluation strategy. If promotion could be listed first, options could be foreclosed (Figure 5).

Presently, promotional pieces are too often considered the initial, if not primary, tourism development strategy; producing a better brochure is often the first response to marketing challenges and the first action considered by any community or agency wanting to "get into recreation and tourism." When the promotional piece of marketing occurs prior to product planning, product development, and service delivery planning, it lacks focus and content and betrays an inadequate understanding of the recreation production process. As non-touristic areas are being promoted as the place to go, discovered by more and more people, and more heavily developed, they change character and lose their existing appeal and productive capacity (Plog 1991). The distinctiveness of host communities, public lands, and community facilities and programmes are inevitably lost. The resulting composition of available benefit opportunities changes accordingly. Current customers, community residents as well as guests, are displaced by new customers having different benefit desires.

When providers set market forces in motion by starting with tourism promotion, they miss out on many opportunities for responsively managing recreation-tourism attractions. Providers thereby preclude development of a strategy for ensuring optimum kinds and levels of visitation. Not having identified customer desires, providers lose the flexibility needed to target their most highly-valued products, and, having opened the door to use and development, they risk losing their distinctive market niche. The promotion of recreation-tourism opportunities must clearly be reordered to the back of the line (Figure 5).

Figure 5. Recreation-Tourism Collaborative Planning Framework

Step 1: IDENTIFICATION OF ISSUES & PROBLEMS
- Community Attitudes Inventory
- Issues Identification with all Partners

Step 2: COMMUNITY ATTRACTIONS AND SERVICES
- Natural Resources
- Cultural Resources & Local Cultures
- Recreation Resources
- Hospitality Resources
- Attractions
- Adequacy of Lodging-Restaurant and Transportation Services

Step 3: VISIONING PROCESS
- Community Values/Attitudes Inventory
- Desired Future Community: Lifestyles & Quality of Life Issues
- Identification of Product "Niche"
- Management Goals & Objectives

Step 4: RECREATION-TOURISM PRODUCTS
- **Public Land & Community Resource Protection, Enhancement and Development**
  - *Maintenance of Resource Quality*
  - *Recreation Attractions*
  - *Monitoring & Protection*

- **Infrastructure Protection, Enhancement and Development**
  - *Accommodations*   - *Transportation/Traffic*
  - *Restaurants*   - *Medical/Police/Fire*

Step 5: VISITOR SERVICES, FACILITIES & INTERPRETATION
- Visitor-Guest Services
- Interpretive Plan
- On-site Support Facilities

Step 6: MARKETING & PROMOTION
- Identify Markets
- Establish General Marketing Strategy & Techniques
- Establish a Promotion Program

Step 7: FUNDING & FINANCING
- Types & Sources of Funding /Revenue
- Budget/Funding Program
- Fund Leveraging
- Financial Projections

Step 8: MONITORING AND EVALUATION
- Implementation Assessment
- Visitor/Customer Reassessment

Step 9: IMPLEMENTING COLLABORATIVE MANAGEMENT STRATEGY
- Partnership Management Roles
- Cooperative Management Agreement(s)

BBM is also shifting recreation-tourism paradigms in the area of marketing, information, and education by changing the content of product messages and how they are presented. It does this by *refocusing* marketing away from "lure piece"-driven sales and promotion to match customers with products that meet their desires (Knopf 1990). It involves providing prospective consumers with definitive enough information about products, and the market niche they occupy, so they are enabled to find the exact areas meeting their desires. This requires all the skills of the interpreter's art to inform visitors and residents about the precise character of physical, social, and managerial setting inputs as well as of activity and benefit opportunity outputs. Embracing BBM is profoundly shifting the marketing approach taken by both the tourism industry and the recreation service partners.

The traditional tourism industry's reliance on "lure pieces" is legendary. The industry's well-named promotional standard is designed with all the cunning of an angler's lure. As all good anglers know, lures are designed to deceive. Likewise, lure pieces are designed to entice increasingly greater numbers of visitors, not necessarily get them to the areas offering what they really want. These efforts are a poor substitute for thoughtful marketing plans designed to help potential visitors find the exact areas that can satisfy their leisure desires for a variety of value-added improved conditions. By way of contrast, benefits-based marketing is about truth in advertising (Figure 6).

A commitment to manage for benefits means offering customers a reasonable hope of finding out what benefit opportunities are being provided, instead of "showing off" attractions in alluring, four-colour brochures. The well-known movie "Field of Dreams" popularized the phrase "If you build it, they will come." In recreation and tourism management, just because recreation opportunities are built and people visit does not mean that everyone will benefit. BBM insists on going further: "If you provide desired benefit opportunities—and answer what, where, and how to get them—they will be realized."

A genuine concern for customer service will also incorporate in the marketing message user ethics messages to prepare visitors well before their arrival for the behavioural expectations of providing partners, host community residents, and previous visitors who have already acquired a sense of ownership of the attractions. Target messages need to go beyond the current resource-based emphasis of "Tread Lightly" and "Leave No Trace" back country and wilderness education programmes. To promote responsible use and enjoyment and desired Benefit achievement, they must convey a leisure ethic that recognizes the interdependent sustainability of biophysical and socio-cultural systems (see Figure 6:

Figure 6. Some Key Marketing Essentials of BBM

Design: Marketing is telling prospective visitors what providers have agreed to provide
   • It must not precede development of a vision for the community's future.

Content: Marketing is telling prospective visitors about the diversity of recreation-tourism
   opportunities available
   • It must contain definitive information on the range of available opportunities.

Ethics: Marketing is preparing prospective visitors for what to expect when they arrive
   • It must inform people about the expectations which the three distinct community
   groups have of their behaviour: local residents, other visitors already there, and the
   providers.

Some Key Marketing Essentials of BBM also "Sustaining Improved Conditions," next section) and that harmonizes the expectations of community residents and visiting customers and collaborating recreation-tourism providers.

Last but not least, for all of the above reasons, BBM's role in shifting recreation-tourism paradigms is stimulating renewed commitment to inform and educate both customers and recreation-tourism managers and service delivery staff about the BAL and its practical application in BBM. In this regard, several helpful publications are now available, most of which explain the nature of BBM are now available: *The Benefits of Leisure* (Driver, Brown & Peterson 1991), *The Benefits of Parks and Recreation: A Catalogue* (Parks and Recreation Federation of Ontario 1992), *Benefits of Recreation Research Update* (Sefton 1994), *The Benefits of Local Recreation and Park Services* (National Recreation and Park Association 1992), and *Beyond Fun and Games: Emerging Roles of Public Recreation* (National Recreation and Park Association 1994). At the time of this writing, at least three user guides on implementing BBM and a text on understanding and implementing BBM are being written. One of the guides has just been published by the Alberta Recreation and Parks Association (Peterson 1996). None of these publications should be viewed as "cook books." The huge paradigm shifts embodied in BBM cannot be reduced to a series of mechanical steps; BBM is not simply another management tool.

Sustaining improved conditions

Increasingly concerned about quality of life issues and the potential loss of both resource and community distinctiveness, rural communities and public land managers are becoming more concerned about their ability to sustain delivery of opportunities for visitors and residents alike to realize desired benefits. At risk is not only their economic future but, of equal or greater importance, their quality of life and the distinctive character of the recreation-tourism amenities that make any community both an attractive place to live and to visit.

First, in the area of sustaining improved conditions, BBM is shifting recreation-tourism paradigms by *relating* the interdependency of biophysical and socio-cultural systems. The issue here is maintaining the integrity and interdependent productivity of land and resources and of distinctive communities and their cultures. Some sustainable ecosystem management proponents, for example, have maintained that everything begins with the land and its resources; that we cannot have healthy communities unless we first have healthy and productive natural ecosystems. It is equally true that the productive quality of lands and resources cannot be sustained unless the society and culture of those charged with caring for those lands is also healthy and stable (Thompson & Driver 1995; Blahna 1995). In the author's experience, academics, managers, and business entrepreneurs predisposed either to resource preservation or to development and growth have great difficulty accepting that there is indeed an interdependent sustainability of both systems.

Thus, public land management agencies committed to ecosystem management must begin not only with the identification of desired future conditions for natural systems, but also with the development of a self-determining vision for their community's own desired future. Collaborative, community-based partnerships will not be nurtured where land managers insist that resources come first. Neither will they be nurtured where community leaders predicate resource conditions upon a community's desired future. Likewise, private sector recreation-tourism businesses must live up to their responsibility to build a community-based infrastructure of attitudes and ideas (Murphy & McGinniss 1992).

BBM is also shifting recreation-tourism paradigms in the area of sustaining improved conditions by *reorienting* public and private recreation-tourism providers towards long-term monitoring and evaluation. Such ongoing evaluation must address the quality of biological, physical, social, and cultural features upon which the sustained delivery of identified benefit opportunities depends, as well as actual benefits achieved. This represents a significant expansion of the tourism industry's traditional focus on short-term economic gain. Here, too, an adequate understanding of the recreation production process facilitates the emerging ideal (see Figure 1). Recreation-tourism providers can only influence the realization of benefits by properly managing setting inputs. A firm commitment to an ongoing programme of monitoring benefit achievement, and supporting BBM research, is essential if we are ever going to establish definitive input-output linkages. In Colorado's Ruby Canyon-Black Ridge area, for example, initial plan recommendations commit managers to an ongoing programme of customer research to evaluate whether desired benefit opportunities are being provided and the degree to which desired benefits are actually being achieved. Under the BBM conceptual framework, monitoring and evaluation must employ socio-cultural benefit measures as well as biophysical resource, facility, and programme measures. Continued collection of benefits-based social data will be a litmus test of both public and private recreation-tourism providers' commitment to implement a BBM conceptual framework. It requires bridging BBM philosophy and practice. Without it there is no use talking about sustaining delivery of desired benefit opportunities.

CONCLUSION

BBM is bringing the leisure profession back to its roots. BBM is recreation management framework that builds on existing activity- and experience-based frameworks, but goes beyond them by explicitly addressing the value which recreation adds to people's lives. The recreation movement was rooted in the notion that leisure adds value to people's live and is therefore good. This value-added focus, however, cannot be restored without considerable change to traditional recreation management paradigms which remain focused predominantly on the physical recreation system and recreation activities. Recreation management must get beyond the simple promotion of leisure benefits to actually change the way we do business, designing our programmes to add explicit value to the customer. Without shifting both the models that guide thinking about recreation and tourism and actual practice, the implementation of BBM will be ill-fated.

What is required? More than academic esotericism and the exercise of semantics. Verbs employed to describe BBM's paradigm shifts convey a sense of active change: *recognize, recast, redirect, require, redefine, reposition, reorder, refocus, relate, and reorient.* Moving beyond mere rhetoric, these changes are impacting positively the entire service delivery system. Full implementation of BBM is changing profoundly the way all contributing leisure opportunity providers work, within the context of community-based collaboration. It demands commitment to the ongoing assessment and monitoring of both visitor and resident expectations. It is enabling leisure service providers to gear management actions towards the realization of explicitly defined, value-added outcomes for participants as well as for local residents. It is changing visitor information programs and practices, and significantly improving the accuracy and objectivity of their marketing messages by detailing targeted benefits. It is also moving both public and private sector partners to sustain the delivery of value-added benefits by maintaining the physical and cultural integrity of recreation systems and accompanying service delivery systems.

Appendix A. Sample Portion of Quantitative BBM Survey Instrument

C. EXPERIENCES AND BENEFITS

1. We would now like to know more about the Experiences and Benefits you realized from the most satisfying activity(ies) you just listed for Zone #_____

  a. Please rate how DESIRABLE each of the Experiences listed were to you for that Activity (or those Activities) within this Zone, and...

  b. The degree to which you were able to REALIZE or ATTAIN each of the Experiences listed:

Individual Experiences:	a. DESIRABILITY							b. ABILITY TO ATTAIN			
	Very Undesirable	Moderately Undesirable	Somewhat Undesirable	Neither Undesirable nor Desirable	Somewhat Desirable	Moderately Desirable	Very Desirable	Not At All Able	Somewhat Able	Moderately Able	Totally Able
• Developing your skills and abilities	-3	-2	-1	0	+1	+2	+3	1	2	3	4
• Having others think highly of you for doing this	-3	-2	-1	0	+1	+2	+3	1	2	3	4
• Testing your endurance	-3	-2	-1	0	+1	+2	+3	1	2	3	4
• Enjoying the closeness of friends	-3	-2	-1	0	+1	+2	+3	1	2	3	4
• Enjoying risk-taking adventure	-3	-2	-1	0	+1	+2	+3	1	2	3	4
• Having your family enjoy being together	-3	-2	-1	0	+1	+2	+3	1	2	3	4
• Quickly accessing outdoor areas close to home	-3	-2	-1	0	+1	+2	+3	1	2	3	4
• Enjoying meeting new people with similar interests	-3	-2	-1	0	+1	+2	+3	1	2	3	4
• Learning more about things here	-3	-2	-1	0	+1	+2	+3	1	2	3	4
• Savoring area aesthetics, including scenery	-3	-2	-1	0	+1	+2	+3	1	2	3	4
• Enjoying reflecting on your personal values	-3	-2	-1	0	+1	+2	+3	1	2	3	4
• Doing something creative	-3	-2	-1	0	+1	+2	+3	1	2	3	4
• Contemplating man's relationship with the land	-3	-2	-1	0	+1	+2	+3	1	2	3	4
• Enjoying physical exercise	-3	-2	-1	0	+1	+2	+3	1	2	3	4
• Getting some needed physical rest	-3	-2	-1	0	+1	+2	+3	1	2	3	4
• Releasing or reducing some built-up mental tensions	-3	-2	-1	0	+1	+2	+3	1	2	3	4
• Escaping everyday responsibilities for a while	-3	-2	-1	0	+1	+2	+3	1	2	3	4
• Feeling good about being isolated	-3	-2	-1	0	+1	+2	+3	1	2	3	4
• Enjoying being away from your family for a while	-3	-2	-1	0	+1	+2	+3	1	2	3	4
• Finding pleasure in helping direct others' activities	-3	-2	-1	0	+1	+2	+3	1	2	3	4
• Having others nearby who could help you if needed	-3	-2	-1	0	+1	+2	+3	1	2	3	4

REFERENCES

Allen, L.A. 1996, March. A primer: Benefits-based management of recreation services. *Parks and Recreation*, 31, (3) 65-76.

Allen, L.A. 1995. Benefits: The next step. Paper presented at *NRPA Congress for Recreation and Parks, Education and Training Session*. San Antonio.

Blahna, D.J. 1995. Integrating social and biophysical factors in ecosystem management: Quest for the philosopher-king. In J.L. Thompson, D.W. Lime, B. Gartner and W.M. Sames (eds.) *Proceedings of the Fourth International Outdoor Recreation & Tourism Trends Symposium and the 1995 National Recreation Resource Planning Conference*, pp. 507-512. University of Minnesota, St. Paul.

Bruns, D. 1995. New paradigms for outdoor recreation and tourism management in government. In J.L. Thompson, D.W. Lime, B. Gartner and W.M. Sames (eds.) *Proceedings of the Fourth International Outdoor Recreation & Tourism Trends Symposium and the 1995 National Recreation Resource Planning Conference*, pp. 425-430. University of Minnesota, St. Paul.

Bruns, D., M. B.L. Driver, M. Lee, D. Anderson, & P.J. Brown. 1994. Pilot tests for implementing benefits-based management. In *The Fifth International Symposium on Society and Resource Management*, pp. 192-193. Colorado State University, Fort Collins.

Bruns, D., S. Richardson, & T. Sullivan. 1995. Recreation-Tourism Partnerships for Sustainable Adventure Travel. In *The Fifth International Symposium on Society and Resource Management*, pp. 134-135. Fort Collins: Colorado State University.

Bruns, D. & P. Stokowski. 1996. Sustaining opportunities to experience early American landscapes. In B.L. Driver, D. Dustin, T. Baltic, G. Elsner and G. Peterson (eds.) *Nature and Human Spirit: Expanding Land Management Ethics*, pp. 321-338. State College: Venture Press.

Chapman, M. 1993. Observations—From the back of the pumpkin truck. Paper delivered at the University of Colorado Natural Resources Law Centre conference *New Era for Public Lands, the Points West Lecture Series for the Centre for the New West*. Boulder, Colorado.

Crompton, J.L. 1993. Repositioning recreation and park services: An overview. In *Trends*, Vol. 30, No. 4. Washington, D.C.: National Park Service, 2-5.

Driver, B.L. 1995. Benefits-based management. Colorado Outdoor Recreation Resource Project, General Meeting. Denver.

Driver, B.L. 1994. The recreation production process: The benefits-based approach to amenity resource policy analysis and management. In *Friluftsliv: Effekter og goder*, pp. 12-30. Dn-notat 1994-7, Direktoratet for Naturforvaltning.

Driver, B.L. & P.J. Brown. 1991. Research on leisure benefits: An introduction to this volume. In B.L. Driver, P.J. Brown, and G.L. Peterson (eds.) *Benefits of Leisure*, pp. 3-11. State College: Venture Publishing.

Driver, B.L. & P.J. Brown. 1978. The opportunity spectrum concept and behavioral information in outdoor recreation resource supply inventories: A rationale. In G.H. Lund et al. (eds.) *Proceedings, Integrated Inventories of Renewable Natural Resources*, pp. 25-27. Fort Collins: Rocky Mountain Forest and Range Experiment Station, USDA Forest Service General Technical Report RM-55.

Driver, B.L., P.J. Brown, G.L. Peterson, & D. Bruns. 1991. Background Paper No. 1 for Leisure Benefits Application Workshop. Unpublished paper.

Driver, B.L. & D. Bruns. 1997. Underlying concepts and uses of the benefits approach to leisure. In Tim Burton and Ed Jackson (eds.) *Leisure Studies at the Millennium*. State College: Venture Publishing Inc. (in Press).

Driver, B.L., H.E.A. Tinsley & M.J. Manfredo. 1991. The paragraphs about leisure and recreation experience preference scales: Results from two inventories designed to assess the breadth of the perceived psychological benefits of leisure. In B.L. Driver, P.J. Brown, and G.L. Peterson (eds.) *Benefits of Leisure*, pp. 263-286. State College: Venture Publishing.

Godbey, G. 1995. Why the paradigm shift to the BAL? In *Abstracts of the Paper and Poster Presentations at the 1995 Leisure Research Symposium, 1995 National Recreation and Parks Association Congress.* NRPA, Arlington. 41.

Knopf, R.C. 1990. Marketing public lands: Is it the right thing to do? *Parks and Recreation Magazine,* 25(3), 57-61.

Lee, M. 1995. A benefits-based approach to leisure services. In J.L. Thompson, D.W. Lime, B. Gartner and W.M. Sames (eds.) *Proceedings of the Fourth International Outdoor Recreation & Tourism Trends Symposium and the 1995 National Recreation Resource Planning Conference,* pp. 348-356. University of Minnesota, St. Paul.

Lee, M. & B.L. Driver. 1992. Benefits-based management: A new paradigm for managing amenity resources. Paper presented at *The Second Canada/US Workshop on Visitor Management in Parks, Forests, and Protected Areas,* University of Wisconsin, Madison.

Lennon, T. 1992. Keynote Address. At Basecamp Opportunities for the 90's: Adventure Travel in South Central Colorado. Colorado Springs.

Murphy, R. & G. McGinniss. 1992. Rural Culture and Values. In: *Small Towns: Culture, Change and Cooperation,* pp. 63-81. Salt Lake City: Western Governors' Association.

National Recreation and Park Association. 1994. *Beyond "Fun and Games": Emerging Roles of Public Recreation.* Arlington.

Peterson, C. 1996. *Benefits Based Recreation, Awareness Into Action: A Guide Book,* Alberta Recreation and Parks Association, Edmonton.

Plog, S.C. 1991. *Leisure Travel: Making it a Growth Market...Again!* New York: John Wiley and Sons, Inc.

Sefton J. 1994. *Benefits of Recreation Research Update.* Alberta Centre of Well-Being, Edmonton.

The Benefits of Parks and Recreation. 1992. Gloucester: The Parks and Recreation Federation of Ontario, 22-82.

Thompson, J.G. & B.L. Driver. 1995. Integrating the Social and Biophysical Components of Sustainable Ecosystem Management: The Need to Create a Culture of Civility. In J.L. Thompson, D.W. Lime, B. Gartner and W.M. Sames (eds.) *Proceedings of the Fourth International Outdoor Recreation & Tourism Trends Symposium and the 1995 National Recreation Resource Planning Conference*, pp. 503-506. University of Minnesota, St. Paul.

USDA Forest Service. 1993. Report of the National Workshop: The Power of Collaborative Planning. FS-553, Washington, D.C.: USDA Forest Service.

COMBINING CALIBRATED DIGITAL IMAGERY AND DISCRETE CHOICE EXPERIMENTS: AN APPLICATION TO REMOTE TOURISM IN NORTHERN ONTARIO

Wolfgang Haider
Simon Fraser University

Jordan J. Louviere
University of Sydney

Donald A. Anderson
StatDesign

Brian Orland
University of Illinois

Terry C. Daniel
University of Arizona

Michael Williams
Intelligent Marketing Systems

INTRODUCTION

This paper presents a novel approach to researching user group preferences in a natural resource management context. Two established yet hitherto separate methodologies, discrete choice experiments (DCE) and calibrated digital imagery (CDI), are combined in an innovative way. DCEs, originally developed in transportation and market research, also have been applied successfully to researching issues in tourism, recreation, and resource management (Louviere & Timmermans 1990; Haider & Ewing 1990). Traditionally DCEs have relied predominantly on stimulus presentation in written form. While this form of presentation is appropriate for most applications, it may not be the most efficient, precise, and lucid vehicle of stimuli presentation in some circumstances, such as documenting possible changes in a landscape. This was the research problem encountered in the project described below, where the focus is on identifying and measuring the effects of timber management on remote tourism in northern Ontario.

This paper focuses primarily on the development of the research instrument. First remote tourism in northern Ontario and its land use conflict with timber management will be discussed. Then, based on the results of a pilot survey we will explain the need to pursue the integration of CDI and DCE, and conceptualize the research question accordingly. The main part of the paper focuses on the research design and the steps taken to successfully accomplish the task. Finally, some preliminary results will be presented, including a brief explanation of how the results can be used to build a decision support system.

THE ISSUE: REMOTE TOURISM AND TIMBER MANAGEMENT IN NORTHERN ONTARIO

Resource-based tourism makes a significant contribution to the regional economy of northern Ontario. Approximately 1,400 outfitting businesses (50 per cent of the Canadian total) operate throughout the region, of which about 25 per cent are remote operations (Fisheries & Oceans 1989). It is estimated that in the North Algoma region alone the total spending on operations, capital improvements and acquisitions by 22 remote tourism operations amounted to $8.1 million in 1988, providing 380 person years of employment (Econometric Research Ltd. and Ontario Ministry of Tourism and Recreation 1990).

Remote accommodations are not accessible by road, and rely on access by float-plane or, in some cases, train. Remote lodges consist of several cabins grouped around a main facility. They vary considerably in size and quality, offering either American plan or housekeeping arrangements. Outpost camps are plywood or log cabins with few amenities (bedrooms might be separate from living areas), and are located on a lake by themselves, or in a secluded portion of a larger lake.

Because of the emphasis on proximity to nature and perceived wilderness, this form of tourism is particularly sensitive to any kind of disturbance by other land uses, of which timber management is the most common. The major effects of timber management on resource-based tourism are:

• noise, generated by harvesting equipment and logging road traffic;

• aesthetics, if cut areas are visible from ground, lakes, or air; and,

• access, if newly constructed forest roads provide access for road-based anglers and hunters to previously remote areas (ESSA 1987).

This land use conflict has been documented in the Class Environmental Assessment of Timber Management on Crown Land in Ontario (Environmental Assessment Board 1994), ongoing local timber management planning processes (Duinker 1991), and, recent academic literature (McKercher 1992). Despite long-standing recognition of the problem, little empirical research has been conducted on resource-based tourism and recreation in northern Ontario. In order to increase the general understanding about the land use conflict from a tourism perspective, and eventually to improve existing timber management guidelines, the Ontario Ministry of Natural Resources (OMNR) has embarked on a long-term research program to study the effects of timber management on resource-based tourism in northern Ontario. Research efforts are complicated by the lack of basic data which could be used for more detailed analysis beyond a synoptic description of the phenomenon. For example, no complete listings and basic descriptions of tourism operations exist, yet operations are distributed over a vast area and vary enormously in size and quality.

A pilot survey

A pilot survey of visitors to remote operations in North Algoma in the summer of 1991 provided some basic understanding and description of remote tourism, and also provided an opportunity to test the methods for their usefulness in measuring the sensitivity of clients to the presence of logging activities (Haider & Carlucci 1994). Mirroring what is typical for most remote tourism businesses in northern Ontario, almost 90 per cent of the respondents originated in the United States. Almost half the respondents stayed for seven days, with shorter trips of three or four days also popular. Typically, group sizes varied between three and six individuals per party, depending on cabin configurations. The significance of social aspects of the trip are emphasized by the fact that about 40 per cent of all respondents travelled with friends, about 20 per cent with family, and 25 per cent with a combination of family and friends. Single clients or other types of group arrangements occur infrequently.

Given the nature of the remote tourism product, it is not surprising that fishing and motor boating were the most popular outdoor activities of all client groups (over 95 per cent participate frequently in fishing), followed by wildlife viewing and photography (over 40 per cent participate frequently and another 40 per cent occasionally). All other activities were of much less importance, but may be significant in specific circumstances, such as the opportunity to portage or boat to another lake for a different fishing experience. The survey also inquired about the importance of wilderness aspects combined with fishing quality as the essence of the remote experience especially important for outpost clients.

The questionnaire also asked about awareness and possible effects of nearby timber harvest operations during the respondent's past vacation. The paucity of positive responses could be interpreted as an indication of successful mitigative measures applied during timber harvest, but more likely resulted from limitations in the sampling approach because respondents consisted only of 1991 visitors. Therefore the survey was unable to account for possible visitor losses in previous years.

In anticipation of that shortcoming, the second part of the survey contained a DCE, a stated preference research technique. Results of the DCE indicated that this experimental technique is well suited to model the range of salient attributes of a remote tourism experience such as accommodation characteristics, travel distances, and fishing quality, but failed to provide meaningful estimates for the variables describing timber management effects.

CONCEPTUALIZATION OF RESEARCH PROBLEM

Upon review of these results, it was concluded that the major deficiency in the pilot DCE was the presentation of the timber management effects in the form of written profiles. All these effects actually relate to visual phenomena, such as type of forest, width of buffer zone, location of a major road, size and age of cut. During a workshop in 1991 the improvements that CDI could provide to traditional DCEs were recognized and the feasibility of joint projects was established.[1]

By applying a multi-attribute research technique, one is able to understand and forecast the likely consequences of timber management practices on the demand for remote tourism in northern Ontario. In particular, the OMNR needs to understand how typical forest management practices like clearcutting, cut patterning and buffering affect tourist choices of remote facilities in northern Ontario. The primary objectives of this study were:

• to measure the extent of the likely effects; and,

• to develop an approach to forecasting the likely consequences of timber management practices on remote tourism demand in northern Ontario.

These objectives can be met by focusing on the tourists' decision-making process, in which they decide whether to participate in a remote experience, and if so, which remote experience they choose. Thus, if timber management practices influence tourist decisions, their influences might be explained as one or a combination of the following:

• primary demand for the remote tourism experience itself, possibly triggering the decision by tourists to no longer consider remote tourism as a desirable form of vacation because of the changed experience;

- choices between Ontario and other geographical locations with which it competes, e.g., Quebec, Manitoba, British Columbia, Alaska; and,

- choices among remote locations within Ontario.

The first two effects would have far reaching consequences for both Ontario and its remote tourism industry in general. The third impact would be felt differently by the various operators and would have implications for both specific areas and operators. Understanding these types of consequences requires a rigorous analysis of the decision-making process of tourists in the target market for remote experiences in northern Ontario. We required a research approach that would allow us to gain insight into tourist decision-making and choice processes, and more importantly would enable us to quantify the likely effects of changes in timber management practices on the choices tourists will make. At the same time, the research approach also needed to account for other competing areas and activities from which tourists could choose in order to understand fully if and how tourists will substitute other destinations or activities for the northern Ontario experiences in response to potential changes in timber management practices.

METHODS

In their respective fields, discrete choice experiments and calibrated digital imagery each have proven to be powerful techniques, enabling a precision of prediction and estimation of human values hitherto impossible.

Discrete choice experiments

The discrete choice experiment, also known as Customer Decision Analysis (CDA) (Louviere 1988; Louviere & Woodworth 1983; Anderson & Wiley 1992; Anderson et al. 1991), is a multi-attribute experimental research technique with origins in economics (random utility theory, see McFadden 1974) on one side, and psychology (information integration theory, see Anderson 1980) and market research (conjoint analysis, see Green and Srinivasan 1978) on the other. Two separate statistical design steps are required for optimal statistical estimation of effects: first, as in conjoint analysis, a fractional factorial design is used to generate an appropriate set of scenarios or profiles, describing the management issue or activity under consideration; second, individual profiles are combined to create choice sets, which are included in a questionnaire, and respondents either choose the most preferred alternative of every set, or do not choose.

Calibrated digital images

The idea of using images calibrated to known resource attributes to derive human values is not new. Malm et al. (1981) used image processing techniques to develop images of pollution plumes in the Grand Canyon based on the output of numerical models of atmospheric dispersion. Those images were used to derive human values for the impacts predicted on scenic resources in the Canyon. That study established the effectiveness of computer techniques, but used computing resources beyond the means of typical natural resource agencies. Orland (1988) described the availability of micro-computer based tools capable of the same range of image manipulations, but at much lower cost. The basic technique in use was to digitize photographic images and then use either editing or image processing software to make changes to the base image to represent anticipated changes. The use of those tools has evolved and become more sophisticated, and they have been used in a variety of settings for eliciting human responses to changes in the natural landscape (see Orland 1993 for a review of application types). Specific applications with forestry relevance include Baker and Rabin's (1988) study of the visual effects of limb rust damage on national forest settings in northern Utah, and Orland and others' (1993) study of the impacts of insect damage and silvicultural responses on the scenery of the Dixie National Forest in southern Utah.

THE STUDY DESIGN

Attribute selection

Results from the pilot study (Haider & Carlucci 1994), as well as from information gathered in focus group interviews in four cities (Detroit, Chicago, Minneapolis, Toronto) (Daniel & Orland 1993), were combined with expert knowledge from government and industry to narrow down the list of salient attributes to a manageable number. Table 1 lists 12 verbal attributes describing the type and quality of the accommodation,[2] fishing quality and regulations, travel distance, as well as noise associated with timber management operations, and cost of the package. It also refers to two images which represented a typical view in

Table 1. Attribute List

• ACCOMMODATION
American Plan lodge $440 (590)
American Plan lodge $530 (725)
American Plan lodge $620 (860)
American Plan lodge $710 (995)
American Plan lodge $800 (1130)
Housekeeping lodge $280 (360)
Housekeeping lodge $350 (465)
Housekeeping lodge $420 (570)
Housekeeping lodge $490 (675)
Housekeeping lodge $560 (780)
Outpost camp
(no running water) $295 (395)
Outpost camp
hot shower) $395 (545)
• SETTING
Frequent wildlife along shore
Occasional wildlife along shore
• CROWDING
No other lodges or anglers on the
    lake
No other lodges, occasional other
    anglers fly in or portage in
Another lodge on the lake, but no
    other anglers fly or portage in
Another lodge on the lake, and
    occasional other anglers fly or
    portage in
• WALLEYE
Good
Excellent
• NORTHERN PIKE
Good
Excellent
• LAKE TROUT
Not available
Good

• BASS
Not available
Good
• LIMITS
6 fish possession limit, no size restrictions
6 fish possession limit, only
1 trophy size
3 fish possession limit, only
1 trophy size
Catch-and-release only, one trophy can be kept
• EXPECTATIONS
Mostly moderate size, occasional trophy
Mostly moderate size, often a trophy
Moderate to large in size occasional trophy
Moderate to large in size, often a trophy
• NOISE
No shore noise
Occasional noise near the lake
Occasional noise in the distance
• DRIVING TIME (home to airbase)
375-525 miles (easy day drive)
575-725 miles (long day drive)
775-925 miles (day and a half drive)
975-1,125 miles (two day drive)
• FLY-IN TIME
15 minutes
30 minutes
45 minutes
60 minutes
• DISTANT IMAGE
[4 levels, selection based on scaling of image bank]
• SHORELINE IMAGE
Pristine
See-through buffer
Logged hill in background

Table 2. Attribute List of Visual Variables Contained in Oblique Aerial View.

BUFFER
30-100 m
500 m
1,000 m
3,000 m

RESIDUALS
None
Hardwood (single, dispersed)
Conifer (patches)
Conifer (single)

ACCESS ROAD(distance from lake)
None
50-100 m
500-700 m
2,000 m or more

FOREST TYPE
Conifer
Mixed wood

SIZE OF CUT
Small (15% of area)
Large (50% of area of more)

SHAPE
Regular (straight lines)
Irregular

BLOCKS
One
Multiple

AGE
Fresh (brown)
Green

approximately six to ten kilometres distance and a typical shoreline view respectively. Table 2 contains the eight attributes relating to timber management, all of which were represented in one oblique aerial scene. The number of levels for each attribute varied between two and eight.

Experimental design

When fitting a statistical design to these attributes, the following criteria must be met:

• every level of every attribute should appear an equal number of times;

• within a choice set (in the present case consisting of pairs of alternatives A and B), the combination of levels of every pair of attributes should appear with equal frequency; and,

• the combination of levels of each attribute from alternative A, when paired with any from B, should appear with equal frequency.

These conditions are met by considering each of the set of profiles making up Alternatives A and Alternatives B respectively as separate orthogonal resolution III fractional factorial designs, and the pairings are organized in such a manner that the overall design is itself an orthogonal design (Dey 1985).

The final design required 128 pairs of A and B alternatives, or 256 distinct remote destination profiles to meet the third condition above. These 128 pairs were blocked into eight sets of 16 pairs each such that each set of 16 satisfied the first condition above. Each block represents one questionnaire version, so that one respondent completed 16 choice tasks only. Figure 1 is a schematic layout of that overall design. Columns represent attributes, and rows represent choice sets, organized into blocks. Note the 32-level attribute in column 31, which enabled us to tie the complex oblique aerial scene containing the eight logging related attributes to the main design efficiently. Without that design adaptation, 256 digitally calibrated oblique aerial scenes would have been required, which would have made the study prohibitively complex and expensive. By developing a sub-design for the oblique aerial scene and linking it to the main design in a 32-level attribute, we were able to limit the number of distinct images to 64, or 32 pairs (Figure 2).

The structure of the design for oblique images also allowed us to introduce pristine images. This was important because we needed to compare any of the timber management scenarios to a no treatment situation. This was accomplished by systematically replacing treatment scenes with pristine scenes in such a manner that, over the full design, each of the 32 treated image pairs appear twice as they are, once with the alternative A side replaced with a pristine image, and once with the alternative B image replaced with a pristine image. At the same time this iteration was held constant within each block so that each respondent, seeing a total of 16 choice sets, would evaluate exactly eight treated pairs and eight pairs comparing a treatment with no treatment, in effect satisfying the statistical design criteria.

Applying calibrated digital imagery

In a previous study of ski resorts (Daniel & Orland 1993), collages of images were used to represent typical conditions of hypothetical scenery and visitor facilities. For that purpose individual images were pulled from a library. Any one image represented only one attribute, and different attribute levels were documented with different original images. Images were scaled to verify their validity in representing the attribute and attribute level. The present case, though, presented a much greater challenge because a larger number of attributes were represented visually, and an additional level of complexity was added by the interactions among those attributes in the visual display. For example, size of forest cutting operation cannot be separated from the forest type, the shape and location of the cut, what is left as residual, or the stage of recovery of the cut. This distinction made it necessary to combine these attributes in one scene, and to edit the single image accordingly to match specifications from the factorial design so that the appropriate attributes could be viewed and evaluated concurrently.

The first step in image creation was to create a library of source imagery. A major concern was to replicate and standardize the views typically experienced by remote anglers when travelling to their destinations. During the summer of 1992 more than 2,000 oblique photos of forest conditions were collected, using float planes chartered for the task and flying from four representative areas in northern Ontario. As much as possible, plane altitude was kept at approximately 600 metres (2000 feet) for general photos, and at approximately 300 metres (1000 feet) for details of ground conditions. All photos attempted to include the horizon within the frame to ensure consistent angle of declination and coverage area. Photos were taken using acrylic bubble windows mounted on the right side of the aircraft and affording a wide angle of view.

Figure 1. Schematic Layout of Research Design

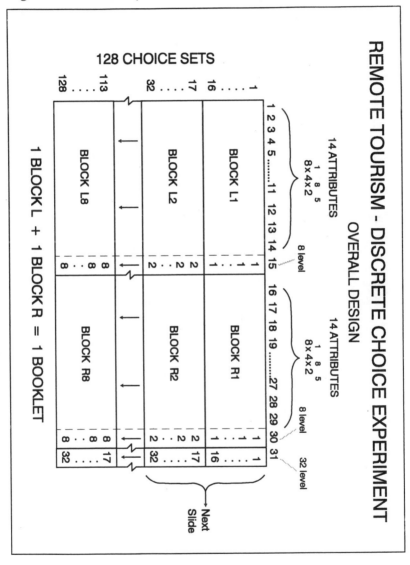

Figure 2. Design-Oblique Image

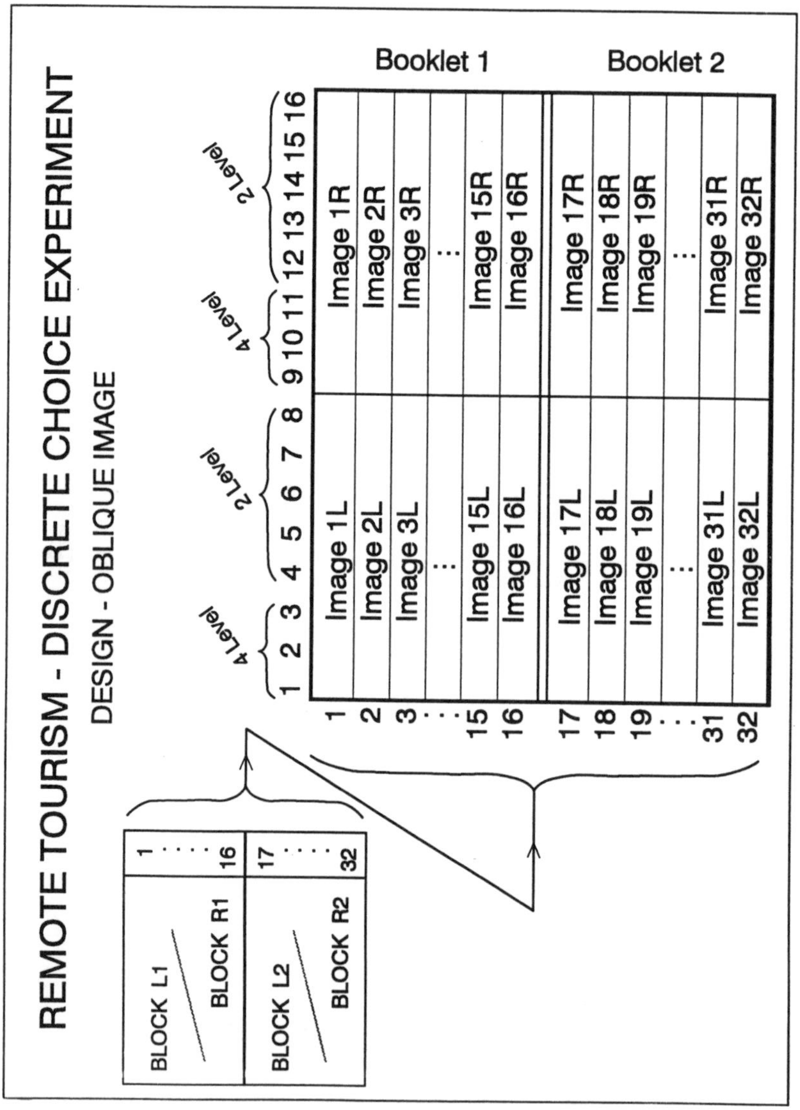

Photos were taken with a hand-held 35-mm camera with auto focus and auto exposure. The majority of photos were taken at a 50-mm focal length setting. A moderate telephoto lens of 85-mm focal length was used at times for finer ground detail. Film was Kodak Ektachrome EPP, a 100 ASA semi-professional colour film with reasonable speed and good colour rendition. A polarizing filter was used at all times and camera direction of view was held between 15 and 60 degrees of a line directly opposing sun bearing. These latter two measures were to maximize colour saturation.

Before undertaking any collection of photographs, the study team was briefed by OMNR scientists on the salient attributes of forest condition and current silvicultural practices. Areas containing the treatments sought by the study team were located via maps and remote sensing imagery. Flight routes were planned to intersect such regions of interest but were frequently altered as new opportunities were presented. Accompanying OMNR staff tracked flight routes on large scale maps for later verification of ground conditions corresponding to key photos.

Four hundred images were selected from the entire set based on an appraisal of image quality as well as suitability for filling the experimental design requirements. These images were reviewed to verify that there was ample representation of the required attributes and levels in the set. Individual attributes and levels were identified in images and delineated on sketches. This provided the image editors with a library of typical conditions and notes on where to find those in the total set.

These baseline images were transferred to Kodak Photo-CDs. Standard Photo-CDs hold about 100 images at five resolutions from 192 x 128 to 3072 x 2048 pixel and 24-bit colour depth (16.7 million colours achievable). The middle resolution, 768 x 512, was used for this project, a compromise between quality needed and the size and concomitant complexity of large image files. Orland (1993, 1988) has described the evolution of typical uses of these PC-based imaging tools, the basic techniques, and issues of image validity and utility.

At first, all images underwent histogram equalization to achieve the best consistent contrast and colouration throughout the image set. It was clear at the outset that the study design would necessitate considerable image editing and the use of an extensive number of source images. From that source image bank 32 base images were selected, based on photographic quality, and water and horizon composition. Each of these base images was to be used twice in the experiment to avoid repetition for any one respondent. The other source images provided prototypical samples for the various forest treatments that appeared as attributes in our experimental design. Holding the attributes forest type, buffer width, and roadway constant for each base image generated further efficiencies. Decisions regarding attribute selection and other design issues were made during one further workshop that brought together project researchers and ministry foresters. Once the design issues were resolved, the assembly of the images was a somewhat mechanical process of taking image portions and combining them to fit the design specifications.

To verify further the shared understanding of forest conditions, one staff member from OMNR was present in the imaging lab in Illinois for a week-long intensive workshop to choose base images and to identify prototypical attributes and attribute levels, as well as to direct image editors in course of the composition process.

After the first attempt to meet design specifications, all images were sent to OMNR in draft form for review and feedback. Reviewers marked the printed images and provided instructions for the editing process. A similar review process was repeated.

Both rounds of reviews were conducted by a team of researchers and ministry foresters in a rigorous manner. Written profiles stating the attribute levels of each profile were compared with the corresponding image by every reviewer individually, as well as in a round-table discussion. The entire set of images was arrayed for each attribute in turn in piles corresponding to every attribute level, to check whether an attribute level was truly well-represented in the emerging images. For example, all 30-100 metre buffers were compared to all 500 metre buffers, ensuring a discrete representation of each attribute level. After two rounds of review all 64 scenes matched the design description in a satisfactory manner so that no further modifications were required, even though the imaging lab was prepared to do so.

For distant and shoreline images it was felt sufficient to ensure that the levels represented were clearly separated and scaled appropriately. Our approach was similar to that employed in the earlier study of ski resort values, in that the images were treated as symbolic of the kinds of conditions encountered. Since there was no attempt to represent a complex range of attributes, such as that for the oblique views, we felt this was justified. The alternative, to identify and scale a further 32 pairs of images to represent these two attributes, was too expensive and time-consuming to consider for this study.

SURVEY INSTRUMENT AND DATA COLLECTION

The final instrument consisted of a spiral binder booklet for each of the eight versions, and each booklet contained 16 choice sets. Each profile took up one page so that the two profiles making up one choice set faced each other. Each profile contained three images. The top image (approximately 5" x 3") represented the oblique aerial view with the eight logging related attributes. Two further images (approximately 3" x 2") represented a typical scene in four to six miles distance from the destination lake, and a typical shoreline scene of the destination lake respectively (Figure 3). The verbal descriptions referring to the accommodation, the setting, fishing quality and regulations were printed on the same page. In effect, the photo album resembled an actual tourist brochure in both appearance and content. Separate booklets were prepared for outpost camps and lodges because results in the pilot survey indicated only little substitution between these two forms of accommodation.

Respondents were presented pairs of remote destination profiles, and were asked to choose between alternatives A and B, which in effect forced respondents to make trade-offs between the various attributes. If neither A nor B were acceptable, respondents always had the option of choosing some other fishing vacation such as another remote destination in Canada (not in Ontario), road based camping on Crown land, a road based camp in Ontario or the U.S., or a fishing trip somewhere else.

Tourists were sampled at seven travel trade shows in Minnesota, Illinois, Wisconsin and Michigan in the winter of 1994. Space was leased for booths at each trade show and an attractive, appealing display was developed to attract potential fly-in anglers visiting the show. Respondents were intercepted at these shows, pre-screened for familiarity with the remote tourism product, equipped with an appropriate survey instrument. They completed the entire task at the booth. Over 1,000 completed questionnaires were obtained balanced over the region sampled. In addition to the choice experiment, relevant socio-demographic and past behaviour questions were included in each survey.

PRELIMINARY DATA ANALYSIS

The choice data obtained from the sample are currently being analyzed using statistical methods appropriate for discrete multivariate response data. By definition, choices are discrete because the tourist can choose to be in only one remote location at a time, or the tourist can decide not to choose. In the present case, multinominal logit models are estimated using maximum likelihood for a number of strategically important market segments.

Figure 3. Example of Profile

Area immediately around your facility on the destination lake

Accommodation:
    Outpost camp (running water, hot shower)
    4-day $590, 7-day $845
    No other fishermen on the lake
    15 minutes fly-in time

Setting:
    Occasional wildlife along shore
    No shore noise

Fishing:
    Good walleye fishing
    Excellent northern pike fishing
    No lake trout fishing
    No bass fishing

Limits & Expectations:
    Catch and release only, one trophy can be kept
    Mostly moderate size fish, occasional trophy

Distance:
    575 - 725 miles (long day drive)

Example: view 4 - 6 miles away

Example: shoreline view

Due to lack of space, not all part-worth utilities derived from the multinominal logit models can be listed here. Table 3 lists the estimates for selected visual attributes for the lodge and outpost models, and the discussion below is exemplary of the kind of findings one can expect in the course of further analysis.

For residuals and roads, no significant differences were observed between the lodge and outpost clients; therefore, the estimates are identical. Respondents clearly preferred patches of conifers left as residuals. Single conifers were already significantly less preferred, and no residuals and hardwood left standing were evaluated as the most inferior options. A primary or secondary logging road within one hundred metres of the lake was perceived as severely distractive, while respondents were indifferent to all other levels of roads. For buffer attributes, differences emerged between lodge and outpost clients. Furthermore, a significant interaction between buffer and age of cutover was also observed and included in the model. As expected, clearcuts closer to the lake (narrow buffer) are evaluated more negatively than cuts further away, and older (greened over) cuts are preferred over young (brown) cuts. Increasing buffer width proved to be of lesser importance to lodge clients, who in turn documented a higher sensitivity with regard to age of cut. In the situation where the width of buffer is only 100m, the difference between old and young cutovers diminishes only for the outpost clients, who perceived both as equally negative, while lodge clients preferred the older cutovers as significantly more acceptable.

Among the written attributes the following items emerged as highly significant: price of accommodation, abundance of walleye and northern pike, possession limits (notably with the highest preference for six fish, of which only one can be trophy size), noise, driving time (only the furthest distance is perceived as truly negative). As explained above, the design also enabled us to consider a truly pristine situation separately from the wide range of logging scenarios covered by the experimental design. Not surprisingly, the pristine situation is preferred significantly.

The preliminary analysis produced no significant differences between the three major market areas surveyed (Michigan, Illinois/Wisconsin, and Minnesota). However, significant differences were observed between respondents with a remote experience and those without. For example, inexperienced respondents were much more likely to opt for a four day package as opposed to a seven day package, and were also less consistent in their evaluation of logging related attributes.

Table 3. Results - Selected Part-Worth Utilities

	LODGE		OUTPOST	
BUFFER	Green	Brown	Green	Brown
30-100m	.029	-.167	-.076	-.134
500m	.087	-.107	.088	.032
1,000m	.094	-.100	.088	.032
3,000m	.094	.070	.204	.318
RESIDUALS				
none		-.056		-.056
hardwood (single)		-.081		-.081
conifer (patches)		.143		.143
conifer (single)		-.005		-.050
ACCESS ROADS				
none		.066		.066
50-100m		-.179		-.179
500-700m		.066		.066
2,000m or more		.066		.066

The most powerful aspect of the analysis is that it is possible to calculate the probability of choice for any one of the possible combinations that can be derived from the attribute file by feeding the respective part-worth utilities into the multinominal logit expression. While tedious when done by hand, this aspect can be used to build a behaviourally based interactive decision support system for PCs, which allows managers easily to simulate and evaluate a wide range of potential scenarios and use the predicted change in tourist choices to answer some strategic questions about the likely impact of timber management practices. With the decision support system, one also can obtain some competitive analysis by allowing Ontario locations to compete with one another or with locations in Alaska or elsewhere. With the introduction of various user groups and market segments, the explanatory power will be enhanced further.

DISCUSSION

Making photographic images fit the fractional factorial design plan is rather different from the traditional method of developing profiles in written form. The technology placed significant demands on the researchers' ability to represent systematically a range of forest conditions visually, and at the same time to communicate them effectively to an audience of non-specialists, while the attributes needed to remain meaningful to experts and managers.

Verbal phrases can be readily combined into descriptive sentences and ranges of attribute levels can be substituted into a matrix of other sentence parts as verbs or conjunctions, etc., without disrupting the meaning of the sentence (e.g., the lake is one km away, . . . is two km away, . . . is more than three km away). Visual images carry, in addition to the attribute desired, orientation, shape, scale and texture, all referring to a particular, real place. There is no equivalent of the conjunction in making images, and therefore creating complete coherent images is much more difficult than creating a working sentence.

The consequence is that while a verbal phrase can be used as a surrogate for a general concept of forest attributes, a picture implies a specific location and thus cannot stand as a surrogate for multiple situations. Given our intention to develop visual protocols to represent ranges of resource attributes, it was essential to address the constraints posed by images early in the design process.

Our response was to ensure that no picture of a place should appear more than once in a set of images seen by a single respondent. Our belief was that if any base image were seen repeatedly by one respondent representing different mixes of forest attributes, then the focus of attention might shift from judgment of the benefits of one resort destination over another, to a game where the respondent tried to guess what was going on, and to find any errors and omissions in the images themselves. This belief is untested; we acted out of a conservative impulse to avoid any unanticipated problems.

Weighed against this is the issue of experimental control. Seeing representations of the same resource attribute in different contexts brings into question the validity of how attributes are represented. Our decision was to validate the attribute representations using an expert review panel of forest managers and scientists.

The image editing processes are time-consuming and expensive. Despite the extensive preparation work, it was difficult for the image editors to achieve a good fit between image parts. It also was taxing intellectually to synthesize the multiple concurrent demands of the study design into a single image. However, at this time the realism achievable by more direct data-driven visualization tools is not good enough to support choices involving the appearance of scenic resources. However, as computer modelling and visualization become a bigger part of resource management, it is evident that more efficient and less expensive sources of imagery for studies such as this will follow.

While a strictly economic viewpoint would dictate that potential users wait until costs fall, this application demonstrated that many of the conceptual and methodological hurdles perceived initially can be overcome and technologies can be combined successfully. The lessons learned along the way will make for more effective use in future settings in the attempt to include human values in the decision-making process of natural resource management.

NOTES

[1] The workshop was hosted by the Ontario Ministry of Natural Resources, and involved key proponents of the discrete choice experimental approach (Donald Anderson, Jordan Louviere, Harry Timmermans) and calibrated digital imagery (Terry Daniel, Brian Orland). Their first collaboration was a study for the U.S. Forest Service North Central Forest Experiment Station on the contribution of scenery to the value of ski resort experiences in the Wasatch Mountains outside Salt Lake City (Daniel & Orland 1993).

[2] Please note that the attribute 'accommodation' combines type of accommodation and price of the package.

REFERENCES

Anderson, D.A., A. Borgers, D. Ettema, & H. Timmermans. 1991. Estimating availability effects in travel choice modelling: A stated choice approach. *Transportation Research Record* 1357: 51-60.

Anderson, D.A. & J.B. Wiley. 1992. Efficient choice set designs for estimating availability cross-effects models. *Marketing Letters* 3/4: 357-370.

Anderson, N.H. 1981. *Foundations of information integration theory*. New York: Academic Press.

Baker, F.A. & D. Rabin. 1988. Using computer graphics to assess the visual impact of limb rust in Ponderosa Pine. *Utah Science*. Utah Agricultural Experiment Station, Logan: UT. 49(4): 98-102.

Daniel, T.C. & B. Orland. 1993. *Visual simulations for recreation choice modelling*. US Forest Service Co-op Agreement.

Dey, A. 1985. *Orthogonal fractional factorial designs*. John Wiley and Sons.

Duinker, P.N. 1991. *Tourism and timber in the Granite-Hill/Obakamiga Lakes area near Hornepayne: Approaches to breaking the impasse*. Thunder Bay, Ont: Lakehead University, Dept. of Forestry, unpublished report.

Econometric Research Limited and Ontario Ministry of Tourism and Recreation. 1990. *Economic impact of the remote tourism industry: North Algoma*. Econometric Research Limited and Ministry of Tourism and Recreation. Toronto.

Environmental Assessment Board. 1994. *Reasons for decision and decision - Class Environmental Assessment by the Ministry of Natural Resources for timber management on Crown Lands in Ontario*. Toronto.

ESSA (Environmental and Social Systems Analysts Ltd.). 1987. *Effects monitoring strategies for timber management guidelines in Ontario: Final report of moose, fish, and tourism technical meetings*. ESSA: Toronto.

Fisheries and Oceans. 1989. *Recreational fishing: A service industry profile*. Economic and Commercial Analysis Report No. 35, Government of Canada.

Green, P.E. & V. Srinivasan. 1978. Conjoint analysis in consumer research: Issues and outlook. *Journal of Consumer Research*, 5(2): 102-123.

Haider, W. & L. Carlucci. 1994. *Remote tourism in North Algoma*. Centre for Northern Forest Ecosystem Research, Fisheries and Tourism Research Unit, Ontario Ministry of Natural Resources: Thunder Bay, Ontario.

Haider, W. & G.O. Ewing. 1990. A model of tourist choices of hypothetical Caribbean destinations. *Leisure Sciences* 12(1): 33-47.

Louviere, J.J. 1988. *Analyzing decision making - Metric conjoint analysis*. Sage Publications Inc. Newbury Park, CA. p. 95.

Louviere, J.J. & H. Timmermans. 1990. Stated preference and choice models applied to recreation research: A review. *Leisure Sciences* 12(1): 9-32.

Louviere, J.J. & G. Woodworth. 1983. Design and analysis of simulated consumer choice or allocation experiments: An approach based on aggregate data. *Journal of Marketing Research*, 20:350-367.

Malm, W., K. Kelley, J. Molenar & T.C. Daniel. 1981. Human perception of visual air quality (Uniform haze). *Atmospheric Environment*, 15 (10/11), pp. 1875-1890.

McFadden D. 1974. Conditional logit analysis of qualitative choice behaviour. In P. Zamembka (Ed.) *Frontiers in econometrics*. pp. 105-142. New York: Academic Press.

McKercher, B. 1992. Tourism as a conflicting land use. *Annals of Tourism Research* 19: 467-481.

Orland, B. 1993. Synthetic landscapes: A review of video-imaging applications in environmental perception research, planning, and designs. In D. Stokols and R. Marans (eds.) *Environmental simulation: Research and policy issues*. pp. 213-252. New York: Plenum.

Orland, B. 1988. Video-imaging: A powerful tool for visualization and analysis. *Landscape Architecture*, 78(4): 78-88.

Orland, B., T.C. Daniel, J. Hetherington & J.L. Paschke. 1993. *Visualization of forest management issues on the Dixie National Forest*. Final Report. U.S. Forest Service, Forest Pest Management—Region 4 and Methods Application Group (FPM-Mag).